Jerusalem, the Covenant City

Hugh Kitson

Hatikvah Ltd
PO Box 2025
Steyning
West Sussex BN44 3QW
United Kingdom

Distributed by New Wine Ministries

ISBN: 1 874367 93 0

Edited by Sandy Waldron
Book and videocassette cover:
Painting *Millennial Jerusalem* by Laurel Sternberg
Title design by Liz Baxter and Robyn Browne
Videograph of people looking skywards, by Divine appointment
Overall cover design by Robyn Browne
Maps prepared by Peter Hamilton

Typeset by CRB Associates, Reepham, Norfolk
Printed in England by Clays Ltd, St Ives plc

Jerusalem, the Covenant City is a one-and-three-quarter hour documentary film for videocassette distribution. Based on the original film produced by the author in 1981 for David House Fellowship, it explores the past, present and future destiny of Jerusalem in the light of recorded history, the prophetic Scriptures and current events.

Contents

Foreword

There are many cities in the world which could lay claim to have had powerful influence upon humankind – cities that have in some way affected the course of history and contributed to the present-day world culture. Jerusalem stands alone. She has never had the attributes which other capital cities have had and which have made them great financial and political centres. In fact, Jerusalem was nothing until God chose her. From that moment Jerusalem became a witness to another world, a spiritual world, to the Kingdom of God. Throughout her history from that moment when God chose her until this day, she became the embodiment of God's original purpose for the human race. She represented on this earth in a literal manner the Almighty and the living God, His purpose, His word, His overwhelming love and faithfulness, His truth and righteousness. Above all she was the testimony to the salvation of God, to the fact that God Himself is both the Saviour and the Redeemer of fallen and hopeless humankind. She was, in fact, the city alone destined to be the place where the work of redemption would be completed, where the Messiah would save His people from their sins. No other city in history or on the contemporary scene can lay claim to such a vocation. Even when in ruin, her desolate stones bore witness to a divine calling, to a destiny which by the grace and faithfulness of God alone, she would finally reach. For if her stones are, as it were, the crystallised tears and travail of the redeemed through the ages of time, those same stones radiantly shine with the promise of a new heaven and a new earth in which righteousness dwells.

This Jerusalem still has a way to go before her sorrow and suffering is over for there is even more conflict and more war to be endured before the Messiah Jesus returns to her in great power and glory. Yet it matters not how intense the battle, nor how universal the antagonism, nor how powerful the enemies of God's purpose may be, God's Messiah will come, His purpose will be fulfilled and the continuous warfare over Jerusalem will end. Then and only then will Jerusalem, which has stood throughout the ages of time, finally fade into the eternal glory of that Jerusalem which descends from above.

Hugh Kitson has done a superb job in communicating these truths concerning Jerusalem. It is a book which contains a wealth of spiritual insight. In my estimation, it is well nigh impossible to hold a balanced and practical understanding of the last phase of world history without understanding the central place which Jerusalem and Israel occupy in the divine purpose. I believe, therefore, that this book is both timely and important.

Lance Lambert

Author's Note and Acknowledgements

As the Christian Era has embarked upon its third millennium, Jerusalem has entered its fourth millennium as the religious, cultural and national capital of the Jewish people. This fact of history is unpalatable to the Moslem world, most of the western world and, strangely enough, to much of Christendom too – even though its establishment is recorded in the Bible they use.

The conflict over the status of Jerusalem will one day set the world ablaze. Why else would the capital city of a nation with a population of only six million people (just one-tenth of one per cent of the world's population) have the third largest press corps in the world permanently stationed there? Perhaps the world's media are subconsciously aware that the destiny of the whole world is centred around the destiny of Jerusalem.

The ancient Jewish Scriptures predicted that world events would be focused around Jerusalem prior to the coming of the Messiah to reign on earth. The New Testament supports this prediction too.

This book is primarily a prophetic Bible study of Jerusalem. While acknowledging that parts of the Bible are written in symbolic or allegorical language, I believe the Divine Author intends to communicate with the human race generally – not exclusively to professional scholars or theologians, neither of which I am. For the most part, the Scriptures say exactly what they mean, and they mean exactly what they say. Consequently, for the purposes of this book, my method of interpretation has been to take Scripture, and particularly prophecy, at face value. There are prophetic passages, however, that are not so clear and Bible scholars differ in their interpretations of the meaning. In most cases, I have presented the alternatives to the reader. The 'Seventieth Week' of Daniel is one example of this.

Because the Bible is not simply a book of the past, but also a book of the present and the future, it is not possible to accept what the Scriptures say without making some fairly controversial observations about the political situation as it exists in the Middle East today.

Because of the volatility of the Middle East, dramatic events can occur very rapidly. At the time this manuscript was being completed, the Final Status negotiations of the Oslo Accords were under way, and not without a few hiccups. Israel and Syria had reopened a faltering dialogue after a four-year stand-off, and consequently 18,000 residents of the Golan Heights – and many more Israelis – were 'up in arms'.

Analysts of the 'peace' process, both on the Arab side and the Jewish side, are nearly all agreed about one thing: the bottom line is Jerusalem. The ancient prophets of Israel tell us that whatever the outcome of either of these sets of 'peace' negotiations, there will be bloodshed, and eventually war. Furthermore, there is enough documentary evidence to demonstrate conclusively that Yasser Arafat has no intention of living peacefully with Israel, whatever the outcome of the Oslo Accords. A leader who I met in one of the Jewish communities in Judea said: 'The PLO Trojan Horse has been pulled inside our borders.'

One cannot rule out the possibility that something totally unforeseen may happen. Nevertheless, this book must go into print some time, and therefore the latest crisis or conflict may not be included. This, however, will make little difference to the overall theme of *Jerusalem, the Covenant City*.

Whatever happens, though, it is my unshakeable belief that nothing will deter the purposes of the God of Israel, as communicated by Him through the prophets in the Bible, from ultimately coming to pass.

Many people have contributed to *Jerusalem, the Covenant City*. Firstly, the concept is based on a documentary film of the same title I produced in 1981 for David House Fellowship based in Melbourne, Australia. I am indebted to that organisation and all who were part of David House Fellowship at that time and in subsequent years.

Secondly, I would like to thank my colleagues on the Board of Hatikvah Film Foundation in two countries for their guidance, encouragement and support, as a new version of the film *Jerusalem, the Covenant City* and this book were in the making. This non-profit organisation was founded in Australia to oversee the production of the film, and is now based in England.

Thirdly, there are several people who read the manuscript at various stages. I am most grateful for their criticism, suggestions, wise counsel and encouragement. Each of these people has made a valuable contribution to this book: our former Pastor and very dear friend in Australia, Rev. Cyril Pritchard; my long-standing friend, Rev. Jim Gibbon, who is the Pastor at Attadale Baptist Church in Perth, Western Australia; Bruce D. Reekie, who is author of the excellent book *The Holy Spirit and Israel*; David Dolan, who is a journalist based in Jerusalem and the author of three books, including *Israel at the Crossroads*; and Lance Lambert, who is the author of several books about Israel and regarded by many as one of the foremost authorities on affairs in the Middle East as they relate to end-time biblical prophecy.

Fourthly, I would like to thank the authors of the many books and publications I have drawn on. They are all mentioned in the footnotes. I would especially like to thank Herman Goldwag, Murray Dixon and Malcolm Hedding, who have made contributions to this book and have been a source of encouragement along the way.

Fifthly, I would especially like to thank my wife, Noreen, and son, Matthew, for their understanding and practical assistance while I was working on this project. My thanks go to Diana Durden who, with my wife, proof-read the manuscript just before going to publication. We would like to thank Eunice Hellin for her ministry of hospitality and practical assistance during our frequent visits to Jerusalem.

Last, and most of all, I would like to thank the God of Abraham, Isaac and Jacob, without Whom this book would be meaningless – in fact it could never have been written. *Jerusalem, the Covenant City* is dedicated to His glory, and to the glory of His Anointed One, the Holy One of Israel.

Hugh Kitson
April 2000

Introduction

On 13 September 1993, the Israeli Prime Minister, the late Yitzhak Rabin, shook hands with the leader of the Palestine Liberation Organisation, Yasser Arafat, on the lawn of the White House in Washington. A Declaration of Principles for the negotiations for a Peace Accord had been agreed upon. Within days Yasser Arafat was openly declaring his ultimate goal – an item excluded by mutual agreement from the Declaration of Principles at that time – a sovereign Palestinian State with Jerusalem as its capital.

Earlier that year, on 28 Iyar 5753 in the Jewish calendar, Israelis celebrated the twenty-sixth anniversary of the re-unification of the Holy City under Jewish sovereignty. The celebration was highlighted by the ratification of The Jerusalem Covenant in which the Jewish people all over the world reiterated their identification with, and pledged their continued love for, Jerusalem.

The God of Israel shows His special love for Jerusalem, and expresses it many times in the Scriptures. One example is found in Ezekiel:

> *'"Thus says the Lord God to Jerusalem ... 'Yes I swore an oath to you and entered into a covenant with you, and you became Mine.'"'*   (Ezekiel 16:3, 8)

No other city in the world has been as significant in the history of humankind as Jerusalem. It was there, four thousand years ago, that Abraham and Isaac offered a sacrifice on what became God's Holy Mountain. It was there, three thousand years ago, that David reigned as King of Israel, and it was there that Solomon dedicated the magnificent Temple of the Lord, and the glory of God descended from heaven to enshroud and fill it. It was there that Yeshua, the Messiah, lived, taught, died and rose from the dead. And it will be to there that He shall return, in all His glory, to establish the Messianic Kingdom foretold in the Scriptures – an era so longed for by the Jewish people and Christians alike.

No other city has been prophesied and wept over as much as Jerusalem. No other city has seen as much conflict and bloodshed as Jerusalem. Now, a new conflict looms as Islam and the PLO stake a claim for the Holy City and attempt to revise its history. The eyes of the world are focusing on Jerusalem as the prophecy of Zechariah comes to pass – *'Jerusalem shall become a burdensome stone for all nations'* – which will culminate in the last great conflict before Messiah's return.

Chapter 1

The Status of Jerusalem in the Bible

The Uniqueness of Jerusalem

Jerusalem is one of the oldest walled cities in the world that has been continually inhabited. When compared with some other major cities of the world, it is not especially beautiful. Geographically, it does not have much going for it either. It has neither a port, nor a river, nor is it situated on a great trade route. It does not even have a natural abundant source of water. In fact, in a physical sense, Jerusalem does not seem to have much going for it at all.[1]

Ironically, there is no other city in the world that has captured the passion of men and women as Jerusalem has. Arguably, more wars and battles have been fought over Jerusalem through its long and chequered history than over any other city in the world. The city has been completely destroyed and rebuilt more than fourteen times – usually over the site of a previous destruction.

Without doubt, it is Jerusalem's religious significance that makes it famous. It could be said that today Jerusalem's economy is founded on religion, and the tourist trade that it brings. It has often been described as 'the city holy to three religions'. But is it this that makes Jerusalem unique as a city?

It is true that the three monotheistic faiths have a significant interest in the Holy City. But, for the Muslim, it is only the third holiest city after Mecca and Medina and it is worth noting that, although it could be inferred, there is no direct mention of Jerusalem by name anywhere in Islam's holy book, the Koran.

Jerusalem has been described as the cradle of Christianity, though some denominations in Christendom do have other centres of equal or greater importance, for example Rome.

For Evangelical Christians, Jerusalem's significance in this age is both historic and prophetic. It is the place where the person Christians believe to be the Messiah,[2] Jesus of Nazareth, died, rose again and ascended into heaven – and also the city to which He shall return to reign as King over all the earth.

But, for the Jewish people, Jerusalem has been at the very heart of their national and spiritual identity ever since King David established the city as Israel's capital just over three thousand years ago. Indeed, when it comes to Judaism, Jerusalem is at its very heart. Judaism cannot be divorced from Jerusalem, any more than it can be divorced from the Jew.

But it is not even this special bond between the Jew and Jerusalem – and special it is – that makes the Holy City so unique. What makes Jerusalem so unique is that the God of Israel – the God of Abraham, Isaac and Jacob – has declared the city to be His own, as we shall shortly see.

Another related factor that makes Jerusalem unique is its place in the world's bestselling book, the Holy Bible.[3] The name 'Jerusalem', which literally means 'possession of peace' is found more than 800 times in the Old and New Testaments. But other names, too, are used in Scripture to refer to the Holy City. These include: Ariel, City of God, City of David, City of Judah, Jebus, City of Righteousness, City of Truth, City of the Great King, Holy City, Faithful City, Salem and Zion. Some of these names appear only once, while others appear a few times; the name 'Zion' appears more than 150 times. Altogether there are about one thousand direct references to the city of Jerusalem in the Old and New Testaments.

Perhaps more important than any other aspect is Jerusalem's prophetic significance in the Bible, which is the main focus of this book. There are fulfilled prophecies in the Bible about many other cities that existed in the ancient world, some of which still exist today – Damascus, for instance, which still has a major prophecy to be fulfilled. However, in this respect Jerusalem is unique: there is no other city in the world that has had its past history so graphically recorded in the Bible **before** it actually happened! The events surrounding the rebirth of the nation of Israel and the re-establishment of Jerusalem as the capital of that nation in the modern era are a living example of this. Even more amazing is the fact that as we stand at the dawn of the third millennium of the Christian Era (CE), we find, too, that Jerusalem's **future** history has been graphically foretold in the ancient Scriptures. Looking at Jerusalem's past history and the present mounting conflict over its status, the meaning of its name – 'possession of peace', or 'City of Peace' – may seem to be entirely inappropriate, but, like so many names found in the Bible, it is prophetic. Indeed, it is the only city in the world that has been promised a glorious and eternal future.

Another aspect of Jerusalem's uniqueness, which we will discover in more detail as we go through this book, is that the Holy City is geographically at the very heart of the outworking of the covenants which the Creator of the universe has made with the human race.

The Uniqueness of the Jewish People

Nations frequently choose a person or a group of people to represent them in the international arena, whether it be in art, sport, trade or politics. In a similar way, historically, the Creator chose an ethnic group of people, commonly known today as the Jewish people, to represent Him in the world, in other words to be His executive officers (priests) – hence the frequent reference to Jews as the 'chosen people'. Speaking through Moses in the Book of Exodus, the Creator said to them:

> *'Now therefore, if you will indeed obey My voice and keep My covenant, then you shall be a special treasure to Me above all people; for all the earth is Mine. And you shall be to Me **a kingdom of priests** and **a holy nation**.'*
>
> (Exodus 19:5–6 – author's emphasis)

This covenant makes the nation of Israel unique among the nations of the world. History shows us that for most of the time the Israelis failed to keep this covenant, often referred to as the Mosaic Covenant, and consequently incurred God's displeasure. But because Israel as a nation failed to live up to God's expectations as His executive officers on the earth, that role has temporarily been given to the Church.

Does that mean that Israel's calling has been forever revoked? In Chapter 10, as we look at the ultimate consummation of the covenants and promises, we will find that the answer to that question is a definite 'NO!' for the New Testament tells us that concerning Israel *the gifts and the calling of God are irrevocable'* (Romans 11:29).

Several hundred years before Moses lived, the Creator of the Universe, to whom the Bible often refers as *'the God of Israel'* or *'the God of Abraham, Isaac and Jacob'*, had made another covenant which would give the Hebrew people, the Jews, a unique status. Known as the Abrahamic Covenant,[4] it stated that the descendants of Abraham, Isaac and Jacob would be the ethnic group of people through whom the Lord would bless all the other nations of the earth.

The Abrahamic Covenant

> *'Now the Lord said to Abram:*
> *"Get out of your country,*
> *From your kindred*
> *And from your father's house,*
> *To a land that I will show you.*
> *I will make you a great nation;*
> *I will bless you*
> *And make your name great;*
> *And you shall be a blessing.*
> *I will bless those who bless you,*
> *And I will curse him who curses you;*
> *And in you all the families of the earth*
> *   shall be blessed."'*   (Genesis 12:1–3)

At the time God spoke these words to Abram, as he was then

called, he was moving from Ur of the Chaldees in the general direction of the Land of Canaan. The Lord made this covenant with Abraham, as the 'Head of State' of a nation that was to be created through his descendants. So it is not simply a covenant that God made with Abraham, but a covenant which would also be valid for his descendants right through to the present day, and beyond.

We will examine two components of the Abrahamic Covenant. The first contains a promise of God that has had a profound effect upon the course of the history of the world.

Curse or Coincidence?

This promise is the small phrase in verse 3 – *'I will curse him who curses you'*. It is a fact of history that every nation that has come against or persecuted the Jewish people has sooner or later come undone. For instance, all the ancient tribal inhabitants of the Land of Canaan have disappeared from history, along with the mighty Assyrian, Babylonian, Persian and Roman Empires.

In the Christian Era there was the crumbling of the great Spanish Empire after the Spanish Inquisition, and the fall of the Turkish Empire. In the twentieth century there was the destruction of Germany in 1945, and the demise of the Soviet Union in 1991. All of these countries have incited anti-Semitism and have Jewish blood on their hands.

Just as dramatically, there has been the humiliating defeat of the Arab armies which have tried to annihilate the State of Israel on several occasions since 1948. Yet in spite of all these attempts to rid the world of the Jews over thousands of years, the Jewish people live on as an identifiable entity. Is this all coincidence, or is it the supernatural outworking of the Abrahamic Covenant? [5]

The Abrahamic Covenant and the Inheritance of the Land

Secondly, let us look at the component of the Abrahamic Covenant that focuses upon the land that was to be the everlasting inheritance of the Jewish people. Prophetically and spiritually, not only is the outworking of this covenant the very basis of the conflict in the Middle East today, but it ultimately impinges upon the status of Jerusalem as well. Let us look at what the covenant is saying.

Apart from the text quoted earlier from the first three verses of Genesis 12, the Abrahamic Covenant is further elaborated on in Genesis 13:14–17 and chapters 15–17. The borders of the inheritance which, incidentally, are much wider than all of modern-day Israel, and includes the pieces of real estate known today as 'The West Bank' and the Golan Heights, are defined in Genesis 15:18–21. At the very heart of the Jewish inheritance was the land inhabited by the ancient Jebusites, i.e. Jerusalem. The Lord went on to say:

> *'Also I give to you and your descendants after you the land in which you are a stranger, all the land of Canaan, as an everlasting possession; and I will be their God.'*
>
> (Genesis 17:8)

Because Abraham was to have two sons, Ishmael and Isaac, and the Lord knew there would be contention over the inheritance, He went on to identify which son would inherit the promises of the covenant:

> *'But My covenant I will establish with Isaac, whom Sarah shall bear to you at this set time next year.'*
>
> (Genesis 17:21)

The everlasting nature of this covenant is reiterated in Psalm 105:8–11.

> *'He has remembered His covenant forever,*
> *The word which He commanded, for a thousand*
> * generations*
> *The covenant which He made with Abraham,*
> *And His oath to Isaac,*
> *And confirmed it to Jacob for a statute,*
> *To Israel for an everlasting covenant,*
> *Saying, "To you I give the land of Canaan*
> *As the allotment of your inheritance."'*

This passage reveals that, not only has God made an **everlasting** covenant with the descendants of Abraham, Isaac and Jacob – i.e. the Jewish people – regarding the Land of Israel, but He has backed it with His *'oath'* (v. 9). The God of Israel has unconditionally bound Himself **forever** to this covenant in the strongest and clearest possible language. Surely this should put the issue of the possession of the land beyond dispute. In his book *The Destiny of Israel and the Church*, Derek Prince lists forty-six occasions in the Old Testament (including the above reference) where God reiterates His oath concerning the Abrahamic Covenant.[6]

To ensure there is no doubt whatsoever, the Bible repeatedly emphasises the fact that the Land of Canaan is identified as the inheritance of the Jewish people forever. Indeed, the Abrahamic Covenant is the 'Title Deed' to the 'Promised Land'. It must surely be assumed that if the whole of the land legally belongs to the Jews for all time, then so must Jerusalem.

There are many other Scriptures in the Old Testament that inseparably bind the City, the Land and the People together. This concept is at the heart of what is known as Zionism.

The Origin of Zionism

The press and television media often portray Zionism as a great evil. Propaganda coming from Islamic sources usually goes even further and attempts to portray Zionism as being racist or, even worse, an extension of Nazism. 'The Zionist aggressors,' they say, 'are out to murder us and steal our land.' A more recent and equally damaging comparison equated Zionism with the Serbian Milosevic regime, which sought to 'cleanse' Kosovo of its Moslem ethnic Albanian population. The western media do little to counter this blatant untruth, which in turn has created a gross distortion of what Zionism really is. In fact the modern Zionist dream for millions of Jewish people, whose ancestors were ejected from their land nineteen centuries ago, and who have suffered incredible persecution, is simply to return to the land of their forefathers and to live in peace. Admittedly, there is a very small minority of Jewish extremists who have evil intentions towards their Arab neighbours, but unfortunately the media give this tiny group a disproportionate amount of attention.

In recent years this distorted portrayal of Zionists and Zionism has caused a shift in political thinking in Israel itself. Consequently – and particularly on the left side of Israeli politics – Zionism today is regarded as passé. Many secular Israelis, in contrast to the religious orthodox, try to portray Israel as having entered a 'post-Zionist' era.

Another widely-held view today is that Zionism had its origins at the end of the nineteenth century through a man called Theodore Herzl, whom we will say a little more about in Chapter 4. However, it may come as a surprise to many in Christendom – and perhaps even a shock to some – to discover that the origin of Zionism is actually found in the Bible. It may come as an even greater surprise to learn that the author of Zionism is none other than the God whom Christians worship. One could almost say that the Lord has a Zionist passion which is second to none!

Zion – the City, the Land, and the People – a Divinely Ordained Unity

When the name 'Zion' is used in Scripture, it is used affectionately, passionately, intimately. The *Tanakh*[7] refers to Zion in three ways. Firstly, Jerusalem is identified as Zion:

> '*The* Lord *loves the gates of Zion*
> *More than all the dwellings of Jacob.*
> *Glorious things are spoken of you,*
> *O City of God!'* (Psalm 87:2–3)

> '*Great is the* Lord, *and greatly to be praised*
> *In the city of our God,*
> *In His holy mountain.*
> *Beautiful in elevation,*
> *The joy of the whole earth,*
> *Is Mount Zion on the sides of the north,*
> *The city of the great King.'* (Psalm 48:1–2)

More particularly, we see that Mount Zion[8] (otherwise known as Mount Moriah) is God's 'Holy Mountain' where the Temple stood.

> ' "Yet have I set My King
> On My holy hill of Zion." '   (Psalm 2:6)

This is a reference to a far greater glory yet to come to Jerusalem, when Messiah establishes His Kingdom on earth. This is a recurring theme relating to Jerusalem's future glory, which we will see as we go through the Scriptures.

Secondly, the Land of Israel is referred to as Zion. Isaiah says:

> ' "The LORD will comfort Zion,
> He will comfort all her waste places;
> He will make her wilderness like Eden,
> And her desert like the garden of the LORD." '   (Isaiah 51:3)

This, of course, is a prophecy we are seeing fulfilled in our generation.

Thirdly, the Lord Himself identifies the Jewish people as Zion:

> ' "I have covered you with the shadow of My hand,
> That I may plant the heavens,
> Lay the foundations of the earth,
> And say to Zion, 'You are my people.' " '   (Isaiah 51:16)

Thus, the God of Israel has ordained that the City of Jerusalem, the Land of Israel and the Jewish People are inextricably bonded together in a covenant relationship.

Zion – God's Chosen Dwelling Place

As we noted earlier, Jerusalem is unique because it is the only city in the world that God has claimed as His own.

> 'For the LORD has chosen Zion;
> He has desired it for His habitation:

> *"This is My resting place forever,*
> *Here I will dwell, for I have desired it. . . .*
> *There I will make the horn of David grow;*
> *I will prepare a lamp for My Anointed.*
> *His enemies I will clothe with shame,*
> *But upon Himself His crown shall flourish."'*
>
> (Psalm 132:13–14, 17–18)

Not only has the Lord chosen Zion, but He has also declared it to be His dwelling place **forever**. Furthermore, this particular declaration has a direct reference to the Messiah. The Hebrew word for 'My Anointed' is the same as the Hebrew word for 'My Messiah'. Psalm 2 identifies the Messiah as Israel's King.

> *' "Yet I have set My King*
> *On My holy hill of Zion."*
>
> *"I will declare the decree:*
> *The LORD has said to Me,*
> *'You are My Son,*
> *Today I have begotten You.*
> *Ask of Me and I will give You*
> *The nations for Your inheritance,*
> *And the ends of the earth for Your possession.' " '*
>
> (Psalm 2:6–8)

What is interesting here is that the Lord identifies Israel's King as His Son. The prophet Joel, speaking of the final restoration of Israel, goes one step further and identifies that the Lord God Himself [9] dwells in Zion:

> *' "So you shall know that I am the LORD your God,*
> *Dwelling in Zion My holy mountain." '*   (Joel 3:17)

The Scriptures not only portray Jerusalem and Mount Zion as the Lord's dwelling place, but also as His throne.

> *' "At that time Jerusalem shall be called The Throne of the*
> *LORD, and all the nations shall be gathered to it, to the name*
> *of the LORD, to Jerusalem." '*   (Jeremiah 3:17)

The prophet Isaiah endorses this:

> *'The Lord of Hosts will reign*
> *On Mount Zion and in Jerusalem*
> *And before His elders, gloriously.'*   (Isaiah 24:23)

This, too, bears testimony to a far greater glory yet to come to Jerusalem when Messiah establishes His Kingdom. We will examine the prophecies concerning the Messianic Age in greater detail in Chapter 11.

The Heavenly Zion

Whereas the *Tanakh* speaks of Zion the city, the land and the people in the natural and earthly realm, which will have its complete fulfilment prophetically, the writer to the 'Hebrews' (i.e. the Jewish believers in the Messiah) refers to the spiritual and heavenly Zion. He introduces a new element not mentioned in the *Tanakh* – the Church – whom he is addressing here.

> *'But you have come to Mount Zion and to the city of the living God, the heavenly Jerusalem, to an innumerable company of angels, to the general assembly and church of the firstborn who are registered in heaven, to God the Judge of all, to the spirits of just men made perfect, to Jesus, the Mediator of the New Covenant.'*   (Hebrews 12:22–23)

These verses say a great deal. The use of the present tense suggests that the heavenly Jerusalem actually exists now even though we cannot see it, and that those who are the saints of God are already part of it. Not only are those saints [10] who have passed from this earthly life actually there now, but those saints who are still here on earth already have their citizenship there. In other words the living saints have their status in the heavenly Zion, even though they are still alive on earth in spirit, soul and body. Bearing in mind what the *Tanakh* teaches, there is also the suggestion that the destiny of the Jewish saints and the Gentile saints is ultimately the same.

As far as Zion is concerned, the Bible tells us something about Jerusalem that makes it unquestionably unique among all the cities of the earth: its status is ultimately in eternity. Indeed, in the Book of Revelation in the New Testament we are given a vision of the New Jerusalem coming down from heaven. We will look at this further in Chapter 12.

For now, let us return to the earthly Jerusalem, and the covenant relationship that the Lord has made with her.

Jerusalem, the Covenant City

The description of this relationship occupies the whole of Ezekiel 16, and speaks of something akin to a marriage covenant. At the beginning of the chapter the Lord addresses Jerusalem, but He is not simply talking to bricks, mortar and Jerusalem stone. He is speaking collectively to Zion – the city, the land, and the people – the divinely ordained unity. This 'marriage covenant' with Jerusalem encompasses most of the other covenants – the Abrahamic Covenant, the Mosaic Covenant, the Land Covenant, and ultimately the New Covenant.

The chapter contains a history of Jerusalem and her people, in miniature. It is written poetically, in the form of an intimate love letter straight from the heart – the heart of God.

> *'Thus says the Lord GOD to Jerusalem: "Your birth and your nativity are from the land of Canaan; your father was an Amorite and your mother a Hittite. As for your nativity, on the day you were born your navel cord was not cut, nor were you washed in water to cleanse you. ... No eye pitied you, to have compassion on you; but you were thrown out into the open field, when you yourself were loathed on the day you were born.*
>
> *"And when I passed by you and saw you struggling in your own blood, I said to you, 'Live!' ... When I passed by you again and looked upon you, indeed your time was the time of love; so I spread my wing over you and covered your nakedness. Yes, I swore an oath to you, and entered into a covenant with you and you became Mine," says the Lord GOD.*

"Then I washed you in water; yes, I thoroughly washed off your blood, and I anointed you with oil. I clothed you in embroidered cloth, ... with fine linen and covered you with silk. I adorned you with ornaments, put bracelets on your wrists, and a chain on your neck. And I put a jewel on your nose, earrings in your ears, and a beautiful crown on your head. Thus you were adorned with gold and silver ... You were exceedingly beautiful, and succeeded to royalty. Your fame went out among the nations because of your beauty, for it was perfect through My splendour which I had bestowed on you," says the Lord GOD.

"But you trusted in your own beauty, played the harlot because of your fame, and poured out your harlotry on everyone passing by who would have it....

" 'Woe, woe to you!' " says the Lord GOD – "that you also built for yourself a shrine, and made a high place for yourself in every street ... you are like an adulterous wife, who takes strangers instead of her husband.

"And I will judge you as women who break wedlock or shed blood are judged; I will bring blood upon you in fury and jealousy.

"[Your lovers] shall stone you with stones and thrust you through with their swords. They shall burn your houses with fire, and execute judgements on you ... and I will make you cease playing the harlot, and you shall no longer hire lovers.

"So I will lay to rest My fury toward you, and My jealousy shall depart from you. I will be quiet, and be angry no more. ... You have paid for your lewdness and your abominations," says the Lord GOD.

For thus says the Lord GOD: "I will deal with you as you have done, who despised the oath by breaking the covenant. Nevertheless I will remember my covenant with you in the days of your youth, and I will establish an everlasting covenant with you. Then you shall know that I am the Lord." '   (Ezekiel 16:3–6, 8–10, 11, 12–15, 23–24, 32, 38, 40–1, 42, 58–60, 62b)

The Lord is addressing Jerusalem with regard to His covenants with the Jewish people, revealing without a shadow of a doubt that the city and the people are bound together in a covenant relationship to God. In the final analysis, in the eyes of the God of Israel – the God whom Christians also worship – the status of Jerusalem cannot be divorced from the Jewish people, or indeed from the Lord Himself. Just as the descendants of Abraham, Isaac and Jacob are the Lord's Covenant People, Jerusalem is His Covenant City.

Those who challenge the status of Jerusalem need to bear this in mind. The prophet Zechariah gives the strongest possible warnings to those who would meddle with the status of Jerusalem: *'He who touches you* [Zion] *touches the apple of His eye'* (Zechariah 2:8) and *'all who would heave it* [Jerusalem] *away will surely be cut in pieces'* (Zechariah 12:3). In later chapters we will further consider these and other warnings in their context. Furthermore, we will discover that the judgement of God is a very real phenomenon for anyone, whether Jew or Gentile, who violates His covenants or attempts to thwart His declared purposes – knowingly or not.

The prophet penned the Book of Ezekiel, and the marriage covenant we have just considered, after he had been taken captive to Babylon. The judgement of God had already fallen for the first time upon Jerusalem for her idolatry, described here as harlotry, just as the Land Covenant promised it would. In this passage in chapter 16, Ezekiel foreshadowed that an everlasting covenant would be established – and indeed it has been. The New Covenant. However, the Jewish nation has yet to embrace it.

In the following chapters of *Jerusalem, the Covenant City* we will chart the course of Jerusalem's history through the biblical era and beyond, right up to the present day as the third millennium of the Christian Era is dawning upon us. We will discover that the prophets of Israel really did write Jerusalem's history in advance, and with astonishing accuracy. In the final chapters we will try to unravel something of what they wrote about Jerusalem's future destiny in this new millennium, and beyond into eternity.

Chapter 2

The History of Jerusalem in the Bible

The King of Salem

The first mention of Jerusalem in the Bible is in Genesis 14, when Abram gives a tithe to a rather mysterious person called Melchizedek, King of Salem, who was a priest of God Most High. Melchizedek is also mentioned in Psalm 110:4, in reference to the Messiah and His priesthood, and again in the New Testament in the Letter to the Hebrews. Many scholars believe the priest encountered by Abram was from an eternal order and was none other than the Messiah in His 'pre-incarnate' form.[11] A study of the person and the priesthood of Melchizedek is beyond the scope of this book, however it is interesting to note that he was the King of 'Salem', the City of Peace, which was later to become known as Jerusalem.

Abraham Visits Mount Moriah

Abraham was the forefather of both the Jewish and Arab peoples, the descendants of Isaac and Ishmael respectively. As we have already noted, the covenant God made with Abraham would continue through Isaac, not Ishmael, although he, too, was not left without a blessing.

> ' "As for Ishmael ... I have blessed him, and will make him fruitful, and will multiply him exceedingly. He shall beget

> *twelve princes, and I will make him a great nation. But My*
> *covenant I will establish with Isaac."'* (Genesis 17:20–21)

Moreover, Abraham's faith was to be tested to see whether
or not he really believed the promise of God. In Genesis 22,
Abraham was given the following instruction by the Lord:

> *' "Take now your son, your only son Isaac, whom you love,*
> *and go to the Land of Moriah and offer him there as a burnt*
> *offering on one of the mountains of which I shall tell you."'*
> (Genesis 22:2)

This reference to Isaac as Abraham's *'only'* son makes it
clear that, as far as God was concerned in regard to the
covenant, Isaac **was** Abraham's only son.

The story here is well known. One can only imagine what
was going through the minds of father and son as they
climbed towards Mount Moriah. Isaac's question about the
whereabouts of the sacrificial lamb displayed a clear note of
anxiety. Abraham replied:

> *'My son, God will provide for Himself the lamb for the burnt*
> *offering.'*   (Genesis 22:8)

This was a supreme exercise of faith, not only for Abraham,
but also for Isaac. Clearly Isaac must have been willing to be
offered as a sacrifice, because as a fully-grown young man
Abraham could not have bound his son without his acquiescence. Just as he was about to kill Isaac, the Angel of the Lord
called out to Abraham and told him not to harm the lad.
Abraham looked up and saw a ram caught in a thicket by its
horns and offered it up to the Lord in Isaac's place.

> *'And Abraham called the name of the place, YHWH Yireh*
> *(The-Lord-Will-Provide); as it is said to this day, "In the*
> *Mount of the Lord it shall be provided."'* (Genesis 22:14)

The divinely-appointed location where all this took place
around four thousand years ago was none other than the site
now known as the Temple Mount in Jerusalem – Mount

Moriah. But what did Abraham mean by *'shall be provided'*? Could he have been prophetically referring to the supreme sacrifice of all time – God's only Son sacrificed for the sin of the whole world – which took place nearby, on this same mountain ridge, some two thousand years later? It was John the Baptist who said, when he saw Jesus of Nazareth approaching him to be baptised:

> *'Behold, the Lamb of God who takes away the sin of the world!'*   (John 1:29)

The Book of Revelation gives us a picture of more than one hundred million angels in heaven saying with a loud voice:

> *'Worthy is the Lamb who was slain*
> *To receive power and riches and wisdom,*
> *And strength and honour and glory and blessing!'*
> (Revelation 5:12)

The Nation of Israel Is Born

Later Isaac married Rebekah and they had twin sons Esau and Jacob. Having procured the birthright by stealth (Genesis 27) Jacob went on to father twelve sons, from whom the twelve tribes of the nation of Israel are descended. Through the elevation of one of the sons, Joseph, to the highest office in the land of Egypt and a subsequent famine, the Lord moved the Children of Israel to Egypt. There, over the next four centuries, their population expanded to two million or more. Because of their growing number and increasing strength as a people, the Egyptians became fearful and subjugated the Hebrews into slavery.

But God had a wider purpose in this great affliction of Israel. If you have never read the story of how the Lord delivered the Israelis from Pharaoh of Egypt, then it is well worth reading the account in the first fifteen chapters of the Book of Exodus. The Lord raised up a man called Moses, who is regarded by most Jewish people as the greatest leader their nation has ever known. In a supernatural encounter, God called to him out of a burning bush, which was not consumed by the fire, and told him to take his sandals off because the ground on which he stood was holy. God gave Moses the task of the leadership of the people of Israel. It was under that leadership that Israel first found its identity as a nation. No man in the history of the *Tanakh* encountered the presence of God as Moses did. Indeed, it was to Moses that *Torah* – the Law – was given, as well as the instructions for the building of the Tabernacle – the meeting-place between God and human beings. This later became the blueprint for the Temple in Jerusalem.

It was prior to *Torah* being given, however, that arguably the greatest miracle in the history of ancient Israel took place. This miracle – the Exodus from Egypt – is commemorated to this day in the Jewish Feast of Passover. As the Israelis were fleeing from Egypt the Lord commanded Moses to stretch out his staff over the waters of the Red Sea, and they parted, allowing all Israel to cross over on the dry sea bed. The pursuing Egyptians perished as the waters flooded in on them. Immediately after that momentous event, as Moses and the Israelis were singing praises to God, they were given prophetic utterance concerning a number of events that would come to pass in the future – including a remarkable prophecy relating to Jerusalem. Although neither Jerusalem nor Mount Zion is directly named here, the inference is obvious:

> ' *"You will bring them in and plant them*
> *In the mountain of Your inheritance,*
> *In the place, O LORD, which You have made*
> *For Your own dwelling,*
> *The sanctuary, O LORD, which Your hands have*
> *established."* '   (Exodus 15:17)

What is so remarkable about this prophecy is that the Tabernacle had yet to be constructed and the Ark of the Covenant had yet to be fashioned by Israel's finest craftsmen. The Promised Land had yet to be entered, Jerusalem had yet to be established as Israel's capital, and the Temple had yet to be built on Mount Zion. Nevertheless, Moses and the Israelis were singing this verse of the song as if it was already an established part of their history. Indeed, in the eyes of the eternal God of Israel, it already was.

Sadly, the demonstration of this level of faith among the Israelis was but a passing moment. Despite the awesome acts of God, the nation was to plunge into unbelief, rebellion and idolatry. Consequently, they were to spend forty years in the Sinai wilderness before being led by Moses' protégé, Joshua, across the Jordan River into their inheritance.

For the next four hundred years or so after entering the Promised Land, the Israeli people were under the leadership of 'the Judges' and, eventually, their first king, Saul. Their fortunes fluctuated as they sought to conquer the land. As had been promised in the covenant made under Moses, when they trusted God and obeyed Him they experienced victory over their enemies. When they were self-confident, rebelled or fell into idolatry they experienced defeat.

The City of David

It was during the reign of King Saul that an unknown young shepherd was anointed in Bethlehem as Israel's future king by the prophet Samuel. The shepherd, whose name was David, was to become Israel's greatest warrior.

Some years later, after the death of King Saul, he was crowned as king over the house of Judah in the city where Abraham had been buried – Hebron – and there he reigned for about seven years. It wasn't until the death of Saul's son, Ishbosheth, that David became king over all Israel. One of his first victorious acts as King of Israel was to capture Jerusalem, which had been the virtually impregnable stronghold of the Jebusites.

'*David took the stronghold of Zion (that is, the City of David)*' – (1 Chronicles 11:5) – and made it the capital of his kingdom. Shortly afterwards the Ark of the Lord, which had been the centrepiece of the Holy of Holies in the Tabernacle, was brought to Jerusalem and King David expressed his desire to build a House for the Lord (2 Samuel 6–7).

Because David was a man of war, God refused him permission to build the House of the Lord, which was to replace the Tabernacle as the permanent resting-place for the Ark.

However, his son Solomon was later given the task. But the Lord did make a covenant with David in which He promised He would establish the dynasty of his kingdom forever. This is commonly known as the Davidic Covenant and is found in 2 Samuel 7:4–17 and 1 Chronicles 17:3–15. We will consider its fulfilment in Chapter 10.

It was during King David's forty-year reign that Israel rose to its zenith as a nation. The Scriptures describe David not only as a warrior, but as a man after God's own heart (1 Samuel 13:14 and 16:7). In the Psalms his heart was often laid bare, revealing his intimate devotion to the Lord his God. However, even David wasn't perfect, and the Bible records two occasions in his life that displeased the Lord greatly. One was his adultery with Bathsheba and the subsequent murder of her husband, Uriah the Hittite (2 Samuel 11). The other occasion is recorded in 1 Chronicles 21 (also in 2 Samuel 24), which tells the story of the census which David took of Israel against the Lord's wishes. As a result of David's sin, God sent a plague which swept through Israel. It was only halted when, at God's command, King David purchased the threshing floor of Ornah the Jebusite, which was on Mount Moriah. There he built an altar to the Lord and sacrificed burnt offerings.

> *'Then David said, "This is the House of the LORD God, and this is the altar of burnt offering for Israel." '*
>
> (1 Chronicles 22:1)

This was the very site where, a thousand years earlier, God had commanded Abraham to prepare to offer Isaac. And so it was on this same divinely chosen site – God's Holy Mountain – that David's son, Solomon, built the House of the Lord.

The House of the Lord

The prosperity with which the Lord had begun to bless Israel during the reign of King David was to continue to multiply in the reign of King Solomon. Not only did the kingdom of Israel enjoy unparalleled wealth, but the nation was at peace with its neighbours too.

After David's death, Solomon extended the borders of Jerusalem to include Mount Moriah within the city walls. In the fourth year of his reign, four hundred and eighty years after the Exodus from Egypt, Solomon commenced building the Temple, which must be considered one of the costliest and most magnificent buildings ever constructed. An account of the construction and furnishing, which took seven years, and a staggering sum of money, is given in 1 Kings 5–7.

In 1 Kings 6:7 we discover:

> *'And the Temple, when it was being built, was built with stone finished at the quarry, so that no hammer or chisel or any iron tool was heard in the Temple while it was being built.'*

If you should ever visit Solomon's quarries underneath the north-eastern area of the Old City, you will see how the stone was carved out to the size required, verifying the biblical account.

When the Queen of Sheba came to Jerusalem, she was overawed both by Solomon's wisdom and by the wealth and the magnificence of the Temple (1 Kings 10:4–7). In 1925, the Illinois Society of Architects estimated that the total cost of Solomon's Temple was the equivalent of an astonishing $87 billion! [12] In US dollar terms at the beginning of the twenty-first century its value could easily exceed one thousand billion dollars!

The *Shekinah* Glory of God

When the Ark of the Covenant was installed in the Most Holy Place in the Temple, the Lord filled the Temple with a cloud:

> *'The glory of the LORD filled the Temple. And the priests could not enter the House of the LORD, because the glory of the LORD had filled the LORD's House.'*
>
> (2 Chronicles 7:1–2)

The Lord then proclaimed:

> ' *"For now I have chosen and sanctified this House, that My name may be there forever; and My eyes and My heart will be there perpetually."* '   (2 Chronicles 7:16)

He reiterated the Davidic Covenant, and warned Israel of the consequences of turning away from Him:

> ' *"... and this House which I have sanctified for My name I will cast out of My sight, and will make it to be a proverb and a byword among all nations."* '   (2 Chronicles 7:20)

Tragically, history tells us that this is exactly what happened. Not once, but twice.

The spiritual decline of the nation began with the King himself.

> *'But King Solomon loved many foreign women ... from the nations of whom the Lord had said to the children of Israel, "You shall not intermarry with them ... For surely they will turn away your hearts after their gods." Solomon clung to these in love.'*   (1 Kings 11:1–2)

The chastisement of God fell upon the house of David (see 1 Kings 11–12), and Israel became divided into two kingdoms after Solomon's death.

The Demise of the Kingdom of Israel

Only two tribes, Benjamin and Judah, stayed with the Davidic dynasty in Jerusalem under the rule of King Solomon's son, Rehoboam. This southern kingdom became known as Judah. The ten northern tribes, which continued to be known as Israel, voted to have a former servant of Solomon as their king – a man called Jeroboam.

Jeroboam, however, was frightened by the prospect of losing the loyalty of his subjects to Rehoboam in the south, and set about preventing them going – as some did – to Jerusalem to worship the Lord, in accordance with *Torah*. To consolidate his position as King of Israel, Jeroboam set up an alternative religious system, with centres of worship at the southern and northern extremities of his kingdom.

> *'The king ... made two calves of gold, and said to the people, "It is too much for you to go up to Jerusalem. Here are your gods, O Israel, which brought you up from the land of Egypt!" And he set up one in Bethel, and the other he put in Dan. Now this thing became a sin, for the people went to worship before the one as far as Dan.'* (1 Kings 12:28–30)

Most of the generations of kings that followed Jeroboam in the north and Rehoboam in the south practised idolatry. Consequently both the kingdoms of Israel and Judah plunged into immorality and social disorder. The Lord continued to plead with them through the prophets:

> *' "Come now, and let us reason together,"*
> *Says the LORD,*
> *"Though your sins are like scarlet,*
> *They shall be as white as snow;*
> *Though they are red like crimson,*
> *They shall be as wool.*
> *If you are willing and obedient,*
> *You shall eat the good of the land;*
> *But if you refuse and rebel,*
> *You shall be devoured by the sword";*
> *For the mouth of the LORD has spoken.'* (Isaiah 1:18–20)

The judgement of the Lord fell upon Israel first, in the year 722 BCE (Before the Christian Era) as the Assyrians decimated the northern kingdom. They took many of the Israelis captive and scattered them to the corners of the Assyrian Empire.

> *'The LORD was very angry with Israel, and removed them from His sight; there was none left but the tribe of Judah alone. Also Judah did not keep the commandments of the LORD their God, but walked in the statutes of Israel which they made.'* (2 Kings 17:18–19)

Judgement upon Judah

A few years later the Assyrians invaded the southern kingdom and took the fortified cities of Judah, and it looked as
though Jerusalem would suffer the same fate. However,
Hezekiah, who was one of only a handful of Judah's twenty
kings to walk with the Lord, was reigning in Jerusalem at
the time. He avoided the capture of the city by giving the
Assyrian king a ransom, which was paid for from the Temple
treasures. When Assyria invaded a second time, the situation
looked even more threatening as the armies of Sennacherib
faced Jerusalem. King Hezekiah tore his clothes, covered
himself with sackcloth and ashes, entered the Temple and
pleaded with the Lord for mercy and deliverance. Judah
witnessed a miraculous victory when the Angel of the
Lord killed 180,000 men in the Assyrian camp, and Hezekiah
was granted peace for the rest of his reign (see 2 Kings
18–20.)

After Hezekiah's death, the Davidic dynasty in Judah
continued for another century or so. All of the successive
kings, except one, lived in rebellion against the God of
Israel and consequently Jerusalem's great wealth all but
disappeared as the Lord allowed the city and its treasures to
be plundered by the Assyrians, the Egyptians and finally the
Babylonians. It was only King Josiah who walked with the
Lord and brought the nation to repentance, thus restoring
the covenant made under Moses. However, this temporary
spiritual revival under Josiah only brought a stay of the
execution of God's judgement that had been prophesied
(2 Kings 22:15–20 and 23:25–27).

> *'And the* Lord *said, "I will also remove Judah from My sight,
> as I have removed Israel, and will cast off this city Jerusalem
> which I have chosen, and the house of which I said, 'My
> name shall be there.'"'*   (2 Kings 23:27)

The prophet Jeremiah also had prophesied:

> *'Judah shall be carried away captive, all of it.'*
>   (Jeremiah 13:19)

The Destruction of Jerusalem by Nebuchadnezzar

The words had scarcely left the prophet's lips when King Nebuchadnezzar of Babylon attacked Jerusalem and took a third of its people captive, including its newly installed eighteen-year-old king, Jehoiachin. This first wave of the Babylonian captivity took place in the year 606 BCE.

In 597 BCE the Babylonian king attacked Jerusalem again, taking more people captive. Among these was the prophet Ezekiel. From Babylon he recorded a vision in which he saw the *Shekinah* glory of God depart from the Temple and the Holy City:

> *'Then the glory of the* LORD *went up from the cherub, and paused over the threshold of the Temple ... And the glory of the* LORD *went up from the midst of the city...'*
>
> (Ezekiel 10:4 and 11:23)

On the ninth day of Av in the year 3174 in the Jewish Calendar (586 BCE in the Gregorian calendar), King Nebuchadnezzar attacked Jerusalem for the third time. His armies completely destroyed the Temple and the city, and took the remaining inhabitants captive to Babylon.

The Babylonian Captivity

The very heart and soul of the Jewish nation had been torn apart. In their captivity, the Jews yearned for Jerusalem.

> *'By the rivers of Babylon,*
> *There we sat down, yea, we wept*
> *When we remembered Zion...*
> *For there those who carried us away captive required of us a*
>   *song,*
> *And those who plundered us required of us mirth,*
> *Saying "Sing us one of the songs of Zion!"*
> *How shall we sing the* LORD*'s song*
> *In a foreign land?*
> *If I forget you, O Jerusalem,*

Let my right hand forget her skill!
If I do not remember you,
Let my tongue cling to the roof of my mouth –
If I do not exalt Jerusalem
Above my chief joy.'   (Psalm 137:1, 3–6)

This psalm was to become the heartfelt cry of every Jewish person for the next two-and-a-half millennia. This lament, which had its beginnings in the Babylonian exile, was to continue through the two thousand years of Israel's longest night, the *Diaspora*.[13] It was a cry that was to continue until that eventful day in the Six-Day War when a divided Jerusalem was reunited under Jewish sovereignty. Then, in the year 5752 in the Jewish calendar, the emotive words of Psalm 137 were incorporated into The Jerusalem Covenant.

The Babylonian exile, however, had a predetermined time span. The prophet Jeremiah, who had predicted the captivity, had also been told by the Lord how long it would last:

'For thus says the LORD: After seventy years are completed at Babylon, I will visit you and perform My good word toward you, and cause you to return to [Jerusalem].'
(Jeremiah 29:10)

Daniel the prophet, also in exile, discovered this prophecy when the seventy years were nearly at an end.

'I, Daniel, understood by the books the number of the years specified by the word of the LORD, given through Jeremiah the prophet, that He would accomplish seventy years in the desolations of Jerusalem.'   (Daniel 9:2)

As a result of this, Daniel gave himself to fasting, prayer and seeking repentance on behalf of the people (Daniel 9:3–19).

The Decree of Cyrus, King of Persia

At the end of the predetermined seventy years, the Persians overthrew the Babylonian Empire. The new Persian King,

Cyrus, allowed the Jews to return to their beloved city to rebuild the Temple. The Bible records:

> *'King Cyrus issued a decree concerning the house of God at Jerusalem: "Let the house be rebuilt, the place where they offered sacrifices; and let the foundations of it be firmly laid."'* (Ezra 6:3 – see also 2 Chronicles 36:21–23)

Not only is this decree recorded in the Bible, but it is also found on an artefact known as the 'Cyrus Cylinder', which contains an account of the conquests of Cyrus when he overthrew the Babylonian Empire. Archaeologists believe that the artefact itself dates back to 538 or 539 BCE.[14]

An even more astonishing fact about the Cyrus Decree is that the prophet Isaiah had specifically named its author and predicted its content more than a hundred years before Cyrus was actually born:

> *'[The LORD] says of Cyrus, "He is My shepherd, and he shall perform all My pleasure, even saying to Jerusalem, 'You shall be built,' and to the Temple, 'Your foundation shall be laid.'"'* (Isaiah 44:28)

The Second Temple

And so, in 537 BCE, the first group of Jews returned to their beloved, albeit ruined city under the leadership of Zerubbabel. In 536 they began to rebuild the Temple, exactly seventy years after the first captives had been deported from Jerusalem. The second Temple, although it took twenty years to complete, had none of the splendour of its predecessor, built by King Solomon. Also, as far as we know, the *Shekinah* glory of the Lord never resided there in the same way.

In 530 King Cyrus died. His successors disregarded the decree he had given, and the Jews met with opposition and trouble in their attempts to rebuild Jerusalem. As a result, much of the city and the walls continued to lie in ruins after the Temple was finally completed and dedicated in 516 BCE.

In 457 a second wave of exiles returned to Jerusalem under the leadership of Ezra. This occurred in the reign of

Artaxerxes I, who permitted them to take back the gold and silver belonging to the Temple. Nevertheless, in Ezra 4:21 it is recorded that Artaxerxes forbade any further building in Jerusalem until he gave the command.

The Command to Restore and Build Jerusalem

In Nehemiah 2 an account is given of Nehemiah interceding with Artaxerxes I for permission to restore and rebuild the walls of Jerusalem. Nehemiah asked for confirmation in writing in the form of letters, and he records:

> *'And the king granted them to me according to the good hand of my God upon me.'*   (Nehemiah 2:8)

The following year Nehemiah arrived back in Jerusalem, with a third wave of exiles, to find the gates of the city burnt and the walls in heaps of rubble. Despite the opposition, construction of the walls was completed in fifty-two days. Nehemiah records:

> *'...when all our enemies heard of it, and all the nations around us saw these things, they were very disheartened in their own eyes; for they perceived this work was done by our God.'*   (Nehemiah 6:16)

Nehemiah, who had been appointed Governor of Judah by the Persian king, led a spiritual revival among those returning from Babylon, as they renewed the Mosaic Covenant and vowed to follow the Lord their God (Nehemiah 8–13).

By the time the city and the walls had been rebuilt, almost two generations had lived and died since Daniel had discovered Jeremiah's prophecy concerning the seventy years' captivity, and the subsequent return of the first Jews to Jerusalem. This event, and the decree of Artaxerxes that allowed it to happen, were to prove prophetically significant.

The Revelation of the 'Seventy Weeks'

The Jewish prophet Daniel had been deported to Babylon with the first exiles in 606 BCE. At the time he was just sixteen years old. As well as playing a significant role in government during the exile, he became God's prophetic mouthpiece to the Gentile and Jewish world – declaring the Lord's contemporary, future and eternal purposes.

In the Jewish Scriptures, for some reason, the Book of Daniel is not included in *Nevi'im* (the Prophets), but in *Kethuvim* (the Writings), along with Psalms, Proverbs, Ezra, Nehemiah, Chronicles and some other books. Yet Daniel's credentials as a prophet are vindicated by history. He accurately predicted the fall of the Babylonian, Persian, Greek and Roman Empires that took place in the centuries that followed. He also predicted the destruction and desecration caused by Antiochus Epiphanes, who defiled the Temple in the second century BCE. Many other prophecies given to him were fulfilled in the minutest detail.

The Scriptures tell us that Daniel's intercession near the end of the seventy-year period of the Babylonian exile played an important part in the fulfilment of Jeremiah's prophecy. As previously noted, Daniel set his face toward the Lord God with fasting, sackcloth and ashes in seeking repentance for his people (Daniel 9:1–19).

While he was praying, Daniel received a visitation from the angel Gabriel. This remarkable encounter is recorded in Daniel 9:20–27:

> [20] *'Now while I was speaking, praying and confessing my sin and the sin of my people Israel, and presenting my supplication before the LORD my God for the holy mountain of my God,*
>
> [21] *yes, while I was speaking in prayer, the man Gabriel, whom I had seen in the vision at the beginning, being caused to fly swiftly, reached me about the time of the evening offering.*
>
> [22] *And he informed me, and talked with me, and said, "O Daniel, I have now come forth to give you skill to understand.*
>
> [23] *"At the beginning of your supplications the command went out, and I have come to tell you, for you are greatly beloved; therefore consider the matter, and understand the vision:*

[24] *"Seventy weeks are determined*
For your people and your holy city,
To finish the transgression,
To make an end of sins,
To make reconciliation for iniquity,
To bring in everlasting righteousness,
To seal up vision and prophecy,
And to anoint the Most Holy.

[25] *"Know therefore and understand,*
That from the going forth of the command
To restore and build Jerusalem
Until Messiah the Prince,
There shall be seven weeks and sixty-two weeks;
The street shall be built again, and the wall,
Even in troublesome times.

[26] *"And after the sixty-two weeks*
Messiah shall be cut off, but not for Himself;
And the people of the prince who is to come
Shall destroy the city and the sanctuary.
The end of it shall be with a flood,
And till the end of the war desolations are determined.

[27] *"Then he shall confirm a covenant*
with many for one week;
But in the middle of the week
He shall bring an end to sacrifice and offering.
And on the wing of abominations shall be one who
makes desolate,
Even until the consummation, which is determined,
Is poured out on the desolate."'   (Daniel 9:20–27)

Examining the Prophecy of the 'Seventy Weeks'

This is perhaps the most far-reaching and comprehensive single prophecy concerning God's timetable for the Jewish people, the Holy City and the coming of the Messiah that is recorded in the *Tanakh*. It is one of the very few prophecies in the Bible which has a definite time-clock attached to it. Another is, of course, Jeremiah's prophecy, which we have just considered, foretelling a seventy-year period for the

Babylonian exile. In Chapter 9 we will discuss a third prophecy with a specific time span which is also found in both Daniel and the Book of Revelation and relates to the end-times.

Let us first of all examine what is meant by the expression 'seventy weeks'. Many Bible scholars believe that the time element here has to do with years rather than days of the week.[15] If this line of interpretation is followed, one 'week' would be equivalent to seven years. Therefore the time period in this prophecy would extend through seventy 'sevens' of years, amounting to a total of 490 years.

Next, let us consider what will be accomplished for Daniel's people, the Jews, and the Holy City, Jerusalem, by the end of the 'seventy weeks'. In verse 24 it is possible to identify six things:

(1) Transgression will be finished, or more literally 'firmly restrained'.
(2) An end to sin will be made, or more literally sins would be 'shut up in prison'.
(3) Reconciliation will have been made for iniquity. This literally means that 'atonement' would have been made for the sin nature of humanity.
(4) Everlasting righteousness, or more literally 'an age of righteousness', will be brought in.
(5) The vision and prophecy will have been fulfilled.
(6) The Most Holy will have been anointed. A more accurate translation of the Hebrew text would be to 'anoint a most holy place'.

Verse 24 sums up the God of Israel's purpose for the Jewish people and the Holy City. It indicates that at the end of the 'seventy weeks' the Messianic Kingdom would be established. Bearing in mind that Daniel was given this vision towards the end of the seventy-year period of the Babylonian captivity and that Jerusalem lay in ruins at that time, in verses 25 to 27 we can identify a number of specific events that would happen within the time frame of this prophecy:

(1) Jerusalem would be restored and rebuilt.
(2) After 'sixty-nine weeks' the Messiah would be killed.
(3) The city (Jerusalem) and the sanctuary (the Temple) would again be destroyed.

(4)   A covenant would be confirmed with or for many.
(5)   In the middle of the final week 'he' would bring about
      the end of the sacrifices and offerings.
(6)   The wrath of God is poured out on the desolator.

There are a number of different theories as to how this prophecy may have been fulfilled, or might yet be – particularly in relation to the final or seventieth week. It is important to state, though, that there is broad consensus among Evangelical[16] Christians concerning the fulfilment of the first sixty-nine weeks, even though there are differences with regard to the detail of the timetable of its fulfilment. The difficulty arises from the fact that after two thousand years, or more, it is virtually impossible to prove beyond doubt the precise date when some of the key historical events related to the prophecy actually took place. Notwithstanding this fact, the conclusion regarding the person at the centre of the prophecy is not only universal, but it is unmistakable.

Let us now consider in more detail the fulfilment of events predicted in this remarkable prophecy.

In verse 25 the prophecy speaks of a command *'to restore and build Jerusalem'*. This command sets the clock ticking – it marks the beginning of the 'seventy weeks'. The possible fulfilment of this is recorded in Nehemiah 2:1, and occurred *'in the month of Nisan in the twentieth year of King Artaxerxes'*.[17] Many historians believe this took place in the year 445 BCE.[18] Daniel's prophecy stated that the street and the wall would be built again in times of trouble, and this is exactly what happened. Nehemiah 4:17 tells us,

> *'Those who built on the wall, and those who carried burdens, loaded themselves so that with one hand they worked at construction, and with the other held a weapon.'*

The 'Seven Weeks' and the 'Sixty-two Weeks'

The next part of the prophecy tells us that from the time of *'the command to restore and build Jerusalem until Messiah the Prince'* there would be 'seven weeks' and 'sixty-two weeks' – a total of sixty-nine 'weeks', or 483 years. The prophecy goes on to say that: *'after the sixty-two weeks Messiah shall be cut off'*. The Hebrew word translated 'cut off' is the common word used in Mosaic Law, which simply means 'to be killed'. The implication of the term is not just that the Messiah would be killed, but that He would die a penal death by execution. The text goes on to tell us the Messiah would be cut off, *'but not for Himself'*.[19] The possible implication here is that His death would be substitutionary, i.e. on behalf of others. The fulfilment of this prophecy is well documented in the New Testament and also by the secular historian, Josephus. The timing of its fulfilment is particularly significant. Where the text says that Messiah would be cut off 'after' the 'sixty-two weeks' (a total of sixty-nine 'weeks', as there has been a previous seven 'weeks') – it can mean either **immediately after** or **some time after** the period of 'sixty-nine weeks' is finished. There are a number of theories concerning what happened at the termination of the 'sixty-nine weeks'. One of the more notable is a theory put forward by Robert Anderson KCB LL.D. He has made some very interesting calculations based on the prophetic year being 360 days in length, as are most years in the Hebrew calendar. Calculating from the first day of Nisan, which he pinpointed as the day that Artaxerxes gave the command to restore and rebuild Jerusalem, he found that the 'sixty-nine weeks', which would amount to 483 years of 360 days each, terminated on the very day that Jesus of Nazareth rode triumphantly through the cheering multitudes into Jerusalem.[20] As we shall see shortly, this event had particular prophetic significance.

Four days later at Passover, at the demand of the Jewish Sanhedrin, Jesus of Nazareth was put to death by the Romans.

Furthermore, verse 26 goes on to tell us that some time after the Messiah was cut off, the city and the sanctuary would again be destroyed.

Who Is the Messiah?

Whether or not we can verify the precision of the dates in Sir Robert Anderson's calculations – or the calculations of others in regard to this prophecy – of one thing we can be certain:

Daniel showed that the Messiah would be here on earth 483 years after the decree to restore and rebuild Jerusalem, and some time before the city was again destroyed. The prophecy also states very clearly that the Messiah would be killed.

Allowing for the different theories in pinpointing the start and finish of the sixty-nine week period *'until Messiah the Prince'* means that the Messiah spoken of by Daniel must have been alive on earth at some time between the years 6 BCE and 33 CE.

In his booklet *The Messianic Time Table*, Messianic Hebrew scholar, Dr Arnold Fruchtenbaum, comes to the following conclusion:

> 'If Messiah was not on earth 483 years after a decree was issued to rebuild Jerusalem, then Daniel was a false prophet and his book has no business being in the Hebrew Scriptures. But if Daniel was correct, and his prophecy was fulfilled, then who was the Messiah of whom he spoke?'

There is only one Person in history whose life on earth coincides with the time frame set out in Daniel's prophecy and who fulfilled the criteria of the prophecy by being put to death. Not only did the Messiah fulfil the criteria of Daniel's prophecy of the 'Seventy Weeks', but He exactly fulfilled over three hundred predictions made by other prophets of Israel. Let us consider some of them.

Zechariah's Prophecy of the Coming King

Although younger, the prophet Zechariah was a contemporary of Daniel. Zechariah was among the first exiles to return from the Babylonian captivity to Jerusalem with Zerubbabel. He was given a number of visions concerning Jerusalem in the last days, which we shall look at later in the book. He was also given a prophecy of Israel's coming King entering Jerusalem:

> ' "Rejoice greatly, O daughter of Zion!
> Shout, O daughter of Jerusalem!

Behold, your King is coming to you;
He is just and having salvation,
Lowly and riding on a donkey,
A colt, the foal of a donkey."' (Zechariah 9:9)

This prophecy was remarkably and precisely fulfilled just over five hundred years later when the person whom Christians believe to be the Messiah, Jesus of Nazareth, rode into Jerusalem on a donkey. This is the event that Christians remember on 'Palm Sunday':

'So the disciples ... brought the donkey and the colt, laid their clothes on them, and set Him on them. A very great multitude spread their garments on the road; others cut down branches from the trees and spread them on the road. Then the multitudes who went before and those who followed cried out, saying:
"Hosanna to the Son of David!
'Blessed is He who comes in the name of the LORD!'
Hosanna in the highest!"' (Matthew 21:6–9)

Luke's Gospel records an exchange with the religious leaders who told Him, *'Rabbi, rebuke your followers.'* But He answered and said to them,

'I tell you that if these should keep silent, the stones would immediately cry out.' (Luke 19:40)

Clearly, the crowds were heralding Him as the Messiah and the rightful Heir to the throne of David that had been vacant for more than six hundred years. The prophet Zechariah certainly identified Him as such. And so Yeshua Hamashiach [21] entered Jerusalem through the gate opposite the Mount of Olives, on or near the site where the Golden Gate now stands.

The Messiah in the Temple

'And when He had come into Jerusalem, all the city was moved, saying, "Who is this?" So the multitudes said, "This

is [Yeshua], *the prophet from Nazareth of Galilee."* Then [Yeshua] *went into the temple of God . . .'*

(Matthew 21:10–12)

In doing so, He fulfilled yet another prophecy in the *Tanakh*:[22]

' *"And the Lord, whom you seek,*
Will suddenly come to His Temple,
Even the Messenger of the Covenant,
In whom you delight.
Behold, He is coming,"
Says the LORD *of Hosts.'*   (Malachi 3:1)

Over the next four days, in the lead-up to Passover, Yeshua taught in the Temple and confronted the religious leaders with their hypocrisy and blindness. All the while they plotted to kill Him. In one of His exchanges with the Pharisees in the Temple, Yeshua with great sorrow foretold the destruction that was to come upon Jerusalem.

'*O Jerusalem, Jerusalem, the one who kills the prophets and stones those who are sent to her! How often I wanted to gather you together, as a hen gathers her chicks under her wings, but you were not willing!*

'*See! Your house is left to you desolate;*

'*for I say to you, you shall see Me no more till you say,* "[Baruch ha ba b'shem Adonai!]" *– "Blessed is He who comes in the name of the* LORD*!"'*   (Matthew 23:37–39)

The Messiah Is Arrested

The corrupt religious leaders, with whom Yeshua had been at loggerheads, were able to have their way, and He was arrested in the early hours of the morning of the Day of Preparation for the Passover. An account of the event is found in Matthew 26, as well as in the Gospels of Mark, Luke and John.

Knowing what lay ahead, Yeshua had celebrated Passover with His disciples during the evening before. Afterwards, as they walked out of the city in the bright moonlight and crossed the Kidron Valley to the Mount of Olives, He told them they were all going to desert Him. Their desertion, according to Matthew's Gospel, would fulfil part of a prophecy found in Zechariah 13:7:

> ' "*Strike the Shepherd,*
> *And the sheep will be scattered.*" '

The exchange that followed between Yeshua and Peter is well known to Christians. Peter insisted that he would never deny his Master, but Yeshua told him that he would deny Him three times before the rooster crowed. A few hours later, as night turned to dawn, this happened precisely as Yeshua predicted. After his denial, Peter wept bitterly.

Earlier that night Judas Iscariot, one of Yeshua's own disciples, had betrayed the Messiah to the chief priests and Pharisees for thirty pieces of silver. This, again, had been prophesied by Zechariah five hundred years earlier (11:12). In the dead of night Judas led a large, heavily-armed contingent of the Temple Guard to the Garden of Gethsemane at the foot of the Mount of Olives. There they arrested the Messiah.

The Apostle John, who was an eyewitness, tells us what happened next:

> '*Jesus therefore, knowing that all these things would come upon Him, went forward and said to them, "Whom are you seeking?"*
> '*They answered Him, "Jesus the Nazarene."*
> '*Jesus said to them, "I AM."*
> . . . '*Then – when He said to them "I AM" – they drew back and fell to the ground.*'
> (John 18:4–6; literal translation from the Greek text)

What the Messiah had said to them, in effect, was what the God of Abraham, Isaac and Jacob had said to Moses from the burning bush. The awesomeness of the name of the Almighty, now given to His Anointed One, hit them with such force and conviction when the Messiah spoke out that they fell to the ground.

Gospel writer Mark records the following remark by Yeshua:

> *'Have you come out, as against a robber, with swords and clubs to take Me? I was daily with you in the Temple teaching, and you did not take Me. But the Scriptures must be fulfilled.'*
> (Mark 14:48–49)

Matthew's account reflects the futility of this heavily armed presence. He records Yeshua's preceding remark:

> *'Do you not think I cannot now pray to My Father, and He will provide Me with more than twelve legions of angels?'*
> (Matthew 26:53)

The implication of this is crucial. For centuries the Christian Church establishment has accused, condemned and persecuted the Jewish people for what they did to the Messiah. While it is undeniable that the religious leaders of Israel at that time, in conjunction with the Roman authorities, were responsible for putting Yeshua to death, this and many other passages of the New Testament clearly teach that He went to 'the cross' of His own volition, to atone for the sins of the world.

The Apostle John confirms this, for he records Yeshua's earlier words to the Pharisees:

> *'I am the good shepherd. The good shepherd gives His life for the sheep. ... As the Father knows Me, even so I know the Father; and I lay down My life for the sheep. ... No one takes it from Me, but I lay it down of Myself. I have power to lay it down, and I have power to take it again. This command I have received from My Father.'* (John 10:11, 15, 18)

Later, as the Jewish Messiah hung with nail-pierced hands and feet on a Roman execution stake, He said:

> *'Father, forgive them, for they do not know what they do.'*
> (Luke 23:34)

If Yeshua, who is Head of the Christian Church, forgave those who crucified Him, then what right has any Christian to condemn the Jewish people for what they did?

> *'For God so loved the world that He gave His only begotten
> Son, that whoever believes in Him should not perish but have
> everlasting life.'*   (John 3:16)

It is obvious, then, that the accusation of the alleged
crime of 'deicide', i.e. 'killing the Son of God', which has
been levelled at the Jewish people by sections of Christendom, has no theological foundation whatsoever – especially
when one takes into account what happened three days later.
Clearly, without the death and resurrection of the Messiah
there would be no atonement for sin for either Jew or
Gentile.

The Christian church establishment at large has distorted
the New Testament, misrepresented the Person of the
Messiah (at least to some degree) and, in His name,
committed the most horrendous crimes against the Jewish
people for at least the last seventeen centuries. The time for
seeking forgiveness is long overdue.

The Apostle Matthew's account of the arrest of Yeshua
concludes thus:

> *'In that hour* [Yeshua] *said to the multitudes, "... all this
> was done that the Scriptures of the prophets might be
> fulfilled." Then all the disciples forsook Him and fled.'*
> (Matthew 26:55–56)

'Strike the Shepherd, and the Sheep Will Be Scattered'

Part of Zechariah's prophecy was fulfilled by the arrest of
Yeshua, but its complete fulfilment would stretch over a long
period of time.

Zechariah clearly identifies who the Shepherd is. In verse 6
of chapter 13 he prophesies:

> *'And someone will say to him, "What are these wounds in
> your hands?" Then he will answer, "Those with which I was
> wounded in the house of my friends."'*

He continues:

> ' "Awake, O sword, against My Shepherd,
> Against the Man who is My Companion,"
> Says the LORD of Hosts.
> "Strike the Shepherd,
> And the sheep will be scattered;
> Then I will turn My hand against the little ones.
> And it shall come to pass in all the land,"
> Says the LORD,
> "That two-thirds in it shall be cut off and die,
> But one-third shall be left in it:
> I will bring the one-third through the fire,
> Will refine them as silver is refined,
> And test them as gold is tested.
> And they will call on My name,
> And I will answer them.
> And I will say, 'This is My people';
> And each one will say, 'The LORD is my God.' " '
>
> (Zechariah 13:7–9)

This prophecy speaks of the calamity that was to befall Israel following the 'striking of the Lord's Shepherd'. It tells us, too, of the ultimate restoration of the sheep to the Lord – which is yet to be completed – and gives us an insight into the heart of God towards His ancient covenant people. Clearly His desire is to bring them to a place where they will be united with Him in heart, mind and spirit. This prophecy also reveals something more about the Shepherd. He is described here as the Man who is the Companion of the Lord of Hosts. Could it be that this Man is the One whom the Apostle John records as saying: *'Before Avraham came into being, I AM'*, and *'I and the Father are one'* (John 8:58 and 10:30, Jewish New Testament)?

The Messiah Is Cut Off

The Messiah's death, predicted by Zechariah and Daniel, was confirmed by other prophets of Israel. Isaiah had declared:

'For He was cut off from the land of the living;
For the transgression of my people He was stricken.'
(Isaiah 53:8)

Isaiah 53, penned nearly 750 years before it was fulfilled, is the most expressive of all the prophecies concerning the death of the Messiah. It is worth commenting that the text of the Isaiah scrolls, discovered among the Dead Sea Scrolls in 1948, was found to be virtually identical to that which we have in our Bibles today. And those particular Isaiah scrolls pre-dated the time of Yeshua by at least one hundred years.

At this point, it is well worth pausing to read Isaiah 53 and then to meditate upon how He suffered for us all.

The Gospel accounts speak of Yeshua's silence during interrogation by both the Jewish religious leaders and the Romans, as foretold by Isaiah:

'He was oppressed and He was afflicted,
Yet He opened not His mouth;
He was led as a lamb to the slaughter,
And as a sheep before its shearers is silent,
So He opened not His mouth.' (Isaiah 53:7)

'And He, bearing His cross, went out to a place called "the Place of a Skull", which is called in Hebrew, Golgotha, where they crucified Him, and two others with Him, one on either side, and [Yeshua] *in the middle.'* (John 19:17–18)

'And when they crucified Him, they divided His garments, casting lots for them to determine what every man should take. ... And the inscription of His crime was written above:
THE KING OF THE JEWS
'...And those who passed by blasphemed Him, wagging their heads and saying, "...save Yourself, and come down from the cross!"

'Likewise the chief priests also, together with the scribes, mocked and said among themselves, "He saved others; Himself He cannot save. Let the Mashiach, *the King of Israel descend now from the cross, that we may see and believe." ...*

'Now when the sixth hour had come, there was darkness over the whole land until the ninth hour. And at the ninth

> *hour* Yeshua *cried out with a loud voice, saying, "Eloi, Eloi, lama sabachthani?" which is translated, "My God, My God, why have you forsaken me?"'*   (Mark 15:24, 26, 29, 30–34)

This is just part of the account of the torment of Yeshua as He hung dying on that Roman execution stake. A thousand years earlier, King David had been given prophetic insight into His suffering and in a psalm had expressed so much of the agony and rejection Yeshua must have felt as He hung there as our sin-bearer. The detail is astonishing.

> *'My God, My God,*
> *Why have You forsaken Me?*
> *Why are You so far from helping Me,*
> *And from the words of My groaning? . . .*
> *All those who see Me laugh Me to scorn;*
> *They shoot out the lip, they shake the head, saying,*
> *"He trusted in the LORD, let Him rescue Him;*
> *Let Him deliver Him, since He delights in Him!" . . .*
> *They gape at me with their mouths,*
> *As a raging and roaring lion.*
> *I am poured out like water,*
> *And all my bones are out of joint;*
> *My heart is like wax;*
> *It has melted within Me.*
> *My strength is dried up like a potsherd,*
> *And My tongue clings to My jaws;*
> *You have brought me to the dust of death.*
> *For dogs have surrounded Me;*
> *The assembly of the wicked has enclosed Me.*
> *They pierced My hands and My feet;*
> *I can count all My bones.*
> *They look and stare at Me.*
> *They divide My garments among them,*
> *And for My clothing they cast lots.'*
>
> (Psalm 22:1, 7–8, 13–18)

As previously suggested, Roman crucifixion was generally carried out by nails being driven through the victim's hands and feet fastening him to an execution stake, usually in the form of a wooden cross. The Apostle John records Yeshua's encounter with His disciples following the resurrection when they were shown the scars where the nails had pierced His hands. All four of the Gospel writers record the fact that the soldiers who crucified Him cast lots for His clothing. Was this psalm merely another 'accident of history' in which the Jewish Scriptures happened to coincide with an event hundreds of years later, or was it a prophetic word given to King David with astonishing detail by the Spirit of the Lord concerning his Greater Son?

Passover Lambs to the Slaughter

Was it another coincidence that, at the same time as Yeshua was being nailed to the cross, the Jewish people throughout Jerusalem, Judea and beyond were slaughtering their Passover lambs, in accordance with the *Torah*? Was it not the shed blood of the lamb upon the door-posts and the lintel that caused the judgement of God to pass over the Israelites? John the Baptist had uttered the prophetic words:

> *'Behold the Lamb of God, who takes away the sins of the world.'* (John 1:29) [23]

and the prophet Isaiah had written:

> *'He was wounded for our transgressions,*
> *He was bruised for our iniquities;*
> *The chastisement for our peace was upon Him,*
> *And by His stripes we are healed.*
> *All we like sheep have gone astray;*
> *We have turned, every one, to his own way;*
> *And the* Lord *has laid on Him the iniquity of us all.'*
> (Isaiah 53:5–6)

The Holy of Holies Revealed, the New Covenant Ratified

It was around three o'clock in the afternoon on the fourteenth day of the month of Nisan. The Land of Israel had been bathed in a mysterious and inexplicable darkness for the previous three hours. The atmosphere would have been tense as the crowds surged through the Temple courtyards on the busiest day of the year. The noise and the smell must have been incredible as the blood flowed from the lambs that were being slaughtered for the Feast of Passover.

Several hundred yards away from the Temple, another crowd was gathered on the ridge of Mount Moriah. They stood in the darkness outside the city wall, at the place called Golgotha. Perhaps they were unaware that the gloom surrounding them was a sign from heaven that had been foretold 750 years earlier by the prophet Amos:

> ' "And it shall come to pass in that day," says the Lord GOD,
> "That I will make the sun go down at noon,
> And I will darken the earth in broad daylight;
> I will turn your feasts into mourning." '   (Amos 8:9–10)

They stared at the tortured figure of the Lamb of God as a sponge full of sour wine was put to His lips.

> 'When Jesus had received the sour wine He said, "It is finished!" And bowing His head He gave up His spirit.'
> (John 19:30)

> 'And behold, the veil of the temple was torn in two from top to bottom; and the earth quaked.'   (Matthew 27:51)

In that moment, yet another of Zechariah's prophecies was fulfilled:

> 'And I took my staff, Beauty, and cut it in two, that I may break the covenant which I had made with all the peoples. So it was broken on that day.'   (Zechariah 11:10–11)

The Mosaic Covenant, which the Lord had made with the people of Israel at the foot of Mount Sinai and which symbolised the separation of humanity from God because of sin, had finally been broken. The massive sixty-foot-high, ten-inch-thick curtain that had separated the Holy of Holies from the Holy Place was torn asunder. Tradition tells us that it had taken three hundred priests to hang it on its hooks and would have taken twelve pairs of oxen to pull it apart. So it was not torn from bottom to top by the might of men, but from top to bottom by the finger of God. And it wasn't something that happened in the dead of night when nobody was around; it happened on the busiest day of the year – *Erev Pesach* – when literally thousands of people and animals were packed into the Temple compound.

'It is finished!' cried Yeshua as He breathed His last and became the atoning sacrifice for the sin of the whole world. The Holy of Holies, into which the High Priest was only allowed to venture but once a year carrying the blood of an innocent creature to atone for the sins of Israel, was now open to all.

Just over thirty years later, one of the New Testament writers spelled out the theological implications of the torn veil:

> '[Messiah] *came as High Priest of the good things to come, with the greater and more perfect tabernacle not made with hands, that is, not of this creation. Not with the blood of goats and calves, but with His own blood He entered the Most Holy Place once for all, having obtained eternal redemption.'* (Hebrews 9:11–12)

And so the Mosaic Covenant had been superseded by the New Covenant. Only the night before His death, when Yeshua had celebrated the Passover Seder with His disciples, He held up the Cup of Redemption after the meal and said:

> *'Drink from it, all of you. For this is My blood of the new covenant, which is shed for many for the remission of sins.'* (Matthew 26:27–28)

The Messiah Conquers Death

Three days later, the New Covenant was confirmed. All four Gospels in the New Testament give the account of the resurrection of Yeshua. A thousand years earlier King David had also foretold that death would not hold Him:

> *'For You will not leave My soul in Sheol,*
> *Nor will You allow Your Holy One to see corruption.*
> *You will show me the path of life;*
> *In Your presence is fullness of joy;*
> *At Your right hand are pleasures forevermore.'*
>
> (Psalm 16:10–11)

The resurrection of the dead is a central belief of both the Jewish and Christian faiths. When Yeshua rose from the dead, He paved the way for Hosea's prophecy to be fulfilled:

> *' "I will ransom them from the power of the grave;*
> *I will redeem them from death.*
> *O Death, where is your sting?*
> *O Hades, where is your victory?" '*   (Hosea 13:14)

Again, is it merely coincidence that the day Yeshua rose from the dead was the Jewish Feast of Firstfruits? The Apostle Paul takes up this theme in his great passage on the significance of the resurrection:

> *'Now* [Mashiach] *is risen from the dead, and has become the firstfruits of those who have fallen asleep ... For as in Adam all die, even so in* [Mashiach] *all shall be made alive.'*
>
> (1 Corinthians 15:20, 22)

The Messiah Ascends to Heaven

Forty days after His resurrection, the disciples of Yeshua were standing with Him on the Mount of Olives, asking Him about the restoration of the kingdom of Israel. Then, while they were watching, a cloud received Him, and He was taken up out of their sight. Two angels appeared and said to them:

> *'Men of Galilee, why do you stand gazing into heaven? This same* [Yeshua], *who was taken up from you into heaven, will so come in like manner as you saw Him go into heaven.'*
>
> (Acts 1:11)

Mark's Gospel tells us that Yeshua was received up into heaven and sat down at the right hand of God. Again, King David was given prophetic insight:

> *'The LORD said to my Lord, "Sit at My right hand,*
> *Till I make Your enemies Your footstool."'*   (Psalm 110:1)

And so the second event in Daniel's prophecy had come to pass. The Man identified in Daniel 9:26 as the Messiah was put to death. The Messiah's death, which was also predicted in other parts of the *Tanakh*, was followed by His resurrection from the dead, and ascension to the right hand of the Almighty.

We have looked at only a handful of the prophecies He fulfilled in His life in the flesh, here on earth. In all, over three hundred prophecies found in the *Tanakh* – all of which were written between 500 and 1500 years earlier – were fulfilled in the conception, birth, life, death and resurrection of Yeshua. If you stop and think about it, the issue of Yeshua's Messiahship is infinitely beyond the mathematical possibilities of chance. Perhaps you might consider it to be more like an absolute certainty?

And yet there are still many more prophecies to be fulfilled when the Messiah returns as the King of Israel to rule the earth from the throne of David in Jerusalem. Then He will return not as the Saviour of the world, but as the Judge of all humanity; not as the Lamb of God, but as the Lion of Judah.

However, the promised Messiah didn't just come to earth, atone for the sin of the human race, and then disappear back into heaven again leaving a power vacuum behind Him. Shortly before He departed for heaven, Yeshua said to His disciples:

> *'Behold, I send the Promise of My Father upon you; but tarry*
> *in the city of Jerusalem until you are endued with power from*
> *on high.'*   (Luke 24:49)

Earlier He had told them:

> *'When He, the Spirit of truth has come, He will guide you into all truth. He will convict the world of sin, and of righteousness, and of judgment.'* (John 16:13, 8)

Just fifty days after that eventful Passover in Jerusalem, the city was once again packed with thousands of Jewish pilgrims who, in accordance with the *Torah*, had come to celebrate the Feast of *Shavu'ot*.[24] The Feast of Pentecost that year was to prove to be as eventful as *Pesach* had, seven weeks earlier. Once again, the New Covenant was confirmed as the Holy Spirit was poured out upon the followers of Yeshua. Jerusalem saw the fulfilment of another prophecy found in the ancient Jewish Scriptures:

> ' *"And it shall come to pass afterward*
> *That I will pour out My Spirit on all flesh;*
> *Your sons and daughters shall prophesy,*
> *Your old men shall dream dreams,*
> *Your young men shall see visions ... "'* (Joel 2:28)

The events of that momentous day are recorded in chapter 2 of the Book of the Acts of the Apostles in the New Testament. When the Law was given at the foot of Mount Sinai three thousand Israelis had perished; now three thousand Israelis received the new life in the Holy Spirit promised in the New Covenant, as they put their faith in their Messiah, Yeshua HaMashiach.

Indeed, that day the Kingdom of God came alive on earth – and remains so to this very day.

Daniel's 'Seventieth Week' Fulfilled?

We have considered the fulfilment of the first sixty-nine 'weeks' prophesied by Daniel which, as we noted, Evangelical Christians universally believe has been fulfilled with the death of Jesus Christ on the cross and the subsequent destruction of Jerusalem and the Temple. But what about the final 'seventieth week'? As previously mentioned, there are a number of different theories about this last seven-year period, but, whatever the theory, there is one crucial question around which they all revolve: has it been fulfilled?

The common view among most pre-millennial[25] Evangelical Christians is that an indefinable gap exists between the sixty-ninth and seventieth 'weeks' – i.e. the final 'week' has yet to be fulfilled at some time in the future. Undoubtedly there is a scriptural precedent for assuming that such a gap can exist between two parts of a prophecy being fulfilled.[26] However, another of the main arguments put forward for suggesting that the 'seventieth week' has yet to be fulfilled is that we haven't seen the complete and literal fulfilment of all six elements mentioned in Daniel 9:24, discussed earlier. In fact only one has been literally fulfilled – *'reconciliation for iniquity'* – through the atonement for sin by the death of the Messiah on the cross. The possible future fulfilment of this final phase of Daniel's prophecy of the 'seventy weeks' is one of the pillars of eschatology for the final years before the return of Yeshua Hamashiach to Jerusalem. We will discuss the eschatological implications of this in Chapter 9, and also in Appendix D.

The other major view is that the 'seventieth week' of Daniel has already been fulfilled. This view is popular among those who hold a 'post-millennial' or 'a-millennial' view of eschatology.[25] They believe that the prophecy of the 'seventy weeks' refers to Israel and, since God has finished with Israel and the covenants of promise now have their fulfilment in the Church, then the prophecy of the 'seventy weeks' must have been entirely fulfilled already. However, there are a number of Hebrew-speaking Messianic Jews who basically hold a 'pre-millennial' view of eschatology and who also believe that the 'seventy weeks' of Daniel were fulfilled in one continuous sequence, but for a very different reason. The argument they put forward is this: having closely studied the Hebrew text of verses 24 to 27 of Daniel 9, they do not believe that any of the English translations of the Bible – including the King James Version – truly reflect what the original Hebrew text actually says. This particularly applies to verses 24 and 27. Consequently, they believe the whole matter of the fulfilment of the 'seventieth week' has been open to misunderstanding, which in turn has led to misinterpretation of what the original text actually means.

Hebrew scholar Herman Goldwag believes that 'week sixty-nine' ended with the baptism of the Messiah, which took place around three-and-a-half years before His death. 'Week seventy' followed straight on from 'week sixty-nine', and Messiah's death, therefore, took place in the middle of the 'seventieth week', thus making the sacrifices and offerings in the Temple obsolete. The covenant spoken of in verse 27 is, in fact, the New Covenant foreshadowed by Jeremiah (31:31–34). This was the covenant identified by Yeshua when He raised the Cup of Redemption during the Passover Seder the night before His death and said:

> *'For this is My blood of the new covenant, which is shed for*
> *many for the remission of sins.'*   (Matthew 26:28)

It was this covenant that was ratified by the shed blood of the Messiah and confirmed by His resurrection and ascension, and the subsequent pouring out of the Holy Spirit at Pentecost. The 'seventieth week' concluded three-and-a-half years later when the gospel went beyond the people of Israel to the Gentiles, as described in chapter 10 of the Book of the Acts of the Apostles.

Herman Goldwag believes that verse 27 is an enlargement of verse 26, rather than something completely different. He understands the latter part of verse 27 to be talking about the destruction of the city and the sanctuary, which was fulfilled in 70 CE, but also to be predicting the ultimate fate of the Roman Empire.

In his book *Daniel's 70 Weeks Prophecy*, Herman Goldwag summarises what has been achieved by the fulfilment of the prophecy:

> 'The exact time of Messiah's first Advent; His mighty
> ministry; His cutting-off (crucifixion) thereby validating
> the New Covenant; His sending of the Holy Spirit "to
> restrain transgression" and empower the believers; His
> shedding of His blood in atonement "for iniquity", so
> making "an end of sins" and consequently bringing in

"everlasting righteousness"; His termination of "sacrifice and offering" by making "His soul an offering for sin" (Isaiah 53:10) as a paschal lamb; His establishing the New Covenant; His fulfilling in Himself many prophecies concerning Him, even to His death, thereby putting a seal (guarantee) on the fulfilment of all prophecies in the Scriptures; the anointing of the most Holy and the preaching of the gospel exclusively to the Jews until the conversion of Cornelius, the first Gentile, were all accomplished in the last (seventieth) "week of years". Thus "seventy weeks of years" were accomplished in one uninterrupted sequence.

'In conclusion, this wonderful prophecy, revealed by God to Daniel through the angel Gabriel, is so outstanding in its inclusion of all the main events concerning Messiah's first Advent, that it is unsurpassed by any other prophecy concerning Jesus Christ. It focuses our attention on the greatest drama ever to take place on the world scene.'[27]   (see Appendix A)

The Messiah's Prophecies Concerning Jerusalem

During His triumphal entry into Jerusalem, Yeshua was hailed by the multitudes as the Son of David. Not long before that He had been involved in a heated exchange with the religious leaders who sought to kill Him. His knowledge of the Jewish Scriptures was thorough and He would have known the detail of the covenant – the Land Covenant – His heavenly Father had made with the Israelis fifteen hundred years earlier in the Sinai desert.

But now, as the crowds cheered Him on, Yeshua had the glorious vista before Him of the city about which His Father had said:

> ' *"This is My resting place forever;*
> *Here I will dwell, for I have desired it."* '   (Psalm 132:14)

Perhaps He had all these things in His mind as He paused on the Mount of Olives. As tears began to fill His eyes and to roll down His cheeks, He uttered a prophetic cry:

> *'If you had known, even you, especially in this your day, the things that make for your peace! But now they are hidden from your eyes. For the days will come upon you when your enemies will build an embankment around you, surround you and close you in on every side, and level you and your children within you, to the ground; and they will not leave in you one stone upon another, because you did not know the time of your visitation.'*   (Luke 19:42–44)

Later, when talking privately to the twelve disciples about what would happen to Jerusalem and its inhabitants, He told them:

> *'They will fall by the edge of the sword, and be led away captive into all nations. And Jerusalem will be trampled by Gentiles until the times of the Gentiles are fulfilled.'*
>   (Luke 21:24)

The Destruction of Jerusalem by the Romans

Less than four decades later, in 66 CE, the Jewish Zealots rebelled against the Romans, eventually taking control of Jerusalem and Judea. Enraged by the Jewish revolt, the Roman Emperor, Nero, sent his best commander, Vespasian, with Rome's finest legions to crush the rebellion.

By the year 69, after years of bitter fighting, the Romans had retaken control of all areas except Jerusalem. Vespasian, who had just succeeded Nero as Emperor, put his son Titus in charge of the Jerusalem campaign.[28] The siege that followed was both terrifying and protracted, and many of Jerusalem's inhabitants died of starvation.

Finally, the Romans broke through the walls on the ninth day of Av in the Jewish calendar – the anniversary of the city's previous destruction by the Babylonians – in the year 3830 (70 CE). The prophecies concerning the destruction of Jerusalem given by Yeshua (Luke 19:42–44 and 21:20–24) were fulfilled to the letter.

The Jewish historian, Josephus, says that Titus had given specific orders that the Temple was to be left intact. However, a Roman soldier, acting on impulse, threw a torch through an archway of the Temple, and the tapestries inside caught alight. In the resulting inferno, the gold that was used to line the walls in this magnificent structure melted and disappeared into the crevices between the stones.[29] Afterward, the Romans tore the stones apart to retrieve the gold, thus fulfilling Yeshua's prophecy concerning the Temple given forty years earlier:

> *'Assuredly, I say to you, not one stone shall be left here upon another, that shall not be thrown down.'*   (Matthew 24:2)

Jerusalem was bathed in Jewish blood. Those who could escape the Roman armies fled. Most were either executed or taken off as slaves. A band of nine hundred Jews held out at Masada above the shores of the Dead Sea for a further three-and-a-half years, in a last heroic attempt to withstand the Romans. They committed mass suicide rather than be taken captive and enslaved. Altogether, more than one million Jewish people are estimated to have perished in the destruction of Jerusalem and the desolation of Judea.

Chapter 3

Jerusalem and the *Diaspora*

The *Diaspora* Begins

The links that bound Zion together had been shattered. The people had lost their Promised Land and beloved city once more.

The nation that had been without a reigning monarch upon the throne of David for nearly seven hundred years was now without the Temple, without offerings and sacrifices, and without the priesthood with all its garments, thus fulfilling the prophecy of Hosea:

> 'For the children of Israel shall abide many days without king or prince, without sacrifice or sacred pillar, without ephod or teraphim.' (Hosea 3:4)

Once more the City of Jerusalem and the Land of Israel became a desolation, with all but a small number of its people scattered like chaff before a mighty wind to the ends of the earth. As predicted by Daniel and the other prophets of Israel, the longest nightmare in Israel's history began. This nightmare had not only been predicted in *Nevi'im* (the Prophets) but *Torah* (the Law) as well. The Land Covenant warned:

> ' "... you shall be plucked from off the land which you go to possess. Then the LORD will scatter you among all peoples, from one end of the earth to the other, and there you shall serve other gods, which neither you or' your fathers have

known – wood and stone. And among those nations you shall find no rest, nor shall the sole of your foot have a resting place; but there the LORD will give you a trembling heart, failing eyes, and anguish of soul. Your life shall hang in doubt before you; you shall fear day and night, and have no assurance of life. In the morning you shall say, 'Oh, that it were evening!' And at evening you shall say, 'Oh, that it were morning!' because of the fear which terrifies your heart, and because of the sight which your eyes see."'

(Deuteronomy 28:63–67)

These horrific words, uttered by Moses 1500 years before the Romans destroyed Jerusalem, paint the most graphic picture of the fate that was to befall the Jewish people for the next nineteen centuries – culminating in the most terrible holocaust the world has ever known.

The Bar Kokhba Uprising

Although Jerusalem lay in ruins, the Romans did not actually forbid the Jews to settle in the area, and several dozen Jewish communities were established in Judea. Sixty years after the overthrow of Jerusalem, Shimon Bar Kokhba led a successful uprising against the Roman garrison stationed in what was left of Jerusalem. Hailed by some as the Messiah, he retook the city and held it for nearly three years.[30]

The Romans then recaptured Jerusalem in 135 CE and this time the city was utterly destroyed. The Roman Emperor, Hadrian, determined to prevent any further revolt, ordered the removal of any trace of the city that was so dear to the Jewish people. On 9 Av – the anniversary of the two previous destructions of the Holy City – Jerusalem was plowed over, and a new Roman city, called Aelia Capitolina, was built on its site, the Jews being forbidden to enter their beloved city.

Judea was given the Latin name 'Syria Palaestina' – anglicised to 'Palestine'[31] – to erase any Jewish connection to the land which the God of Israel calls His own. As a further act of desecration, a temple to the pagan god Jupiter was erected on Mount Moriah, where the House of the Lord had stood.

'The Desolation of Jerusalem'

Hundreds of years in advance, the Lord had given the prophets of Israel a graphic picture of the desolation that was to befall the Holy City in 135 CE. The prophet Micah had foretold:

> *'Zion shall be plowed like a field,*
> *Jerusalem shall become heaps of ruins,*
> *And the mountain of the temple*
> *Like the bare hills of the forest.'*   (Micah 3:12)

and Jeremiah had prophesied:

> *'How lonely sits the city*
> *That was full of people!*
> *How like a widow is she,*
> *Who was great among the nations!...*
> *Judah has gone into captivity,*
> *Under affliction and hard servitude;*
> *She dwells among the nations,*
> *She finds no rest;*
> *All her persecutors overtake her in dire straits.*
> *The roads to Zion mourn...*
> *Her adversaries have become the master.'*
> (Lamentations 1:1, 3, 4, 5 in part) [32]

These prophetic words paint the sad picture of Jerusalem's destiny for the next nineteen centuries or so. Indeed, as prophesied by Yeshua, the Gentiles trampled upon Jerusalem.

For more than two centuries after the Romans laid waste the Holy City, Jews were forbidden to settle in their ancient capital. A reprieve came in 362 CE when Emperor Julian – known as Julian the Apostate – succeeded Constantine and not only allowed the Jews back into Jerusalem, but encouraged them to rebuild the Temple, where he said he would join them in worship. [33] As the builders went to the foundations, an earthquake struck, apparently igniting reservoirs of trapped gases below the ground and destroyed all the building materials. Further attempts to rebuild the Temple were abandoned when Julian's short reign came to an end after twenty months. [34]

The Byzantine Period

During the fourth century CE, under Constantine, Christianity became the official religion in the Roman Empire. Christian churches replaced the pagan temples and Jerusalem became a religious centre for pilgrims. During this period the Church deliberately distanced itself from the Jewish roots of its faith. Much of the Church's dogma and practice departed from the teaching of the New Testament and 'Replacement Theology'[35] gained a stronghold, opening the door to anti-Semitism within the Church. After the Roman Empire was divided late in the fourth century, Eastern Byzantine rulers stepped up persecution of the Jews by trying to force them to convert to Christianity.

In the year 614 CE, the Persians captured Jerusalem with the help of the Jews, who were allowed to govern the city for three years.

In 629, the Byzantine Emperor Heraclius recaptured the city and took reprisal against the Jews for their 'treachery'.

Islamic Rule in Jerusalem

Many of the Jews survived to see Caliph Omar, a follower of the prophet Mohammed, overrun Jerusalem in 638, vanquishing the so-called 'Christian' empire. Seventy Jewish families were allowed to settle in a quarter of the city adjacent to the Western Wall. In 692, Caliph Abdul Malik completed the Dome of the Rock on the site where most Israeli archaeologists believe the Temple stood. Some years later, Caliph Walid II built the Al-Aqsa Mosque just south of the Dome of the Rock on the Temple Mount. The Islamic rulers, keenly aware of the importance of Jerusalem to both Jews and Christians, were fairly tolerant of their non-Moslem subjects, who continued to outnumber the Moslems in the land until the Crusaders were defeated five centuries later. The Moslems made it quite clear, however, that their 'religion was superior to the two older faiths, and would rule Jerusalem until Allah's judgement day'.[36]

Jerusalem Changes Hands Again and Again

In 1096 CE Pope Urban's Crusader armies arrived in the Holy
Land to expel the Moslem 'infidels'. In 1099 the Crusaders
plundered the city. It was a tragic period for Jerusalem's
inhabitants – untold numbers of both Moslems and Jews
were slaughtered by the Crusaders, and those that escaped
were forbidden to enter the Holy City. Ninety years later, the
Crusaders were defeated by the forces of the Kurdish general
Saladin who conquered the city in 1187. Islamic rule was re-
established in Jerusalem, which was then declared to be the
third holiest place in Islam, after Mecca and Medina.
However, the Jews were allowed to resettle in the Holy City
in what became known as the 'Jewish Quarter' near the
Western Wall. In 1212 a large contingent of Jewish people
arrived, including 300 rabbis from England and France.

From then until the War of Independence in 1948, the
Jewish Quarter in the Old City of Jerusalem was continuously
inhabited by a remnant of the sons of Abraham, Isaac and
Jacob.

In 1259 Tartar invaders ransacked Jerusalem, and then the
following year the Mameluk tribes took over and occupied
the Holy City. For the next two and a half centuries, the Holy
Land was ruled from either Cairo or Damascus. The tribes
frequently fought each other, and consequently the land was
never able to recover from its earlier wounds. If Zion had
been able to cry out, the words of the prophet Jeremiah
would have been their lament:

> ' "Is it nothing to you, all you who pass by?
> Behold and see
> If there is any sorrow like my sorrow,
> Which has been brought on me . . .
> The adversary has spread his hand
> Over all her pleasant things;
> For [Jerusalem] has seen the nations
>   enter her sanctuary." '   (Lamentations 1:12, 10)

Jerusalem was conquered yet again in 1516 by the rapidly
expanding Turkish Moslem Ottoman Empire under the
leadership of Suliman the Magnificent.

The City Walls Rebuilt, the Golden Gate Sealed

In 1535 Suliman rebuilt the walls of Jerusalem as they stand today. On the eastern side of the city he constructed a gate leading on to the Temple Mount, known as the Golden Gate. It was through the gate that previously stood on or near the site of this present Golden Gate that Yeshua, riding on a donkey, had entered into the Temple courtyard 1500 years earlier. Suliman had intended to enter through the Golden Gate with great pomp. For some reason, he suddenly changed his mind and ordered that the gate be sealed and should remain shut. The Book of Ezekiel contains a remarkable prophecy about the sealing of the eastern gate.

> *'Then He brought me back to the outer gate of the sanctuary which faces toward the east, but it was shut. And the* LORD *said to me, "This gate shall be shut; it shall not be opened, and no man shall enter by it, because the* LORD *God of Israel has entered by it; therefore it shall be shut."'*
>
> (Ezekiel 44:1–2)

Today, all gates of the Holy City are in daily use except the Golden Gate. Could it be that the Golden Gate has been sealed until the entry of the Messiah into Jerusalem? The prophet Ezekiel goes on:

> *'"As for the prince, because he is the prince . . . he shall enter by way of the vestibule of the gateway and go out the same way."'*
>
> (Ezekiel 44:3)

We shall see.

'Sackcloth and Ashes'

The Ottomans' occupation of Jerusalem was to last four hundred years. During the nineteenth century CE, the American author Mark Twain visited the Holy Land and vividly described what he saw.

> 'Palestine sits in sackcloth and ashes ... desolate country whose soil is rich enough but is given over

wholly to weeds ... we never saw a human being on the whole route ... There was hardly a tree or shrub anywhere ... Nazareth is forlorn ... Jericho the accursed lies a smouldering ruin ... Bethlehem and Bethany, in their poverty and their humiliation, have nothing to remind one that they once knew the high honour of the Saviour's presence.'

Of Jerusalem he wrote:

'Jerusalem is mournful, and dreary and lifeless. I would not desire to live here.'[37]

'It Is Very Desolate'

Another nineteenth-century pilgrim was a Scottish pastor by the name of Robert Murray M'Cheyne, who visited the Holy Land in June 1839 with a party of men including Andrew Bonar, who later wrote his biography. Like many Evangelical Christians of that era, Rev. M'Cheyne had a very clear view of the destiny of the Jews in the purposes of the God of Israel. He had once written, 'We should be like God in His peculiar affections; and the whole Bible shows that God has ever had, and still has, a peculiar love to the Jews.'[38] As they trekked through the Judean hills up to Jerusalem, he wrote his impressions down in his journal:

'The terracing of all the hills is the most remarkable feature of Judean scenery. Every foot of the rockiest mountains may in this way be covered with vines. We thought of Isaiah wandering here, and David and Solomon. Still all was wilderness. The hand of man had been actively employed upon every mountain, but where were these labourers now? Judah is gone into captivity before the enemy. There are few men left in the land; not a vine is there. "The vine languisheth." We came down upon Garieh, a village embosomed in figs and pomegranates. Ascending again, we came into the valley of Elah, where David slew Goliath. Another long and steep ascent of a most rugged hill brought us into a strange scene – a desert of sunburnt rocks. I had read of this and knew that Jerusalem was near. I left my camel and went before, hurrying over the burning rocks. In about half an hour Jerusalem came in sight. "How doth the city sit solitary that was full of people!" Is this the perfection of beauty? "How hath the LORD covered the daughter of Zion with a cloud in His anger!" It is, indeed, very desolate. Read the two first chapters of Lamentations, and you will have a vivid picture of our first sight of Jerusalem. We lighted off our camels within the Jaffa Gate. Among those who crowded round us, we observed several Jews. I think I had better not attempt to tell you about Jerusalem. The plague is still in Jerusalem, so that we must keep ourselves in quarantine. The plague only communicates by contact, so that we are not allowed to touch any one, or let any one touch us. Every night we heard the mourners going about the streets with their dismal wailings for the dead. On Monday we visited the [Church of the Holy] Sepulchre, and a painful sight, where we can find no traces of Calvary. Same evening rode up to the Mount of Olives: past Gethsemane, a most touching spot. Visited Sir Moses Montefiore, a Jew of London, encamped on Mount Olivet; very kind to us. [Next day] went round most of the places to be visited near Jerusalem, – Rephaim, Gihon, Siloa's brook, "that flowed past the oracle of God;" the Pool of Siloam; the place where Jesus wept over the city; Bethany, – of all places my favourite; the tombs of the kings. Such a day we never spent in this world before. [Next day] in the evening walked to Aceldama, – a dreadful spot. Zion is ploughed like a field. I gathered some barley, and noticed cauliflowers planted in rows. See Micah 3:12. Jerusalem is indeed like heaps. The quantities of rubbish would amaze you, – in one place higher than the walls. Judah's cities are all waste, except Bethlehem.' [39]

R.M. M'Cheyne had written to his congregation back in Scotland, 'We will seek the good of the Jews; and the more we do so, the happier we will be in our own soul. You should always keep up a knowledge of the prophecies regarding Israel.'

'My Lord Has Forgotten Me'

By this time the Holy City, which the Lord had declared to be *'His dwelling place forever'*, had suffered nearly eighteen centuries of desolation, war and bloodshed as Gentile invaders, one after the other, had trodden her down. If the stones of Jerusalem could have cried out, as Yeshua had said they one day would, they possibly would have asked what had become of the everlasting covenant that the God of Israel had made with Jerusalem? (Ezekiel 16)

Under the influence of the Spirit of the Lord, Isaiah had prophetically penned these sentiments, together with the Lord's answer:

> *'Zion said, "The LORD has forsaken me,*
> *And my Lord has forgotten me."*
>
> *"Can a woman forget her nursing child,*
> *And not have compassion on the son of her womb?*
> *Surely they may forget,*
> *Yet I will not forget you.*
> *See, I have inscribed you on the palms of My hands;* [40]
> *Your walls are continually before Me.*
> *Your sons shall make haste;*
> *Your destroyers and those who laid you waste*
> *Shall go away from you....*
> *As I live," says the LORD.*   (Isaiah 49:14–18)
>
> *' "For a mere moment I have forsaken you,*
> *But with great mercies I will gather you.*
> *With a little wrath I hid My face from you for a moment;*
> *But with everlasting kindness I will have mercy on you,"*
> *Says the LORD, your Redeemer....*
> *"For the mountains shall depart*
> *And the hills be removed,*
> *But My kindness shall not depart from you,*
> *Nor shall My Covenant of peace be removed,"*
> *Says the LORD, who has mercy on you.'*   (Isaiah 54:7, 8, 10)

The prophet Jeremiah echoes these sentiments:

> *'For the Lord will not cast off forever.*
> *Though He causes grief,*
> *Yet He will show compassion*
> *According to the multitude of His mercies.'*
>
> (Lamentations 3:31–32)

By the middle of the nineteenth century the Jewish people accounted for the largest single ethnic group living in Jerusalem.[41]

Yet all over the world millions of Jews in the *Diaspora* continued to yearn for their beloved city, which was somehow still beyond their reach. Zion had been at the centre of their daily prayers throughout those eighteen centuries. However, for non-Jews, apart from being the destination of a number of Christian and Moslem pilgrims, Jerusalem was little more than a byword among the nations of the world. It was nothing more than an overgrown, disease-ridden village in the Judean wilderness – a backwater of no consequence in the world.

But the fortunes of the Forsaken City were about to change. Prophetic writings that had lain dormant for so long were about to come to life. The Lord's appointed time to favour Zion was drawing nigh.

Restoration Foretold by the Prophets of Israel

The restoration of Jerusalem to the Lord's favour was promised by the prophet Zechariah:

> *'"The Lord will take possession of Judah as His inheritance in the Holy Land, and will again choose Jerusalem."'*
>
> (Zechariah 2:12)

and again:

> *'"Thus says the Lord:*
> *'I will return to Zion,*
> *And dwell in the midst of Jerusalem.*

> *Jerusalem shall be called the City of Truth,*
> *The Mountain of the LORD of Hosts,*
> *The Holy Mountain.'"'*   (Zechariah 8:3)

The Canaanic, or Land Covenant, which foretold the *Diaspora*, went on to prophesy the regathering of the nation of Israel,

> *'"...the LORD your God will bring you back from captivity, and have compassion on you, and gather you again from all the nations where the LORD your God has scattered you ... Then the LORD your God will bring you to the land which your fathers possessed, and you shall possess it. He will prosper you and multiply you more than your fathers."'*
> (Deuteronomy 30:3, 5)

The prophet Isaiah, who had foreshadowed the restoration of Jerusalem after the Babylonian captivity, also predicted a second regathering that would herald the Messianic Age.

> *'It shall come to pass in that day*
> *That the LORD shall set His hand again the second time*
> *To recover the remnant of His people who are left...*
> *He will set up a banner for the nations,*
> *And will assemble the outcasts of Israel,*
> *And gather together the dispersed of Judah*
> *From the four corners of the earth.'*   (Isaiah 11:11, 12)[42]

Two whole chapters of Ezekiel – chapters 36 and 37 – are devoted to the restoration of the land to the people and the people to the land – and ultimately to the Lord their God, the God of Israel.

The prophet Hosea – who, as we saw earlier, had foretold that Israel would abide many days without a king, a sacrifice and an ephod – goes on to say in the very next verse,

> *'Afterward the children of Israel shall return, seek the LORD their God and David their king, and fear the LORD and His goodness in the latter days.'*   (Hosea 3:5)

The prophet Jeremiah endorses this:

> ' "For it shall come to pass in that day,"
> *Says the* LORD *of Hosts,*
> *"That I will break his yoke from your neck,*
> *And will burst your bonds;*
> *Foreigners shall no more enslave them.*
> *But they shall serve the* LORD *their God,*
> *And David their king,*
> *Whom I will raise up for them. . . .*
> *Jacob shall return, have rest and be quiet,*
> *And no one shall make him afraid.*
> *For I am with you," says the* LORD, *"to save you;*
> *Though I make a full end of all nations where I have*
> *scattered you,*
> *Yet I will not make a complete end of you.*
> *But I will correct you in justice,*
> *And will not let you go altogether unpunished." '*
> (Jeremiah 30:8–11)

And again, the prophet Isaiah:

> 'For Zion's sake I will not keep silent,
> for Jerusalem's sake I will not remain quiet,
> till her righteousness shines out like the dawn,
> her salvation like a blazing torch.
> The nations will see your righteousness,
> and all kings your glory . . .
> You will be a crown of splendour in the LORD's hand,
> a royal diadem in the hand of your God.
> No longer will they call you Deserted,
> or name your land Desolate . . .
> for the LORD will take delight in you,
> and your land will be married.
> As a young man marries a maiden,
> so will your sons marry you . . .
> I have posted watchmen on your walls, O Jerusalem;
> they will never be silent day or night.
> You who call on the LORD, give yourselves no rest,
> and give Him no rest till He establishes Jerusalem
> and makes her the praise of the earth.' (Isaiah 62:1–7, NIV)

There are many other promises in the Old Testament that foretell the restoration of Jerusalem and the kingdom of Israel, but what of the New Testament?

Restoration Foretold by the Apostles

The New Testament is not silent. Just before Yeshua ascended into heaven, His disciples asked Him,

> ' *"Lord, will You at this time restore the kingdom to Israel?"*
> *And He said to them, "It is not for you to know the times*
> *or seasons which the Father has put in His own authority."* '
> (Acts 1:6–7)

Yeshua did not say, 'It won't happen, it's all over for the kingdom of Israel', He said, *'It is not for you to know the times or seasons which the Father has put in His own authority.'*

However, even after this explanation, the fact that the Apostles were still expecting the kingdom to be physically restored is evident later in the Book of Acts.

Preaching to a Jewish audience in Jerusalem, many of whom had witnessed the events surrounding the death and resurrection of the Messiah, the Apostle Peter said:

> ' *"Those things which God foretold by the mouth of all His prophets, that the Messiah would suffer, He has thus fulfilled. Repent therefore and be converted that your sins may be blotted out, so that times of refreshing may come from the presence of the Lord, and that He may send* [Yeshua HaMashiach], *who was preached to you before, whom heaven must receive until the times of restoration of all things, which God has spoken by the mouth of all His holy prophets since the world began."* '
> (Acts 3:18–21)

A few years later, the Apostles were gathered together in Jerusalem to discuss the status of Gentile believers. The Apostle Jacob,[43] addressing the assembly, quotes from the word of the Lord through the prophet Amos:

> ' *"After this I will return*
> *And will rebuild the tabernacle of David which has fallen*
>   *down.*
> *I will rebuild its ruins,*
> *And I will set it up,*
> *So that the rest of mankind may seek the* L ORD,
> *Even all the Gentiles who are called by My name,*
> *Says the* L ORD *who does all these things."* '
>
>   (Acts 15:16–17, quoting Amos 9:11, 12)

This gathering of the Church leaders, who were all Jewish, took place in Jerusalem about twenty years before the destruction of the city by the Romans. Most of them would have actually listened to Yeshua as He described the Holy City's future destruction. Yet they still believed that one day the ruins of David's tabernacle – the kingdom of Israel – would be rebuilt.

The most explicit promise in the New Testament concerning the future for the Jewish people in the purposes of God is found in the Apostle Paul's Letter to the Romans.

The Apostle devotes three whole chapters of this Letter to explaining God's destiny for Israel. I strongly recommend that the reader study Romans 9, 10 and 11. In chapter 11 Paul paints a picture of the Gentile church as being 'wild olive branches' which have been grafted into a cultured olive tree. He goes on to warn the Gentile believers not to be arrogant towards the Jews, or they would incur God's displeasure. Sadly, this is a warning that has been ignored by most of the Church through its history. Paul goes on to predict Israel's salvation:

> 'For I do not desire that you should be ignorant of this mystery, lest you should be wise in your own opinion, that hardening in part has happened to Israel until the fullness of the Gentiles has come in.
>   *And so all Israel shall be saved, as it is written:*
> *"The Deliverer will come out of Zion,*
> *And He will turn away ungodliness from Jacob;*
> *For this is My Covenant with them,*
> *When I take away their sins."* '
>
>   (Romans 11:25–27, quoting Isaiah 59:20–21 in part)

Chapter 4

Jerusalem and the Rebirth of the Nation

The Birth of the Modern Zionist Dream

During the Passover Seder every year, for more than eighteen centuries, millions of Jews throughout the *Diaspora* had uttered the prayer, 'Next year in Jerusalem'. So central was Jerusalem to the heart of Judaism that the more devout orthodox would beseech the God of Israel with the 'Amidah' prayer three times every day. This prayer was a heart-cry to God to bring them home to their ancient beloved city – Jerusalem.

By the mid-nineteenth century of the Christian Era the destiny of the Jewish people was starting to move in a more promising direction. Not only was the hope, the desire and the dream of a return to the land of their forefathers intensifying, but it was beginning to become a reality.

The pogroms in Czarist Russia were making life increasingly unbearable for hundreds of thousands of Jewish people who had been living in that part of the world for centuries. In the latter part of the nineteenth century thousands of Jews began to vote with their feet. Many headed for America, but some decided to return to the land of their forefathers, which had been renamed 'Palestine' by the Romans.

Among them was a Lithuanian Jew with the name of Eliezer Perlman, who had been born in 1858. In order to avoid conscription into the Russian army, and almost certain death, he moved away from his home and assumed the name Eliezer Elyanof. His upbringing and education was sponsored by a kind family who remained close to him throughout his life. It was during his teenage years that young Eliezer read a Hebrew translation of the story of *Robinson Crusoe*. This seemingly insignificant event in his life gave him a passion for the Hebrew tongue of his forefathers. In late adolescence he moved to Germany, and then Paris to complete his education.

It was from Paris that this young man was to put into print an appeal which was to cause much controversy among his own people. It was an appeal that encapsulated the dream that had throbbed in the hearts of millions of Jewish people for eighteen centuries – and for eighteen centuries it had been a dream beyond their reach. What young Eliezer had written, which would later be published in Jewish journals all over Europe, first appeared in 1879 in a Warsaw newspaper called *Hashahar*:

'If, in truth, each and every nation is entitled to defend its nationality and protect itself from extinction, then logically we, the Hebrews, also must have the same right. Why should our lot be meaner than all the others?

Why should we choke our hope to return and become a nation in our deserted country which is still mourning its lost children, driven away to remote lands two thousand years ago? Why should we not follow the example of all nations, big and small, and do something to protect our nationality from extermination?

If we care at all that the name of Israel should not disappear from this earth, we must create a centre for the whole of our people, like a heart from which the blood would run into the arteries of the whole, and animate the whole. Only the settlement of *Eretz Israel* can serve this purpose.

Now the time has come for us, the Hebrews, to do something positive. Let us create a society for the purchase of land in *Eretz Israel*; for the acquisition of everything necessary for agriculture; for the division of the land among Jews already present and those desiring to emigrate there, and the provision of the funds necessary for those who cannot establish themselves independently.' [44]

The article was accredited to a certain Eliezer Ben Yehuda. Young Eliezer had adopted a new name which means 'Son of Judah'.

In 1881 the pogroms in Russia had prompted the first major *aliyah*[45] to Palestine, and the small Jewish population that had lived in the Holy Land uninterrupted throughout the period of the *Diaspora* began to swell. That same year, as a young man in his early twenties, Eliezer Ben Yehuda made *aliyah* to the land of his forefathers and made his home in Jerusalem. By this time, the majority of Jerusalem's population was Jewish.

A 'Dead' Language Reborn

Not only did the Zionist vision pulsate through Ben Yehuda's being, but he had another vision too. His life's work, which was to make that vision a reality, was to leave its indelible mark on the future nation of Israel. With at least seventy different languages in common usage among the Jews of the *Diaspora*, Eliezer Ben Yehuda believed that there had to be one common language if a future State of Israel was to survive. He fervently believed that language had to be the ancient tongue of the prophets and kings of Israel – Hebrew.

Although still used for prayer, liturgy and rabbinical debate, for over two thousand years Hebrew had ceased to be the everyday language of the masses. Consequently many words had become lost. Ben Yehuda, almost single-handedly and in the face of much opposition, set about modernising the ancient tongue. His vision was to make it possible for several million people to order groceries, drive cattle, make love and curse their neighbours in a language which, until his day, had been fit only for Talmudic argument and prayer.

Eliezer Ben Yehuda spent forty-one years of his life, up until his death, compiling the most comprehensive dictionary ever produced for any language.[46] In restoring and modernising the ancient language, he painstakingly searched out thousands of words that had been lost. In addition, words had to be created for things that didn't exist in Bible times. He resisted the temptation to borrow words from European languages, but searched the roots of the Hebrew language, and other Semitic languages, to come up with suitable Hebrew words.

The legacy of his work, which lives on today, is arguably the fulfilment of a prophecy found in the Book of Zephaniah:

> ' "For then I will restore to the peoples a pure language, that they all may call on the name of the LORD." '
>
> (Zephaniah 3:9) [47]

The Zionist Dream Gains Momentum

By 1896 Eliezer Ben Yehuda had lived in Jerusalem for fifteen years, and seventeen years had elapsed since his appeal for a Jewish homeland had first been published in Jewish journals throughout Europe. That year a Hungarian Jew from Vienna by the name of Theodore Herzl published a small book entitled *Der Judenstaat* (The Jewish State). In it he wrote: 'The idea I have developed in this pamphlet is a very old one: it is the restoration of the Jewish State.'

Herzl was a man of action and would later become recognised as the 'Father of Modern Zionism'. The following year, in 1897, he convened the First Zionist Congress in Basle, Switzerland, where the Zionist Organisation was founded. The Congress adopted a resolution defining the aim of Zionism: 'The aim of Zionism is to create for the Jewish people a home in Palestine secured by public law.' [48]

At the end of the Congress, Herzl made an entry in his diary, dated 3 September 1897: 'In Basle I founded the Jewish State ... maybe in five years, certainly in fifty, everyone will see it.' [49] His words were to cause mirth among many, but they were to prove prophetic.

However, Theodore Herzl had a humble Gentile friend who knew people in high places. This man was an ordained Church of England minister who believed that the Bible clearly prophesied the rebirth and restoration of Israel in her ancient homeland. His name was William Hechler.

Among Hechler's circle of friends in England was Lord Shaftesbury, a man influential in the British government. On one occasion Hechler delivered a personal message to Abdul Hamid II of Turkey from Queen Victoria, requesting the

Ottoman Sultan to act more sympathetically towards the
Jews of Palestine. On the European continent, William
Hechler was confidante to Frederick, Grand Duke of Baden,
who later introduced him to Kaiser Wilhelm II of Germany.
Hechler introduced Herzl to all these people and, in turn,
they all played a part, to a greater or lesser extent, in the
realisation of Herzl's dream.

However, as the nineteenth century drew to a close and
the twentieth century dawned, the greatest obstacle to the
establishment of a Jewish State in Palestine was the Sultan of
the Ottoman Turkish Empire, Abdul Hamid II. Not only was
he vehemently opposed to the idea of a Jewish homeland in
Palestine, but he made life very difficult for those making
aliyah. As well as imposing prohibitions on Jewish *aliyah*
from time to time, the Turks imposed severe restrictions on
how Jews conducted themselves in their Promised Land, as
Eliezer Ben Yehuda knew only too well. The Turks were not
popular among the Arabs either.

The Visionary and the Deliverer

Although Ben Yehuda and Herzl were about the same age,
shared the same dream and often corresponded, it is believed
that the two men only ever met on one occasion, and that
meeting was not a happy one.

Herzl, on the one hand, was anxious to see the Zionist
State established as soon as possible. He believed it was
paramount to gain the support for Zionism from the nations
of the world, and the starting point of his vision was a
programme of gradual Jewish colonisation of Palestine for
which Turkey, with its enormous national debt, would be
remunerated. Because of their influence with the Turks, he
thought the Jewish homeland would be best established
under the auspices of Germany, and he counted on the
German Kaiser's goodwill to enable it to happen.

Ben Yehuda, on other hand, having lived under Ottoman
rule – as well as having been imprisoned by the Turkish
authorities at one stage – did not believe they would accept
such a bribe. Furthermore he never fully trusted the Germans
and believed that the Zionists would be better off under the

auspices of Great Britain. Besides, as an influential resident of Jerusalem, Ben Yehuda had a more practical vision of the policies needed to make a newborn Jewish nation a viable entity. First and foremost he believed that the Zionist vision had to be fostered and accepted by all parties on the ground in Palestine. He presented Herzl with a five-point plan:

(1) There could never be a Jewish State without a common language. A Hebrew dictionary must be published as soon as possible, for how could a language be properly taught if there were no standards of pronunciation and meaning?

(2) Funds must be raised for the purchase of land from individual Arab owners, land on which new colonies could be founded.

(3) There must be a definite programme for fostering amicable relations with the Arabs. There should be, for example, schools where Jewish and Arab children would study side by side and learn the art of living peacefully together.

(4) There must be a definite programme for adult education so that the older generation already living in Palestine could be enthused with the spirit of the new Zionist movement.

(5) Schoolbooks were needed in Hebrew. It was foolish to try to bring up children entirely on oral instruction, which was too easily forgotten.[50]

Herzl rejected Ben Yehuda's plan on the grounds that none of these matters was a priority at that time, especially that of Hebrew being fostered as the national language. Herzl believed the priority should be to persuade the Turks to sell colonisation rights to the Jews and from there, eventually, to establish a Jewish State in Palestine. However, Herzl was later to learn that not only was the Ottoman Sultan Abdul Hamid II immovable on the issue, but the German Kaiser was more neutral than he originally thought about establishing a Jewish homeland. Furthermore Wilhelm II was not prepared to compromise Germany's good relations with the Ottoman Empire in order to help the Jews. Quite apart from that, there was considerable opposition to Zionism among the Jews of Europe.

Theodore Herzl never saw the rebirth of the State of Israel and in 1904 he died a broken-hearted man at the age of only forty-four.

By the outbreak of the Great War in 1914 over 65,000 refugees had fled from Russia, Romania and Poland to settle in their ancient homeland. The Turks continued to resist the waves of *aliyah*. In 1914 they outlawed Zionism and deported 11,000 Jews, but the First World War, as it became known, was to terminate the 400-year Turkish Ottoman rule over the Lord's land.

The Balfour Declaration

As Prime Minister of Great Britain from 1902 to 1905, Arthur Balfour had met Theodore Herzl and heard his idea for a Jewish homeland. Later, as Foreign Secretary, he also met with Chaim Weizmann, who was later to become the first President of the reborn State of Israel. Lord Balfour, like both Lloyd George, who was Britain's Prime Minister during World War I, and General Edmund Allenby, believed that the biblical statements were the essential factor in any decisions regarding the Jewish people and Palestine. Balfour believed the Jews were exiles who should be given back their homeland in payment for Christianity's 'immeasurable debt'. He wrote:

> 'The position of the Jews is unique. For them race, religion and country are inter-related as they are inter-related in the case of no other religion, and no other country on earth.'[51]

On 2 November 1917, Lord Balfour, as British Foreign Secretary, made public the contents of a letter he had written on behalf of the Cabinet, favouring the establishment of a Jewish homeland in Palestine. The recipient was Lord Rothschild, who represented the Jewish people in Britain. The declaration approved by the Cabinet read as follows:

> 'His Majesty's Government view with favour the estab- lishment in Palestine of a national home for the Jewish

people, and will use their best endeavours to facilitate the achievement of this object, it being clearly understood that nothing shall be done which may prejudice the civil and religious rights of existing non-Jewish communities in Palestine, or the rights and political status enjoyed by Jews in any other country.'

However, this Cabinet motion, which became known as the Balfour Declaration, was a statement of British policy which any subsequent government could have ignored, as it was not submitted to Parliament for enactment nor, at that stage, did it have the status of an international treaty. Not only that, but because most of Palestine was still under the control of the old Ottoman Empire, the British had no means of guaranteeing its implementation anyway.[52]

Jerusalem Falls to the British

Historians have said that World War I prepared the Land for the People, and World War II prepared the People for the Land. By the time of the Balfour Declaration, World War I had just entered its fourth year. At the beginning of the war, the Turks had joined forces with Germany. The Allies, consisting of the British Empire, France and Russia, had declared war on Turkey in order to protect their interests in the Middle East. In 1915 Britain and France enlisted Arab support to help break the Turkish stranglehold on the Middle East. In return, the British guaranteed the formation of an independent Arab State in Mesopotamia and on the Arabian peninsula after the war was won.

In 1917, as Lord Balfour was shaping British policy for Palestine, Allied forces composed of British and ANZAC troops, under the command of General Allenby, were pushing north from Egypt into Palestine, in an attempt to wrest the Holy Land from the Turks. On 31 October 1917 the Australian 10th Light Horse mounted infantry Brigade took Beersheba, the gateway to Palestine.

Following the capture of Beersheba, the Allies won victory after victory. On 8 December the Cameron Highlanders and the Australian Light Horse advanced to Jerusalem, which they liberated from the Turks the following day. Two days later, on 11 December, and just forty days after the Balfour Declaration, General Sir Edmund Allenby dismounted from his horse and entered the Holy City through the Jaffa Gate on foot – a strange act for a conquering hero! Notwithstanding the tumultuous welcome given him by Jerusalem's impoverished Jewish inhabitants, General Allenby had a good reason for doing this: as a devout Christian and Bible student, he in no way wanted to eclipse the future entry into Jerusalem of his own Master, Israel's coming King and Messiah.

The capture of Jerusalem by the British was accompanied by an unusual event. The day before, for the first time in history, allied aircraft flew over the Holy City and dropped leaflets signed by General Allenby urging them to surrender. The Moslem inhabitants interpreted these leaflets, which 'came from above', as coming from 'Allah'. They were somewhat confused by Allenby's identity because his name in Arabic was 'Alla-Nebi', which means 'Prophet of God'! This resulted in the surrender of Jerusalem without a shot being fired! As strange as it may seem, this event fulfilled an amazing prophecy by Isaiah:

> ' "*Like birds flying about,*
> *So will the* LORD *of Hosts defend Jerusalem.*
> *Defending He will also deliver it.*
> *Passing over He will preserve it.*" '   (Isaiah 31:5)

Perhaps just as remarkable as the fulfilment of the prophecy itself was the motto[53] of the squadron that dropped the leaflets from the sky: 'I Spread My Wings and Keep My Promise.'

Was this pure coincidence, or, as the Moslems thought, a message from heaven? Indeed, this was one of the most astounding victories of World War I, for this was the only enemy stronghold to be captured in the whole conflict without a single shot being fired by either side. And it was the only time in its long and often bloody history that Jerusalem was taken without bloodshed. Perhaps equally significant was the fact that it happened to fall on the anniversary of the Jewish Festival of *Chanukkah*, which commemorates the liberation of Jerusalem from the tyranny of Antiochus Epiphanes by the Maccabees in 164 BCE.

Allenby's troops ended more than a thousand years of Islamic domination of the Holy Land and the Holy City. The campaign to take Palestine from the Turks cost the lives of about five thousand Allied troops. Without doubt their sacrifice aided the eventual restoration of Israel.

Some Forgotten Pieces of History

In January 1919 Chaim Weizmann, acting on behalf of the Zionist Organisation, reached an agreement with His Royal Highness Emir Faisal, acting on behalf of the Arab Kingdom of Hejaz. This agreement, which was made under the auspices of the British Foreign Office, allowed for Jewish settlement in Palestine 'on a large scale and as quickly as possible ... upon the land through closer settlement and intensive cultivation of the soil.' Furthermore, the parties to the agreement stated that they were 'mindful of the racial kinship and ancient bonds existing between the Arabs and Jewish people, and realising that the surest means of working out the consummation of their national aspirations is through the closest possible collaboration in the development of the Arab State and Palestine, and being desirous of further confirming the good understanding which exists between them.' [54]

The agreement between HRH Emir Faisal and Chaim Weizmann under the auspices of the British Foreign Office also guaranteed the freedom of religion and protection of holy sites for the Muslims – something which the Jewish people have always honoured to this present day. The only rider that His Royal Highness placed on the agreement – which he did in his own handwriting – was that Britain grant the Arabs their independence. However, it did not take long for this momentous agreement to become a forgotten piece of history, even though both the British and the Jewish people fulfilled their side of the bargain.

Just as remarkable as this forgotten agreement, was a statement made by Emir Faisal's father, Sherif Hussein, in the previous year, 1918. Hussein, who was the Arab leader with whom the British government had been dealing, said:

> 'The resources of the country are still virgin soil and will be developed by the Jewish immigrants. One of the most amazing things until recent times was that the Palestinian [55] used to leave his country, wandering over the high seas in every direction. His native soil could not retain its hold on him.' [56]

This statement, made by the most prominent Arab leader in the Middle East at that time, confirms some important truths. Firstly, it confirms that the land was largely un-developed at that time. Secondly, and more importantly, it reveals that the Arabs knew that the country, which was then known as Palestine, was the home of the Jewish people – the people then known as the Palestinians – and that the soil of that country was the native soil for the Jew. Could there have been a realisation, too, that the precious soil would only respond to the tender care of its rightful husbandmen?

Speaking to Zion, perhaps this is what the Lord meant when He uttered these words through the prophet Isaiah:

> *'You shall no longer be termed Forsaken,*
> *Nor shall your land any more be termed Desolate . . .*
> *For as a young man marries a virgin,*
> *So shall your sons marry you;*
> *And as the bridegroom rejoices over the bride,*
> *So shall your God rejoice over you.'*   (Isaiah 62:4, 5)

The Balfour Declaration Ratified

Two years after the end of World War I, at the San Remo Conference in April 1920, the League of Nations gave Britain a mandate to rule Palestine and Mesopotamia. This raised the Balfour Declaration to the legal status of an international treaty (see Appendix F, map 1). As well as protecting the rights of those already resident in the land, Britain was obliged to 'be responsible for putting into effect the declaration originally made on November 2nd, 1917 by the government . . . in favour of the establishment in Palestine of a national home for the Jewish people'. Furthermore, Britain was obliged to use her best endeavours to facilitate Jewish immigration, and to encourage Jewish settlement of the land.[57]

However, despite the Faisal-Weizmann agreement, the Arab nationalist movement, which had its beginnings in the early 1900s, was outraged. Not satisfied with independence confined to Mesopotamia and Arabia, they vowed they would not co-operate with the British Mandate in Palestine until they achieved self-government there as well.

The British Mandate

The first High Commissioner to Palestine appointed by the British government was a Jew by the name of Sir Herbert Samuel. Much to the delight of Eliezer Ben Yehuda, who was nearing the end of his life, one of the first things that Samuel did was to pronounce that there would be three official languages in Palestine: English, Arabic and Hebrew.

Just over a quarter of a century after Ben Yehuda died, Hebrew was to become the mother tongue of the reborn State of Israel, just as it had been the mother tongue of the ancient prophets of Israel.

One year after the San Remo conference, the British Mandate was already in trouble. The Arab nationalists were not only vehemently opposed to a Jewish homeland, but they refused to co-operate with the British. Sir Herbert Samuel was forced to suspend Jewish immigration temporarily. Following a series of Arab riots in Jerusalem the British Colonial Secretary, Winston Churchill, visited Palestine to try and reach a settlement. In 1922 Churchill published a White Paper, which became British policy for the next few years. Although Churchill reaffirmed his support for the Jewish national home, he included four major stipulations:

(1) Divide Palestine down the Jordan River and create an Arab homeland as a part of Britain's Palestine mandate (see Appendix F, map 2).

(2) Restrict the Jewish national home to the area west of the Jordan River.

(3) Avoid a predominantly Jewish state.

(4) Limit Jewish immigration to the economic capacity of
     the country.[58]

This was a far cry from the original aspirations of both the
Balfour Declaration and the Faisal-Weizmann agreement.
The Zionist Executive reluctantly signed it, but the Arab
nationalists flatly rejected it. As part of the settlement Britain
established an Arab homeland in the 77 per cent of Palestine
that lay east of the Jordan River, and Jews were barred from
entering it. This new Arab nation in Palestine became known
as Transjordan.

Palestine remained relatively calm until an outbreak of
violence in 1929 in which 133 Jews and 87 Arabs were killed.
One of the worst massacres was in Hebron, where 59 Jews,
many of them women and children, were slaughtered. As a
result, the British forced an evacuation of all Jews from
Hebron – their oldest city, and the second holiest after
Jerusalem. Three thousand years of almost continuous Jewish
presence in the city where the Hebrew patriarchs were buried
came to an end.

There were to be further White Papers and Commissions,
and suspensions of Jewish immigration into the Holy Land.
Even with these difficulties, the Jewish population of Palestine grew tenfold to approximately 600,000 during the years
of the British Mandate. As the Jewish population grew and
opened up the land both agriculturally and economically,
Arabs and other non-Jews from surrounding areas were also
drawn to the Holy Land. Years later, after the State of Israel
had become a reality, the man who has been described as
Britain's greatest political leader of the twentieth century
would reflect upon the 1922 White Paper, and what he saw as
the resulting benefits for both Jews and Arabs. In 1949
Winston Churchill recalled in a speech to the House of
Commons:

> 'The whole point of our settlement was that immigration
> was to be free but not beyond the limits of economic
> absorptive power. We could not have had it said that
> newcomers were coming in, pushing out those who
> have lived there for centuries. But the newcomers
> who were coming in brought work and employment

with them and the means of sustaining a much larger population than had lived in Palestine and Transjordan. They brought the hope with them of a far larger population than had existed in Palestine at the time of our Lord. One has only to look up to the hills that were once cultivated and then were defaced by centuries of medieval barbarism to see what has been accomplished.

In twenty-five years the Jewish population of Palestine doubled or more than doubled, but so did the Arab population of the same areas of Palestine. As the Jews continued to reclaim the country, plant the orange groves, develop the water system, electricity and so forth, employment and means of livelihood were found for ever larger numbers of Arabs – 400,000 or 500,000 more Arabs found their living there – and the relations of the two races in the Jewish areas were tolerable in spite of external distractions and all kinds of disturbances. General prosperity grew.' [59]

Indeed, not only did prosperity grow – as Winston Churchill observed – but an ecological miracle, unrivalled in the twentieth century, unfolded as the returning Jews transformed the land that had lain desolate for nearly nineteen centuries – just as the ancient prophets had foretold.

> ' "But you, O mountains of Israel, you shall shoot forth your branches and yield your fruit to My people Israel, for they are about to come. For indeed I am for you, and I will turn to you and you shall be tilled and sown. I will multiply men upon you, all the house of Israel, all of it; and the cities shall be inhabited and the ruins rebuilt. ... The desolate land shall be tilled instead of lying desolate in the sight of all who pass by. So they will say, 'This land that was desolate has become like the garden of Eden; and the wasted, desolate, and ruined cities are now fortified and inhabited.' " '
>
> (Ezekiel 36:8–10 and 34–35)

However, as the miracle in the Holy Land unfolded during the 1920s, 1930s and 1940s, the British Mandate in the Holy

Land continued to deteriorate. Britain had a higher interest than fulfilling her international obligation to the Jewish people – oil. Needless to say, Britain succumbed to the Arab pressure to severely restrict, or even halt Jewish immigration into Palestine. Many Jews who attempted to return to their Promised Land were turned away to face what became the worst nightmare in Jewish history. Those pioneers who gained entry to settle the land struggled in the midst of hardship, anti-Jewish violence and, in particular, promises broken by Britain.

The late 1930s saw violence in Palestine rise to hitherto unprecedented levels, resulting in the White Paper of 1939. This document, which repudiated the policy of a Jewish State in Palestine as being unworkable, also put severe restrictions on Jewish immigration into the Promised Land. The British had driven the final nail into the coffin of the Balfour Declaration.

In Europe the situation was deteriorating rapidly as half a million Jews inside Nazi Germany were under increasing threat, together with millions more in neighbouring countries. Tens of thousands wanted to get out, but they had nowhere to go. The previous year, in 1938, a 32-nation conference had been convened at Evian in Switzerland. The attending nations virtually closed their doors to any Jewish immigration. Almost nine million Jews were trapped in the inferno that was about to engulf Europe at the hands of Adolf Hitler.

At least six million of them were murdered. There is no doubt that the number who perished would have been less, had Britain fulfilled her mandate and allowed the many thousands of Jewish refugees, who tried to escape from Europe before and during the Holocaust, to enter their ancient homeland without hindrance.

Even after the war was over, thousands of pitiful refugees, who had escaped the Holocaust, attempted to return to their promised home aboard overcrowded and often unseaworthy vessels, only to be denied entry by the British. In 1947 the western world was shocked by the heart-rending scenes when the *Haganah*-sponsored[60] ship *Exodus* arrived at the port of Haifa and its helpless cargo of Jewish refugees were turned away from their only hope. As a result, the newly-formed United Nations organisation ordered that the whole issue of a Jewish homeland in Palestine be reopened.

The UN Resolution 181

In 1947 a United Nations Special Committee on Palestine (UNSCOP) recommended the partition of the remaining 23 per cent of Palestine into Jewish and Arab States, with Jerusalem as a free international city (see Appendix F, map 3). However, the UNSCOP resolution ignored the fact that Britain had already divided Palestine in 1922 and created an Arab State – Transjordan. The only aspect of this plan that the British supported was the internationalisation of Jerusalem. On 29 November 1947 the partition resolution was submitted to the General Assembly of the United Nations, which passed the resolution thirty-three to thirteen, giving the necessary two-thirds majority. Now opposing the formation of the Jewish State that her government had recommended in the Balfour Declaration thirty years earlier, Britain abstained.[61]

This United Nations Partition plan, better known as UN Resolution 181, is just one event in the fulfilment of a prophecy found in Joel that will ultimately bring the judgement of God upon the nations: *'They divided My land'* (Joel 3:2).[62]

For the Jewish people, however, 1947 signified a light at the end of a long dark tunnel. Just fifty years after Theodore Herzl had written that significant note in his diary, the way was now open to form a Jewish sovereign State in the land that God had promised to Abraham, Isaac and Jacob. The leader of the Palestinian Jews, David Ben-Gurion, voiced his expectation with these words:

> 'I know that God promised all of Palestine to the children of Israel. I do not know what borders He set. I believe they are wider than the ones proposed. If God will keep His promise in His own time, our business as poor humans who live in a difficult age is to save as much as we can of the remnants of Israel.'[63]

Indeed, under the United Nations Partition Plan, the borders were considerably diminished and the Jews would be denied sovereignty over their ancient capital; even so the Zionists gratefully accepted the UN Partition Plan. The Arabs, however, believing they could eliminate any Jewish State as soon as it came into existence and push the Jews into the Mediterranean Sea, rejected Resolution 181 outright. One Arab leader vowed, 'We will strangle Jerusalem.' [64]

The Battle for Jerusalem

A nightmarish siege of the Holy City began. In a desperate attempt to bring essential supplies to the famished Jewish population of Jerusalem, the Jews armour-plated their vehicles to withstand the merciless ambushes of the Arab marauders. Denied adequate arms to defend themselves, and unprotected by the British, many Jews were killed as the convoys ran the gauntlet from Tel Aviv up to Jerusalem. [65]

By April 1948, the 'Arab Liberation Army' had set up two fronts; 7,000 men were positioned in the north and a further 2,000 Moslem Brotherhood volunteers from Egypt, across the Negev desert in the south. They launched assaults against the Jewish quarters in various towns and cities, particularly in Jerusalem. There were also concentrated attacks against outlying *kibbutzim* [66] in the Hebron hills.

Israel Is Reborn

At 8 o'clock on the morning of 14 May 1948 – 5 Iyar 5708 in the Jewish Calendar – the Union Jack was lowered at Government House in Jerusalem. British High Commissioner, Sir Alan Cunningham, left for Haifa where he boarded a British warship. The turbulent British Mandate had ended.

At 4 o'clock that afternoon, the man who was about to become Prime Minister, David Ben-Gurion, and the leaders of the new nation assembled in the Tel Aviv Museum, where the Declaration of Independence of the State of Israel was read out:

'...By virtue of the natural and historic right of the Jewish people and of the resolution of the General Assembly of the United Nations, we hereby proclaim the establishment of the Jewish State in Palestine, to be called *"Medinat Yisrael"*, the State of Israel.'

These words, spoken by David Ben-Gurion in Hebrew, were broadcast by radio throughout the land, except in Jerusalem, which was without electricity. As he finished, the thunderous applause of the listening population, together with echoes of 'Hatikvah', the Jewish National Anthem, resounded through the newly born *Eretz Yisrael* – the Land of Israel.

The rebirth of the nation on that eventful day fulfilled a remarkable prophecy by Isaiah:

> ' *"Who has ever heard of such a thing?*
> *Who has ever seen such things?*
> *Can a country be born in a day,*
> *Or a nation brought forth in a moment?"* '
>
> (Isaiah 66:8, NIV) [67]

David Ben-Gurion concluded with a plea to the Arabs: 'We extend our hand in peace and neighbourliness to all the neighbouring states ... the State of Israel is prepared to make this contribution to the Middle East as a whole.' [68]

A War of Extermination

Despite the United Nations' recognition of the newborn Jewish State, the Arab States declared war. 'This will be a war of extermination and a momentous massacre which will be spoken of like the Mongolian massacre and the Crusades,' said Azzam Pasha on the eve of the Arab invasion.[69]

The following day, Israel was attacked on all fronts by forces which included Egyptians, Syrians, Iraqis, Lebanese and Arab Legionnaires from Jordan.

The Battle for Jerusalem Intensifies

The 85,000 Jews in Jerusalem, already weakened by the Arab stranglehold on the roads which prevented supplies, weapons and ammunition from reaching them, found themselves in a precarious situation. Two thousand Arab Legionnaires, well equipped with artillery and commanded by British officers, moved on Jerusalem from the north and completely surrounded the outskirts of the city. Jewish relief columns from the coastal plain were ambushed in the hills. Lacking arms and ammunition because of the British prohibition that had been in force, the Jews faced the grimmest period in the War of Independence. In desperation, they managed to cut a bypass – the 'Burma Road' – through the Jerusalem mountains, enabling the first trucks loaded with cans of food and water to reach Jerusalem intact.

Meanwhile, King Abdullah's Arab Legion mounted a furious attack on the Jewish Quarter of the Old City of Jerusalem. For two weeks, two hundred Jewish men, women and children held off the assault, virtually without arms or ammunition. Finally, they surrendered, ending sixteen centuries of almost continuous Jewish residence in the ancient alleys beside the Western Wall of the Temple Mount.

It was ironic. On the one hand the doors of their ancient Promised Land were flung wide open for all to come home. On the other hand the gates of the Old City – their ancient capital – were barred to them. For the next nineteen years they even were denied access to the *Kotel* – the Western Wall. So near and yet so far. An Israeli Air Force officer, who was later to follow in the footsteps of his uncle as President of Israel, recalls what it was like:

> 'We, the Israelis who lived for nineteen years with a divided Jerusalem, our dream was constantly one day to find ourselves at the *Kotel* – ourselves in East Jerusalem. We, the breed of pilots used to see it from the air, and I used to fly and look at it, and look at it – and couldn't even touch it.'[70]

Armistice

After several ceasefires and resumptions of fighting, an armistice was signed in April of the following year. Despite losing the Old City to Jordan (who held it under UN trusteeship), Israel had won far more land than the United Nations Resolution 181 had allocated, including West Jerusalem. The war had cost 6,000 Israeli lives and 30,000 wounded, from a population of 600,000.

The Armistice Agreement signed by Israel and Jordan provided the Israelis with free access to places of worship, to the Jewish cemetery on the Mount of Olives and to Hadassah Hospital on Mount Scopus. Jordan never honoured these obligations. Instead, the Jordanians embarked on a campaign of desecration. Ancient synagogues, housing priceless *Torah* Scrolls, were destroyed. The Great Synagogue – the Hurvah – that had been a central part of the life of the Jewish Quarter of the Old City was razed to the ground. Jewish graves on the Mount of Olives were ripped open and bones scattered. Not one of the nations listened to Israel's pleas for justice in the UN, giving Jeremiah's words concerning Jerusalem another poignant ring:

> ' "Is it nothing to you, all you who pass by?
> *Behold and see*
> *If there is any sorrow like my sorrow,*
> *Which has been brought on me . . . " '*
>
> (Lamentations 1:12) [71]

Jordan Illegally Annexes East Jerusalem

In 1950, the year after the end of the War of Independence, King Abdullah of Jordan illegally annexed Judea and Samaria, as well as the eastern part of Jerusalem, which the UN Resolution 181 had originally destined to be a 'free' city. The Jordanian King also dropped the biblical names Judea and Samaria in order to de-legitimise Jewish claims to the territory. Furthermore, the King declared this occupied territory would be known as the West Bank of the Kingdom of Jordan, since it was located beyond the west bank of the Jordan River. The term 'West Bank' has stuck with the world's media to this day.

A Legacy of Lasting Conflict

The Jews of Jerusalem and the infant Israeli State were not the only ones to suffer as a result of the War of Independence.

Around 600,000 Arabs were displaced by the war, which was the equivalent of the entire Jewish population of Israel at that time. Many of the Arabs left Palestine during the last months of the British Mandate. The Arab nations who had tried to eliminate the infant Jewish State roundly blamed Israel for the problem – and still do today. Israel was accused of evicting the Arabs and seizing their homes. This accusation is supported by a number of western nations, and particularly most of the media. While this was true in some cases, particularly in border areas where security was a concern, the overwhelming majority of Arabs who became refugees left their homes of their own accord. Many were encouraged to leave by their own leaders, having been told that they were safer behind Arab lines, and that they would be able to return once the Jews were annihilated. Without doubt, fear of being caught up in the conflict was the main reason for this exodus. About 160,000 Arabs remained in Israel, and were later given equal citizenship rights with Jews.

However, Israel is not to blame for the exodus of Arabs that took place in 1948, or the subsequent refugee problem that has existed ever since. Had the Arabs decided to live with the Jews in the spirit of the Faisal-Weizmann agreement, and had they later accepted UN Resolution 181, then the course of history might have been very different.

At the beginning of 1949, as the War of Independence still raged, Winston Churchill addressed the House of Commons in London with these words concerning the refugee problem:

> 'When the British Government quitted the scene and the Arab armies from Syria, Transjordania and finally in considerable strength from Egypt rolled forward to extinguish the Jewish National Home, all this Arab population fled in terror to behind the advancing forces of their own religion. Their condition is most grievous and I agree that it should certainly not be neglected by the [British] Government. The one great remedial measure is peace and a lasting settlement. The Jews need the Arabs. If we can get peace, the problem of the refugees will be reduced to one third, possibly one-quarter, perhaps it will disappear altogether.' [72]

However, this unfortunate result of the war was never resolved and Churchill's predictions never came to pass. It was to be another thirty years and another three wars before Israel was able to sign a peace treaty with one of her Arab neighbours. In the years and decades that followed, the pitiable Arab refugees were to become an expendable pawn in the Middle East conflict. Israel, on the one hand, refused to take back those who had left in 1948. Apart from being unable to handle the burden of repatriating hundreds of thousands of Arabs, some of whom were quite hostile, Israel had a refugee problem of her own. She had to cope with almost 600,000 Jewish refugees who were expelled from neighbouring Arab countries in the Middle East. And she did.

On the other hand, Israel's neighbours refused to absorb many of the Arab refugees, who were their own kith and kin. In any case a large number of them had migrated to Palestine in previous decades, as the Jews opened up the land. Rather, it suited the purposes of the Arab States to use the refugee problem as a lever against Israel in the international arena.

And so the refugee problem – together with the loss of territory – originally the result of one war caused by the Arabs, became the reason for the next war in 1956. And the next in 1967. And again in 1973.

Indeed, the rebirth of the nation of Israel certainly did create a legacy of conflict in the Middle East. At the time of Israel's Jubilee in 1998, it was often referred to as 'Israel's 50-Year War'. And it hasn't finished yet. This legacy of conflict is no accident of history. It had been forecast by the prophets of Israel, especially with regard to Jerusalem. As we shall see in the chapters that follow, there is a hidden dimension to this conflict. We will also discover that it is part of God's plan to bring about not just the physical restoration of Israel, but ultimately the spiritual restoration of His ancient covenant people to Himself.

Chapter 5

The Reunification of Jerusalem

The Six-Day War

On 5 June 1967, the Middle East erupted into full-scale military conflict for the third time since the rebirth of the Jewish State. Contrary to international law, Egypt had closed the strait at Sharm E-Sheikh, in the Red Sea, to Israeli shipping. The Egyptians also ejected the United Nations peace-keeping force that had been stationed in the Sinai peninsula since the war of 1956. Egypt and Syria had been amassing troops and tanks along Israel's borders, with the clear intention of having a third attempt to wipe out the Jewish State. Israel responded by mounting a pre-emptive strike against both countries. Within hours of the war starting Israel virtually destroyed the Egyptian air force and established air superiority in the entire region. Jordan, having signed a mutual defence pact with Egypt a week earlier, decided to join the war. Ezer Weizman takes up the story:

> 'I think it is a known fact that on the morning of 5th June we did not plan taking Jerusalem, we did not plan to fight the Jordanians ... We even sent a message to His Majesty across the Jordan River that it is not a business with him and us, but between us and the Egyptians.' [73]

Jordan ignored the plea of the Israelis and began to inflict a barrage of mortars and shellfire upon the population of West

Jerusalem from their strongholds in the eastern part of the city. Israel had no choice but to silence the Jordanian artillery.

Two days later, on 7 June 1967, the seemingly impossible happened. The Israelis found themselves in the Old City of Jerusalem. Among them was a young paratrooper, Gershon Salomon, who was in the first unit to make it through to the Temple Mount. He vividly recalls that moment:

> 'My feeling, and every soldier's feeling, was the same upon entering this place for the first time. We went first into the Dome of the Rock, and once inside I started to cry like a little child. Then, all of the soldiers which were around the Rock started to cry. We could not stop ourselves. We stayed on the Temple Mount for long hours – we could not move. You cannot understand this moment for us! This place was the place of the Temple, the heart and soul of the Jewish people. I felt I was very close to Abraham, Isaac, Jacob, King David, and the prophets. It was the most important day of my life, and it follows me every moment of my life ... I felt that we had completed a special mission that all of the generations since the destruction of the Temple in 70 AD asked us to fulfil.'[74]

The holy places were back in Jewish hands. In the midst of the battle for the Holy City that was raging around them, other Israeli soldiers stood below the Temple Mount at the Western Wall, to which they had been denied access for nineteen years, and they, too, laughed and wept unashamedly. The words of an ancient psalm suddenly came to life once again:

> *'When the* LORD *brought back the captivity of Zion,*
> *We were like those who dream.*
> *Then our mouth was filled with laughter,*
> *And our tongue with singing.*
> *Then they said among the nations,*
> *"The* LORD *has done great things for them." '*
>
> (Psalm 126:1–2)

Those words of the Psalmist were to prove prophetic, because around the world there were many, including hardened sceptics, who were taken aback by the magnitude of Israel's victory and acknowledged it as the hand of the Lord. Indeed, He had done great things for Israel. Years later, Ezer Weizman, as the newly elected President of Israel was to concede: 'It's a miracle, it's God's hand, it's a miracle.'

' . . . Until the Times of the Gentiles Are Fulfilled'

Two-and-a-half thousand years of mainly Gentile domination of the Holy City had come to an end, giving a ring of reality to the conclusion of this prophecy by Yeshua:

> *'And Jerusalem will be trampled by Gentiles until the times of the Gentiles are fulfilled.'*   (Luke 21:24)

This milestone [75] in Jewish history anticipates a far more wonderful day of liberation when this prophecy will be completely fulfilled as Yeshua the Messiah takes up the throne of David. Then Jerusalem will never again be trampled over by the Gentiles, for it is written:

> *' "So you shall know that I am the LORD your God,*
> *Dwelling in Zion My holy mountain.*
> *Then Jerusalem shall be holy,*
> *And no aliens shall ever pass through her again." '*
> (Joel 3:17)

Resolution 242

As a result of the Six-Day War of 1967 Israel controlled three times as much territory as she had before the war (see Appendix F, maps 4 and 5). The overwhelming victory for Israel left the Arab world absolutely stunned. But, with the land, Israel had also inherited an Arab population of more than one million people, which concerned Israeli leaders. The government of Prime Minister Levi Eshkol stated their readiness to hand back most of the territory gained in the war if the Arab States finally agreed to end their twenty-year *jihad* against Israel and recognise her right to exist in peace. In September 1967, the vanquished Arab leaders met in Sudan and vowed that they would not negotiate, recognise, or make peace with 'the Zionist enemy'.[76]

Shortly after the Sudan summit, the United Nations passed Resolution 242, which has basically been interpreted as a demand on Israel to withdraw from 'all territories occupied' in the war. However, Resolution 242 did not in fact call for Israel's total withdrawal of all territories taken in the war, which were actually taken in self-defence. On the contrary, it called for negotiations between Israel and her neighbours to establish secure, recognised and defensible new boundaries.[77] Furthermore, Resolution 242 also called on the Arab States to recognise Israel's right to exist in peace, which most of them have refused to do. At the time of writing, only three of the twenty-two Arab States have recognised Israel; the rest are still in a 'state of war' with the Jewish State after more than five decades.[78]

'You Will Arise and Have Mercy on Zion'

Israel's stunning victory in the Six-Day War of 1967 was perhaps the greatest military victory the nation had seen since the days of the kings of Israel. For the first time for more than two-and-a-half thousand years, the whole of Jerusalem was under Jewish sovereignty.[79]

The links that had once bound Zion together, and had been broken, were re-established as the city, the land, and the Jewish people were reunited. Could this be the fulfilment of a prophecy found in Psalm 102?

> *'You will arise and have mercy on Zion;*
> *For the time to favour her,*
> *Yes, the set time, has come.'* (Psalm 102:13)

Jewish rejoicing around the world was great. The most holy site, the Temple Mount, was now in the hands of the sovereign Jewish State. Rabbi Schlomo Goren, then Chief Rabbi of the Israeli Defence Forces, was among the first to reach the Western Wall on 7 June 1967. He assembled a team to survey the Temple Mount with a view to finding the exact location where the Temple had stood.

However, Jewish access to the holiest of all sites – the Temple Mount – was to be short-lived. Four days after the war finished, General Moshe Dayan, the Defence Minister at the time, handed back control of the Temple Mount to the *Waqf*, the Supreme Moslem Council, for fear of inciting riots.

The Israeli government later passed a law forbidding Jews to worship on the Temple Mount. The law was passed as much for religious as for political reasons, as any Jew who ventures onto the site of the Holy of Holies, without first being ceremonially 'cleansed', would defile the site. A sign was posted on the entrance ramp to the Temple Mount, which is still there today. It reads:

> Notice and Warning: Entrance to the area of the Temple Mount is forbidden to everyone by Jewish Law owing to the sacredness of the place.
>
> The Chief Rabbinate of Israel

And so, to this day, Jews are excluded from the Temple Mount, and Moslems control it. The Holy Place, God's Holy Mountain, is still trampled on by the Gentiles. But below the south-west corner of the Temple Mount, Jews kiss and caress the stones of the *Kotel* in greater numbers than ever before. And below the southern edge of the Temple Mount, and throughout the ancient city, Israeli archaeologists painstakingly sift the dust and turn the stones to piece together the past glory of Jerusalem. Surely the Lord's favour is once again beginning to shine upon Zion, as it is written:

> *'For Your servants take pleasure in her stones,*
> *And show favour to her dust.'*   (Psalm 102:14)

The Building Up of Zion

In the wake of the Six-Day War, the Israelis began to resettle the areas of their biblical heartland in Judea and Samaria from which they had been expelled, including Hebron. However, the greatest resettlement has been in and around the capital. In the generation since the reunification of Jerusalem in 1967, the city has enjoyed unprecedented growth unknown since the days of King Solomon. This phenomenal growth and development is a sure sign that the Messiah's advent is near, for it is written:

> *'When the* LORD *shall build up Zion,*
> *He shall appear in His glory.*
> *This shall be written for the generation to come.'*
>
> (Psalm 102:16, 18, KJV)

A more accurate translation of the Hebrew text *ledor akharon* in verse 18 would read:

'This shall be written for **the last generation**.'[80]

During the twentieth century nearly five million Jews returned to their ancient homeland. Today, they continue to arrive home from more than a hundred countries from all points of the globe – north, south, east and west – and many of them have settled in and around Jerusalem, fulfilling other prophecies in the *Tanakh*:

> *' "Thus says the* LORD *of Hosts:*
> *'Behold, I will save My people from the land of the east*
> *And from the land of the west;*
> *I will bring them back,*
> *And they shall dwell in the midst of Jerusalem.' " '*
>
> (Zechariah 8:7–8)

> *' "Behold, I will bring them from the north country,*
> *And gather them from the ends of the earth,*
> *Among them the blind and the lame,*
> *The woman with child*
> *And the one who labours with child, together;*
> *A great throng shall return there. . . .*
> *Hear the word of the* LORD, *O nations,*
> *And declare it in the isles afar off, and say,*
> *'He who scattered Israel will gather him,*
> *And keep him as a shepherd does his flock.' " '*
>
> (Jeremiah 31:8, 10)

There are few, if any, countries in the world which would so readily accept the old, the sick and the infirm as Israel does. In order to house the *Olim*,[81] the Israelis have undertaken massive building projects all over Israel. In Jerusalem itself they include residential areas such as Ramot in the north, Gilo in the south, Ma'ale Adumim to the east and Mevasseret Zion to the west.[82] The words of the prophet Zechariah foreshadowed a time when the Lord would be in the midst of Jerusalem, as a wall of fire around her, and the city would stretch well beyond its walls:

> '"Jerusalem shall be inhabited as towns without walls because of the multitude of men ... in it. For I," says the LORD, "will be a wall of fire all around her, and I will be the glory in her midst."'   (Zechariah 2:4–5)

This prophecy, like the following one, refers to the Messianic Age yet to come, however we can observe that there is an element of fulfilment even today:

> '"Thus says the LORD of Hosts:
> 'Old men and old women shall again sit
> In the streets of Jerusalem,
> Each one with his staff in his hand
> Because of great age.
> The streets of the city
> Shall be full of boys and girls
> Playing in its streets.'"'   (Zechariah 8:4–5)

It is interesting to compare the descriptions of a desolate land and city that both Mark Twain and Robert Murray M'Cheyne gave in the mid-nineteenth century with the sights we see in and around Jerusalem today – especially in the light of the above two prophecies. Following the reunification of Jerusalem in 1967 former Mayor, Teddy Kollek, embarked on a massive programme for the beautification of the Holy City in preparation for the coming of the Messiah. Compare this with:

> 'Beautiful for situation,
> The joy of the whole earth,

> *Is Mount Zion, on the sides of the north,*
> *The city of the great King.'* (Psalm 48:2, KJV)

and

> *'When the* LORD *shall build up Zion,*
> *He shall appear in His glory.'* (Psalm 102:16, KJV)

The Jerusalem Law

Some years after the Six-Day War of 1967, Israel formally annexed East Jerusalem and the Golan Heights, which had been won from Jordan and Syria respectively. However, Judea, Samaria, Gaza and the Sinai Peninsula remained as territories under Israeli military administration. Following the Camp David Accord in March 1979, which US President Jimmy Carter brokered between Israeli Prime Minister Menachem Begin and Egyptian President Anwar Sadat, a formal peace treaty was signed between Israel and Egypt. The whole of the Sinai Peninsula, which included substantial oilfields, was later handed back to Egypt. This transaction accounted for more than 90 per cent of the territory Israel won in the Six-Day War, and the subsequent 'Yom Kippur' War of 1973.[83]

However, contention over the status of Jerusalem still continued.

On 30 July 1980, the Knesset[84] voted overwhelmingly in favour of a Bill proclaiming that 'Jerusalem is the Eternal and Indivisible Capital of Israel'. This Bill, which was an official declaration to the world of what was already an accepted fact in Israel, became known as the Jerusalem Law. The then leader of the opposition Labour Party, Shimon Peres, supported the Bill. 'We are united,' he said, 'namely that Jerusalem must remain as one city as the capital of Israel.' Former Labour Prime Minister Yitzhak Rabin[85] gave the following reason for the Bill:

> 'No doubt, many people in Israel supported the Bill because of certain provocations against Israel in the international arena, including the United Nations, in

Europe and in Egypt – that these provocations were aimed to put a question mark on Jerusalem as a united city.'

Predictably, international opposition to the declaration was intense. The Arab States delivered an ultimatum that all foreign embassies must leave Jerusalem or their oil supplies would be cut off. Thirteen embassies based in Jerusalem[86] promptly vacated the city and relocated in Tel Aviv.

The International Christian Embassy, Jerusalem

When the nations of the world isolated Israel for enacting the Jerusalem Law, it prompted one group to stand with Israel on this issue. The group, comprising Christians from twenty-three nations under the leadership of Dutchman Jan Willem Van der Hoeven, set up the International Christian Embassy in Jerusalem during the Feast of Tabernacles in 1980. The Director of the Embassy, Johann Lückhoff, explained their reasons:

'It is to be a focal point for Christians world-wide, right here in Jerusalem. The Christians show their concern according to Isaiah 40 that says: *'Comfort My people, comfort My people . . . '* And so we at the Embassy want to encourage Christians world-wide to pray for Israel, to pray for 'the peace of Jerusalem' and to show their concern for the Jewish people in as many ways as possible.'[87]

The support given by the Embassy was to touch the heart of the Jewish nation. At the opening of the Embassy on 30 September 1980, Jerusalem's Mayor, Teddy Kollek, commented: 'This has been one of the most moving ceremonies I have ever attended in my life.'[88]

'Watchmen on the Walls'

The opening of the International Christian Embassy in Jerusalem is just one example of the movement of the Spirit of the Lord during the last quarter of the twentieth century. Other examples include the Jerusalem-based organisation Bridges For Peace, which was founded in 1976, and Christian Friends of Israel, which began in 1986. All three of these charities seek to show the love of the Lord to the nation of Israel in a practical way. In fact during the last three decades the Holy Spirit has moved among many Bible-believing Christians around the world to intercede on behalf of the Jewish people and the nation of Israel, especially in anticipation of the establishment of the kingdom of the Messiah on earth, and the birth-pains that will precede it. This prayer for the nation of Israel and the city of Jerusalem was stated as the purpose of the Lord 2,700 years ago by the prophet Isaiah:

> '*I have set watchmen on your walls, O Jerusalem,*
> *Who shall never hold their peace day or night.*
> *You who make mention of the* LORD, *do not keep silent,*
> *And give Him no rest till He establishes*
> *And till He makes Jerusalem a praise in the earth.*'
>
> (Isaiah 62:6–7)

This statement by God through the prophet Isaiah actually contains a mandate to all 'who make mention of the Lord' – in other words every Christian – to pray for the accomplishment of God's purposes concerning Jerusalem.

'A Standard for the People'

Not only is there a dramatic rise in the number of individual Christians who 'pray for the peace of Jerusalem' as the problems Israel faces continue to increase, but the Lord has birthed a growing number of Christian ministries with a focus on both intercession and practical humanitarian assistance.[89] Some of these ministries are actively assisting in the return of *Olim* to their ancient homeland, whether in terms of transportation, in conjunction with the Jewish Agency, or in some form of support when they arrive in Israel. This Gentile involvement in bringing Jewish people home was outlined by the prophet Isaiah:

> *'Thus says the Lord God:*
> *"Behold, I will lift My hand in an oath to the Gentiles,*
> *And set up a standard for the peoples;*
> *They shall bring your sons in their arms,*
> *And your daughters shall be carried on their shoulders.' "*

(Isaiah 49:22)

A Change of Government, a Change of Direction

A significant change in Israeli politics took place in 1992. Atheistic humanism became the ideological mainspring of government as never before in the history of the reborn State. The Labour Party had been in power for the majority of Israel's forty-four years, but the right-wing Likud party had held office for most of the previous fifteen years. On 23 June that year the Israeli people went to the polls in what proved to be the most crucial election up to that time.

The media reported that the Likud government, led by 'hard-line' Prime Minister Yitzhak Shamir, had been defeated in a 'landslide' swing to Labour. The truth of the matter was that the Labour leadership struggled to pull together a coalition to gain an absolute majority in the 120-seat Knesset. The new Prime Minister was Yitzhak Rabin. He was the first *Sabra* (native-born Israeli) to hold that office and, tragically, he was later to become the first Israeli leader to be assassinated. The new Foreign Minister was Shimon Peres. Both men had previously held office as Prime Minister for a brief period.

The 1992 election marked a turning-point for the nation. It was the first Israeli government from either side of politics to depart from the biblical precept that *Eretz Yisrael*[90] belongs to the Jewish people as an everlasting possession, as stated in the Abrahamic Covenant. Yitzhak Rabin had little regard for the Hebrew Scriptures, dismissing them as mere fables. The day after he took office as Prime Minister, he expressed his view of the Jewish people, 'We are a nation just like any other nation.'[91]

The ideology of the Rabin government was to have the effect of bitterly polarising the nation, especially with regard to the inheritance of the Jewish people – *Eretz Yisrael*. It was to have devastating consequences not only for himself, but also for the well-being of the nation.

However, there is one issue that has almost universal consensus among Jews, both in the *Diaspora* and in Israel. It is Jerusalem – the Covenant City.

The Jerusalem Covenant

'Ladies and Gentlemen, I am honoured and pleased that one of my first meetings and gatherings, after having been elected, is with you – Ladies and Gentlemen, who are representatives of world Jewry, that have come to Jerusalem to sign the Covenant – to re-affirm the link of the Jews with Jerusalem, and Jerusalem with the *Diaspora*.'

These words were spoken on 19 May 1993 by Ezer Weizman, who had succeeded Chaim Herzog as President of Israel only a week earlier. He was addressing a gathering of the leaders of world Jewry at a private ceremony in the presidential residence just before they all added their signatures to a historical document.

A year earlier, during the final weeks of the Shamir/Likud government, a letter was sent from Jerusalem to the leaders of Jewish communities in the *Diaspora* all over the world. The letter, signed by the Deputy Minister for Jerusalem Affairs, the Chairman of the World Zionist Organisation and Teddy Kollek, the then Mayor of Jerusalem, invited its recipients to become signatories to *Amanat Yerushalayim* – The Covenant of Jerusalem.

The Covenant was drawn up to commemorate the twenty-fifth anniversary of the reunification of Jerusalem, celebrated on 28 Iyar 5752 – 31 May 1992. Written by Menachem Elon, the Deputy President of the Supreme Court of Israel, the Covenant consists mainly of biblical verses, Talmudic passages and Psalms that refer to Jerusalem. *The Jerusalem Covenant* (see Appendix B) is divided into seven sections, each of which addresses a theme common to Jerusalem. The document includes one portion that deals with Jerusalem's centrality to the Jewish people, while another emphasises Jerusalem as a centre of peace. 'Still another views the city as a meeting ground for the entire world,' Elon said. 'In Isaiah it says, *"All the nations will come to Jerusalem."'* He continued:

> 'That the Covenant has seven sections is not coinciden-tal. The number seven figures prominently in Judaism: Shabbat is the seventh day, for example, and historically there have been seven gates into the walled city of Jerusalem. The sections, like the gates, lead into the heart of the city. The most gratifying thing about the Covenant, is that it has been accepted by all parts of the Jewish nation – Orthodox, Conservative, Reform and Jews who have never set foot in a synagogue. Jerusalem has finally brought about a consensus.'[92]

During the twenty-fifth anniversary year, every Jewish community around the world received two parchment scrolls with the text of the Covenant. At ceremonies held throughout the *Diaspora* during the year, the leaders of each community were invited to sign the scrolls in order to affirm their commitment to, and identification with, Jerusalem. Each community kept one of the scrolls for display, and the other one was brought back to Jerusalem by at least two representa-tives from the community for the *Yom Yerushalayim* (Jerusalem Day) celebrations in 1993. These Covenant scrolls were presented to the President of Israel at a ceremony on Ammunition Hill in Jerusalem. Over one thousand Jewish leaders from seventy countries were present for this special event, held on the evening of *Yom Yerushalayim*, 19 May 1993.

Earlier that day, at the ceremony where he signed the Covenant, President Weizman recalled the event twenty-six years ago which they were now celebrating:

> 'Israel is, was and always will be the centre of world Jewry, and Jerusalem within it. Jerusalem is an eternal city. Jerusalem is a complicated, intricate and phenom-enal city.
>
> Now I am not sure that I always believe in miracles but what happened in '67 was a miracle. It's like the

story of Balaam, [who] went up to curse the Israelites and he went blessing them. So by shelling Jerusalem and hitting Israel, it was a blessing that we had to attack and take the West Bank and Jerusalem with it. It's a miracle, it's God's hand, it's a miracle.'[93]

There are some remarkable aspects to The Jerusalem Covenant, which in many respects has greater significance than the Jerusalem Law passed by the Knesset in 1980. For instance, this historic event, involving the whole of world Jewry at the highest levels, was virtually ignored by the world's media. Consequently, at the time, there was none of the furore that took place when the Jerusalem Law was enacted by the Knesset. This lack of attention in the eyes of the world was possibly providential, as was the event itself. As mentioned earlier, much of the text of the Covenant is from the Hebrew Scriptures which not only reinforce the Abrahamic Covenant in relation to the land and the city, but also reaffirm the promises of God through the prophets. No doubt that is the great strength of the *Amanat Yerushalayim*, which will probably prove to have both spiritual and prophetic significance in the years ahead as the Israelis' hold on Jerusalem is challenged.

However, The Jerusalem Covenant has its weaknesses too. This covenant differs from the covenants of the Bible in a number of respects.

Firstly, The Jerusalem Covenant originated with human beings rather than the God of Israel. Unfortunately, the God of Israel seems to be portrayed as a mystic personality in the background of Israel's affairs, rather than the Sovereign God who is guiding the destiny of the nation and preserving her, and who longs to be recognised for who He is.

Secondly, The Jerusalem Covenant likens itself to the biblical covenant the nation made at the end of the Babylonian exile. But, when compared with the covenant found in Nehemiah 9 and 10, there is one important element missing. The covenant in Nehemiah is primarily a covenant of repentance for the sins of the past in which the people vowed to obey the Lord.

Thirdly, this covenant compromises the holy places, i.e.

the Temple Mount as the exclusive dwelling place of YHWH and His Anointed One. It permits the worship of other gods, including Allah,[94] which the Lord expressly forbids, not only for Israel, but for all people. It is the first of the Ten Commandments. Therefore the sanction of the worship of other gods (religions) in The Jerusalem Covenant is contrary to *Torah*.

There is little doubt, however, that the signing of The Jerusalem Covenant heralded a turning point for Jerusalem, because since its inception, it has surely been put to the test.

A Battle of Rhetoric

As Jews were signing The Jerusalem Covenant all over the world, a war of words was raging over Jerusalem. Eliyahu Tal, Founder and Chairman of the 'International Forum for a United Jerusalem', best summed up the war of rhetoric. A week after the *Yom Yerushalayim* celebrations that year, he commented:

> 'On its 26th anniversary, Jerusalem Day has firmly established itself in the Jewish calendar. This year it was commemorated by a mass rally to Jerusalem of Jewish communities throughout the *Diaspora*, reminiscent of the pilgrimage to Jerusalem during the Temple times.
>
> Heart-warming as this manifestation of Jewish solidarity was, one still had to ask: "What is being done for Jerusalem the rest of the year?"
>
> Selling Jerusalem to the Jews is hardly necessary. After all, it is the only issue that enjoys complete consensus in an otherwise divided Jewish world. Unfortunately, this view is not shared by most of the rest of the world, including our closest friend, the US.
>
> One cannot escape the feeling that the arena has been ceded to Arab propaganda, which has become more consistent and sophisticated over the years ... Arab spokesmen are trying to rewrite the history of the Holy City, without even blushing.
>
> Behind the cloak of academic credence and fine rhetoric lies pure propaganda. Among the assortment

of half-truths and brazen distortions: "the Palestinians are the descendants of the Jebusites, and therefore have an earlier claim to Jebus, i.e. Jerusalem"; "the biblical Philistines are the precursors of today's Palestinians"; "Jesus and St. Paul were Palestinian martyrs," etc.

One could dismiss such statements with an ironic smile, had they not been absorbed by the general media and even penetrated prestigious publications. The damage is almost irreparable.

While branding the Jews as "newcomers" to Jerusalem, [one Arab spokesman] claims he can trace his family tree back to Saladin. Fair enough: so can we. Soon after Saladin's victory in 1187, Jews began to return to the city. The largest contingent, comprising 300 rabbis from England and France, arrived in 1212. Since then, *aliyah* has continued uninterruptedly.

Another cliché coined by the Arabs and adopted by the media is "Arab Jerusalem", when referring to the Old City. How many of Israel's friends, engaged in the ongoing debate over Jerusalem, are aware of the fact that Jews have constituted the largest sector of the city's population since the 1820s? Other similar myths can and should be exposed.

Unfortunately we have played into the hands of our adversaries in more ways than one.

Israel has harmed its cause by adhering to the commonly used definition of Jerusalem as "the city holy to three faiths". This equation is as dangerous as it is inaccurate, since it places the rights of the three religions on an equal footing ... The fact is that Jerusalem is the heart of Judaism, the cradle of Christianity and only the third holiest city to Islam.

There is general agreement that once the Arab-Israeli conflict is on the agenda, the issue of Jerusalem will be the hardest to resolve. Jerusalem was the main note of discord at Camp David; Menachem Begin stated that Jerusalem was indivisible, while Anwar Sadat declared that all Israel's attempts to alter the status of the city [under Islam] were null and void. The gap between these opposing views has not narrowed since then.

The battle over this sensitive political and religious issue is being fought with words and imagery rather than with guns and missiles ... The issue of Jerusalem is one of international proportions, and must be dealt with on a global scale. Both the Vatican and Moslem world will insist on having a say in the matter, and it may be safely assumed that their attitudes will be less than friendly to Israel's position.

'A long hard struggle over Jerusalem lies ahead.'[95]

Indeed it does.

Chapter 6

Jerusalem –
the Capital of Palestine?

The *Intifada*

In the late 1980s a new conflict began in the Middle East. Unlike the previous wars that Israel had fought in its forty years of Statehood, this one was not so much a threat from without, but a threat from within. The first spark that was to ignite what became known as the *Intifada* or 'Uprising' began as a riot on 8 December 1987 at the Jebalya Refugee Camp in the Gaza Strip. The revolt was sparked by the death of four Arabs when their two vehicles collided with an Israeli army truck.[96] The rioting was characterised by the hurling of bricks, stones, steel balls and petrol bombs, and quickly spread throughout the Gaza Strip, Judea and Samaria. Two days after the riots began, Yasser Arafat, the chairman of the Palestine Liberation Organisation,[97] stated on PLO radio from Baghdad:

> 'O heroic sons of the Gaza Strip, O proud sons of the West Bank, O heroic sons of the Galilee, O steadfast sons of the Negev ... the fires of revolution against these Zionist invaders will not fade out ... until our land – all our land – has been liberated from these usurping invaders.'[98]

The following month, Arafat's deputy stated:

> 'The establishment of an independent Palestinian state on the West Bank and the Gaza Strip does not contradict

our ultimate strategic aim, which is the establishment of a democratic state in the entire territory of Palestine, but rather it is a step in that direction.'[99]

Scenes of 'oppressed' Palestinian youths throwing rocks and petrol bombs at the 'mighty' Israeli military 'oppressors' became commonplace viewing on the world's television screens over the next few years, fanning the flames of the *Intifada* into a roaring inferno that Israel could not fight. The Israeli soldiers – often faced with the moral dilemma as to how to deal humanely with rioting children and teenagers who were out to kill if they could – responded with tear gas, rubber bullets and in more serious cases, live ammunition. For the PLO the *Intifada* was a propaganda coup – the world's media successfully turned their image as a terrorist organisation into that of a group of people oppressed and robbed of their land by the mighty aggressor – Israel.[100]

On 15 November 1988, the Palestine Liberation Organisation proclaimed the existence of the 'State of Palestine'. On 2 April the following year, Yasser Arafat was 'unanimously elected' as 'President' of the de facto state. His ultimate aim: a state that would occupy not just Judea and Samaria, Israel's biblical heartland, but the whole of *Eretz Yisrael*, with 'Al Quds' – Jerusalem – as its capital.

Saddam Hussein Backs the *Intifada*

In mid-1990 more fuel was added to the PLO fire. A new recruit now championed their cause, Saddam Hussein, President of Iraq. Claiming to be the 'Nebuchadnezzar' of the modern era, he threatened to 'burn half of Israel' with his Scud missiles, capable of carrying devastating chemical warheads. In August the Iraqis invaded Kuwait, plundered the land and its oilfields, terrorising and murdering sections of the population, all with the collaboration of the two hundred thousand 'Palestinians' living in Kuwait. In an attempt to deflect world opinion away from himself, Saddam Hussein claimed that Israel was the real invader in the Middle East. Despite the wrath of the nations of the world, he refused to budge from Kuwait (which he asserted was a province of Iraq) unless Israel withdrew from all 'occupied territories in Palestine'. His demand included Jerusalem, which he vowed to liberate for the 'Palestinian people'. With this support, the *Intifada* gained a new momentum which led to a tragic incident on the Temple Mount during the Jewish Feast of Tabernacles that year.

Jihad on the Temple Mount

Tension had begun to build up on God's Holy Mountain well before dawn on Monday morning, 8 October 1990. Devout Moslems had come to defend the Temple Mount from a group of about thirty-five Jews who wanted to march to the site where the House of the Lord once stood. This was not the first time that the group, known as the Temple Mount Faithful (TMF), under the leadership of Gershon Salomon, was making an attempt to lay the cornerstone of the third Temple. The first attempt had taken place a year earlier on 16 October. Salomon, a professor in Oriental studies at the Hebrew University in Jerusalem, had been in the first paratroop unit to reach the Temple Mount on 7 June 1967. He gave the following reasons for what they were doing:

> 'On our most holy day, Sukkot, we felt that we must make the first step for rebuilding the Temple. I and my friends, as well as every Israeli and every Jew in all the world, felt that God had performed a great miracle in bringing us back to our historical country ... The land of Israel and the State of Israel is now rebuilding every day more and more, [and so] we felt that we must take the second step, which was the will of God, to build His house again on the Temple Mount. We decided to bring the first cornerstone for this Temple, after 2000 years ... we brought it with us to put it on the Temple Mount, [but] the police and the government decided not to allow us to do it.' [101]

Two years earlier the TMF had lodged an action in the Israeli High Court, in an attempt to compel the government to assert more forcibly Israel's sovereignty over the Temple

Mount. They alleged that the Moslem governing authorities on the Temple Mount (the *Waqf*) were deliberately destroying and concealing ancient visible remains of Solomon's Temple, the second Temple and Crusader structures. They argued that these acts were motivated by a Moslem desire to obliterate all Jewish connections to the site, and thereby to remove the basis for any Israeli claim to the Temple Mount.[102]

A senior *Waqf* official, Adnan Husseini, who was also in charge of engineering projects on the Temple Mount, denied the allegations, stating that there was no sign of any ancient Jewish presence on the Temple Mount. Such a statement is in keeping with the radical Moslem contention that there was never any Jewish occupation of the site before the start of the Moslem period at the beginning of the seventh century CE.[103]

This warm sunny morning in October 1990 was the fifth day of *Sukkot* (the Feast of Tabernacles), when Jewish men of priestly descent come to the Western Wall each year, to say a Levitical benediction over the assembled worshippers. About 25,000 Jews had gathered in the large Western Wall plaza below the Temple Mount. As the priestly ceremony ended, the TMF came marching into the plaza, singing religious and nationalistic songs and waving Israeli flags. Forbidden by the Israeli authorities to march onto the Temple Mount itself, the group made their way out of the Old City through the Dung Gate, heading down towards the Kidron Valley, where King David had built his capital city.

The TMF stopped near the bottom of the valley at the Pool of Shiloah to re-enact an ancient Jewish water purification ceremony. However, just as the TMF marchers left the Old City through the Dung Gate, loudspeakers began to broadcast sermons from inside the Al-Aqsa Mosque at the southern end of the Temple Mount platform, which was packed with Moslem worshippers. Urged to wage *jihad*, or 'holy war', to defend *Haram al-Sharif* (the holy shrine) from the Jews planning to march to the sacred site, crowds of Palestinian men congregating outside Al-Aqsa Mosque and the nearby Dome of the Rock began to collect building blocks, stones and metal bars from various Temple Mount construction sites. They rushed to the western edge of the Mount, followed by thousands more *jihad*-frenzied Arabs. They overwhelmed the forty-four Israeli policemen stationed there who then fled and warned the Jewish worshippers at the Wall below to evacuate the area. Fortunately, by the time the enraged Moslems began hurling their missiles onto the Western Wall plaza below, most of the Jewish worshippers had left. Even so, about a dozen were injured in the barrage.

The bolstered Israeli security forces then re-entered the Temple Mount. In the ensuing battle, seventeen Palestinian Arabs were killed and scores more wounded, in what turned out to be one of the bloodiest incidents of the *Intifada*. Amid the gunfire, a shout was heard, 'Saddam will avenge us!' Many Palestinians in Jerusalem and elsewhere in Israel held a wake on the night of the tragedy, waiting for the Iraqi chemical-tipped Scud missiles to rain down on Tel Aviv, the largest centre of Jewish population. But their hoped-for avenger and saviour did not come through – at least not right away.

The world's media put the blame squarely on Israel for the incident. They ignored the fact that the Moslem leaders were officially informed that the Israeli High Court had banned the TMF from holding their 'cornerstone dedication' on the Temple Mount a week before the incident took place. The Israeli judiciary was in agreement with police that the proposed ceremony would trigger bloodshed at Islam's third holiest site – and Judaism's holiest site. In an attempt to avert this possibility, the High Court's ban was published in all East Jerusalem's Arabic newspapers.[104]

Intelligence reports later substantiated the suspicion that the Temple Mount *jihad* was instigated by Saddam Hussein in order to shift world attention from Iraq's occupation of Kuwait to Israel's 'occupation of Palestine'.[105]

Media Tunnel Vision

Six years later in 1996, again at *Sukkot*, there was to be another incident that resulted in even worse bloodshed than in the 1990 riots. This incident revolved around the Western Wall Tunnel.

The tunnel itself had been excavated over a fourteen-year period during the 1970s and 1980s. It runs northwards from the plaza along the length of the Western Wall under the Moslem Quarter. At the northern end of the wall, the tunnel follows an ancient aqueduct which had been constructed during the Hasmonean period of the second century BCE. Contrary to some rumours, at no point does the recently-excavated tunnel actually go beneath the Temple Mount itself.[106] The Western Wall Tunnel was opened to tourists in July 1991, but because there was no way out at the northern end, the tourists had to turn round and double back to the entrance at the Western Wall plaza. This severely limited the number of tourists who could visit the tunnel at any one time.

At the beginning of 1996 the Peres-led Labour government, which preceded the Netanyahu-led Likud government, had reached an agreement with the Moslem *Waqf* that would benefit both sides. On the one hand, the Israeli government would permit the *Waqf* to create an under-cover worship area in the south-eastern corner of the Temple Mount. On the other hand, the Western Wall Heritage Foundation would be allowed to create an exit at the northern end of the Western Wall Tunnel onto the Via Dolorosa. This deal would enable greater numbers of tourists to pass through the tunnel, and at the same time boost the business of the Arab traders on that street. Although the *Waqf* began paving work to the east of the Al-Aqsa Mosque, for some reason the Labour government did not go ahead with the opening of the northern end of the tunnel. Later in 1996, however, the newly elected Likud government decided they would open it.

A few days before *Sukkot* the Mayor of Jerusalem, Ehud Olmert, symbolically laid a sledge-hammer to the final two feet of stone that needed to be excavated to forge the opening of the tunnel on to Via Dolorosa. What followed is almost unbelievable.

Ignoring the agreement made with the previous Israeli government, an enraged Yasser Arafat immediately held an emergency session of his Cabinet, then announced to the world's media that the Israelis were tunnelling under the Temple Mount near the Al-Aqsa Mosque. 'It is a crime, a big crime against our religion and our holy places. We cannot accept the judaisation of Jerusalem,' he ranted to the rolling television cameras.[107] The suggestion was also made that this 'tunnelling' was undermining the foundations of the mosque. The media reported Arafat's allegations as fact.

Judea, Samaria and Gaza erupted in violence. Palestinian 'police' turned their automatic weapons, supplied by Israel, on the Israeli security forces. Three days of rioting and gun battles left about eighty-five people dead on both sides, and hundreds more wounded.

The nations of the world, along with the media, roundly condemned Israel for the carnage, and accused her of defiling Islam's third holiest site. There was no mention and no recognition of the fact that an agreement had been reached between the Israeli government and the Moslem *Waqf*, nor that the Temple Mount is the holiest site for the Jews. And it was only after several days of needless bloodshed that the media acknowledged that the exit, where the so-called tunnelling had occurred, was some distance from the Al-Aqsa Mosque. In fact it is about half a kilometre away!

The Temple Mount – a Ticking Time Bomb

These two incidents concerning the Temple Mount, which resulted in so much bloodshed, are highlighted because they demonstrate the depth of passion for Jerusalem, and particularly the Temple Mount, in both Jew and Arab. The 1996 incident concerning the Western Wall Tunnel demonstrates the media's willingness to broadcast PLO propaganda without looking into the facts. With accurate and truthful reporting from the outset, the violence would never have been incited. Arguably, because of their tunnel-vision, or selective reporting in that particular case, the world's media – together with Yasser Arafat – have the blood of seventy Palestinian Arabs and fifteen Israeli Jews on their hands.

Both the 1990 and 1996 incidents indicate that Jerusalem, and especially the twenty-five or so acres of land that comprise the platform on which the House of the Lord once stood, is like a powder keg that has the potential to cause the whole Middle East, if not the whole world, to explode into a holocaust.

The *jihad* for Jerusalem and the Temple Mount, however, goes beyond human passion and religious ideology. Behind it is a conflict in the spiritual realm that is being played out in the natural realm – in the arenas of religious fervour, of political manoeuvring, and subsequent military conflict. History shows us that this piece of real estate has already been the most fought over piece of land on the face of the earth. The prophetic Scriptures, as we shall see in Chapter 9, foretell that it will one day fulfil its potential to trigger a global holocaust, as the spiritual forces of darkness pit themselves against the revealed purposes of the God of Israel – the One who said of the Temple Mount:

> ' "This is My resting place forever,
> Here I will dwell, for I have desired it. . . .
> There I will make the horn of David grow;
> I will prepare a lamp for My Anointed.
> His enemies I will clothe with shame,
> But upon Himself His crown shall flourish." '
>
> (Psalm 132:14, 17–18)

Saddam's Fury

At the same time as this tragic event took place on God's Holy Mountain during the Feast of Tabernacles in 1990, the armies of the whole western world were amassing in the Middle East, and particularly along Saudi Arabia's northern border with Kuwait. Their mission: to eject Saddam Hussein from Kuwait, subdue the bellicose tyrant and destroy his formidable military machine, which was a threat to the entire region.

There was one potential hazard to the fragile American-led alliance, which included a number of Arab nations – that Israel might enter the war. As has already been mentioned, several months before invading Kuwait, Saddam Hussein had threatened to 'burn half of Israel' with his Scud missiles. Israel, while in the throes of issuing gas-masks to its civilian population, had warned that if a single missile was fired in the direction the Holy Land, retaliation against Iraq would be swift and devastating. At the time, Israeli Military Intelligence had good reason to believe that Saddam Hussein had developed nuclear as well as both chemical and biological weapons.[108] Iraq had already had its nuclear development severely curtailed a decade earlier when Israel destroyed a nuclear plant.

Saddam knew full well that if he could draw Israel into the war, the Arab nations who stood against him would probably come across to his side to fight 'the Zionist infidel'. For the very same reason, the Allies did their best to persuade Israel to allow them to deal with Saddam Hussein. After months of brinkmanship in which the Iraqi leader defiantly ignored one UN ultimatum to withdraw from Kuwait after another, the Allied airforces led by the United States, began massive bombing raids into Iraq on 17 January 1991. As promised, Saddam Hussein launched his Scud missiles at Israel, as well as at other Allied positions. As each Scud missile screamed across the Holy Land towards its mark, Palestinian Arabs cheered and chanted *'Allahu Akbar!'* – 'God is Great!'

The forty-day Gulf War ended on the Jewish Feast of *Purim*.[109] Apart from the eight-year Iran-Iraq war, this was the first major war in the Middle East since 1948 in which Israel did not fight. A total of thirty-nine Scud missiles landed in Israel causing considerable damage to property. Many of the missiles had malfunctioned, either missing their target, or simply failing to explode on impact. What was absolutely astonishing was that only one Jewish person died as a result of a direct hit by a Scud missile. Many Israelis saw this as a miracle from God. What Saddam had not taken into account when he vowed to avenge the Palestinians and 'burn half of Israel' was an end-time promise that the Lord had made to Israel:

> ' *"No weapon formed against you shall prosper."* '
> (Isaiah 54:17)

After murdering and raping thousands of Kuwaitis, laying waste the country and the oilfields, the Iraqis were finally ejected from Kuwait, their army in tatters. The Allies, however, stopped short of advancing on Baghdad and taking the Iraqi leader captive to put him on trial as a war criminal. Instead, they left him to continue his internal reign of terror – and his constant defiance of the United Nations and the nations of the West.

Many senior Kuwaiti government officials, who had fled when Iraq invaded their country, were now able to return to rebuild the country. One of their first actions was to expel all of the 200,000 Palestinian residents who had sided with Saddam Hussein. This mass expulsion took place without so much as a word of protest from the world's media.

Looking back at the Gulf War, one of the amazing things about it was the speed with which the armies of the world gathered together when Iraq threatened to take over the oilfields of Saudi Arabia. It was almost as if it was a rehearsal for a great event prophesied in the Scriptures, when the armies of the world will gather together for the last great battle – which will be against Jerusalem.

> *'And they gathered them together to the place called in Hebrew, Armageddon.'*   (Revelation 16:16)

Israel Under Pressure

The 1991 Gulf War established the United States as the undisputed leader of the 'New World Order' – in other words, the world's 'policeman'. Having enlisted many Arab nations into an alliance to deal with Saddam Hussein, who was clearly a threat to the stability of the Middle East, pressure was now on US President George Bush to deal with the other 'thorn in the side' of the Middle East – Israel.

Having been constrained from retaliating against Iraq for raining down Scud missiles on *Eretz Yisrael*, Israeli Prime Minister Yitzhak Shamir suddenly found himself being forced to sit around a table with 'the Palestinians' in Madrid. He did manage to extract one significant concession from the Americans, and that was to exclude the PLO, as an organisation, from the conference, in keeping with Israel's policy of not negotiating with terrorists. In fact Shamir flatly refused to recognise the PLO, in any shape or form, as the legitimate representative of the Arab Palestinian people. Earlier that year the Israeli Prime Minister had offered the Palestinians – that is those Arabs who were living in Judea, Samaria and Gaza – some form of limited self-government in which the PLO would not be involved. However, the regions where the Palestinians would receive autonomy would still be under Israel's authority and control. The Palestinians, under pressure from the PLO, refused Shamir's offer.

From both the Americans' and the PLO's point of view, the Madrid Peace Conference of 1991 achieved nothing. The PLO's designs on *Eretz Yisrael*, and Jerusalem, had been kept at bay, but the PLO-driven *intifada* continued unabated and the threat of the violence escalating was always a possibility. Unable to please the Arab nations that had backed him against Saddam Hussein, the American President was unhappy too.

The next year, 1992, saw a change of government both in Israel, as Labour gained power under Yitzhak Rabin, and in the US as George Bush was voted out of the White House, in favour of a slick Democrat called Bill Clinton.

'Peace' Accord

Scarcely had the ink dried on The Jerusalem Covenant in 1993 when the media were proclaiming a new era of peace in the Middle East. The event that created the euphoria was a historic handshake between the Israeli Prime Minister and the leader of the PLO. All of a sudden, the Palestine Liberation Organisation was no longer a terrorist organisation, but the 'legitimate' representative of the 'Palestinian' people. This handshake with Yasser Arafat – as distasteful as Yitzhak Rabin seems to have found it at the time – took place on the front lawn at the White House in Washington on 13 September 1993 before the world's media. A Declaration of Principles (DOP) for a Peace Accord had been signed. The negotiations for this historic agreement had been going on in secret in Norway and had taken everyone, even the Israelis, by surprise.

The DOP – or Oslo Accords, as they became known – was not a peace treaty in itself. It was a timetable for the negotiations of various stages of autonomy for the Palestinian Arabs in the disputed territories. The DOP, as such, made no guarantees concerning either the formation of a Palestinian State or the final status of Jerusalem. In fact, by mutual agreement, the DOP deliberately excluded any such guarantees. These subjects, it was decided, would not be on the agenda for discussion until 1996.

The euphoria on both sides was intense, according to the media. Arabs living in Jerusalem had their Palestinian flags flying from some of the high places of the Old City. In contradiction of the agreement he had just signed, within days Yasser Arafat was proclaiming that Jerusalem would be the capital of a Palestinian State. Even so, there were many Palestinians who were far from satisfied with the Oslo Accords. HAMAS and other Islamic fundamentalist groups were violently opposed to any form of agreement with Israel. They felt as though they had been sold out by the PLO leader's agreement to a phased withdrawal from the disputed territories by the Israelis. HAMAS and their allies were demanding that the Jews immediately relinquish 'all occupied Arab lands' – which in their eyes constitutes all of Israel – and subsequently they stepped up their terrorist campaign in order to derail the peace process.

Many Israelis were far from happy too. The next three years saw a dramatic increase in the number of Israelis killed in terrorist attacks. The murder weapons used included axes, knives and guns – but most devastating of all was the suicide bomber. Jerusalem experienced some of the biggest demonstrations it had ever seen. Jewish settlers in Gaza, Judea and Samaria were denounced by their own government for their 'messianic' aspirations – i.e. their belief that the Abrahamic Covenant gave them the Title Deed to *Eretz Yisrael*, which included the country's biblical heartland where they dwelt.

Moreover, most Israelis were deeply disturbed because the government had far exceeded its electoral mandate and were pandering to an enemy whose clear intention was to destroy them. Many Israelis could still remember Arafat's words in the lead-up to the Gulf War when he sided with Saddam Hussein:

'We will enter Jerusalem victorious and raise our flag on its walls ... We will fight you with stones, rifles and *El-Abed* [the Iraqi Scud missile].'

Even as he shook Prime Minister Rabin's hand on the White House lawn in September 1993, the PLO leader had used the Arab term *marahil* (stages) several times during his speech, sending a coded message to the Arab world that the agreement marked the launch of the Phased Plan.[110]

However, as the PLO and the Arab nations set their sights on disinheriting the Jewish people from the biblical heartland of Israel – the mountains of Judea, Samaria and especially Jerusalem – they ignored an ancient prophecy in which the Lord speaks to the mountains of Israel. The prophecy, found in the Book of Ezekiel, refers to the latter days when the Jewish people would return to the Promised Land:

> *'Thus says the Lord Goɒ: "Because the enemy has said of you, 'Aha! The ancient heights have become our possession,' therefore prophesy, and say, 'Thus says the Lord Goɒ: ... "Surely I have spoken in My burning jealousy against the rest of the nations and against all Edom,*[111] *who gave My land to themselves as a possession, with whole-hearted joy and spiteful minds, in order to plunder its open country."'*
>
> *... Therefore thus says the Lord Goɒ: "I have lifted My hand in an oath that surely the nations that are around you* [the mountains of Israel] *shall bear their own shame."'*
>
> (Ezekiel 36:2, 5, 7)

As the clamour following the historic handshake continued, and terrorist atrocities against Israeli citizens escalated, an Israeli called Binyamin Netanyahu, who had risen to prominence during the Gulf War and later succeeded Yitzhak Shamir as leader of the opposition Likud Party, echoed the fear of many Israelis. His remark, which went largely unreported by the world's media was to prove prophetic.

He said, 'The battle for Jerusalem has begun.'

'*Jihad* for Jerusalem!'

In early May 1994 – while the first phase of Palestinian Arab autonomy was being implemented in Gaza and Jericho, and Israeli Defence Forces were in the process of withdrawing from those areas – Yasser Arafat was in South Africa witnessing the inauguration of Nelson Mandela as that country's first black President.

'You have come to fight and start a *jihad* for Jerusalem, the historic shrine!' he told a packed Johannesburg mosque on 10 May. Israeli agents had breached security and recorded his speech at the closed meeting, which Arafat was addressing. The PLO leader was not too pleased to have his words made public to the world a few days later, when he arrived in Oslo to meet with Israeli Foreign Minister Shimon Peres and former US President Jimmy Carter. The Israeli leadership made it clear that unless there was a satisfactory explanation for this call to *jihad* for Jerusalem – a clear violation of the 'Oslo' agreement between Israel and the PLO – the Accord was finished. A rather sheepish Arafat, reluctantly and unconvincingly, read a written statement explaining that he was not advocating violence against Israel, but that he was using the word '*jihad*' in a religious sense, as a 'peaceful crusade for peace'.

In the past, '*jihad*' was always taken to mean a violent struggle against Israel, and Arafat had always given his support to those who sought to destroy Israel by force. His connivance with Saddam Hussein is well documented, especially when the Iraqi leader had vowed: 'In the name of Allah we shall cause fire to devour half of Israel'. Eleven years earlier the PLO leader had given his support to the Ayatollah Khomeini: 'I pray Allah to guide your steps on the road of faith and *jihad* in Iran which will continue the struggle until we reach the walls of Jerusalem where we will raise the flags of our two revolutions.' Clearly, Arafat's reference to '*jihad*' was anything but a 'peaceful crusade for peace'.[112]

Perhaps the most revealing comment that came out of Arafat's Johannesburg address was the parallel he drew between the Declaration of Principles of September 1993 and the treaty signed between Mohammed and the residents of Mecca at the beginning of his conquest of Arabia. It was through this treaty that Mohammed made 'peace' with the Meccans – who rejected his claim to be a prophet – and withdrew his forces to Medina. At the time of the treaty, the Meccans were stronger than Mohammed's forces. But when the situation was reversed, some two years later, Mohammed reneged on the treaty. He went to war and imposed Islam on the Meccans by force.

This was to set a precedent for Islam, whereby it became acceptable to make an armistice with a stronger enemy, if it is in the interests of the Moslem community. However, when the enemy is perceived to be weaker, war becomes imperative and is demanded by the *Koran.* In that situation Moslems are no longer bound by any treaty previously made. By referring to the Oslo Accord in this way, Arafat was sending a message to the Islamic world that he would renege on any agreement made with Israel when the Palestinian/Arab cause is believed to be in an advantageous position. If this precedent is followed, then the *jihad* for Jerusalem means war, not peace.[113]

Unfortunately for Arafat, the ultimate outcome of this *jihad* for Jerusalem has a predetermined conclusion, for the prophet Isaiah tells us:

> ' *"Wail, O gate! Cry, O city!*
> *All you of Philistia are dissolved;*
> *For smoke will come from the north,*
> *And no one will be alone in his appointed times."*
> *What will one then answer the messengers of the*
>   *[Philistine] nation?*
> *That the* Lord *has founded Zion,*
> *And the poor of His people shall take refuge in it.'*
>   (Isaiah 14:31–32) [114]

The PLO Plot Thickens

In January 1996 Yasser Arafat attended a meeting of Arab Ambassadors in Stockholm, Sweden. He told the meeting that a Palestinian State would soon be established with the blessing of Shimon Peres and Yossi Beilin.[115]

He went on to tell the gathering that 'we Palestinians will take over everything, including all of Jerusalem. Peres and Beilin have already promised us half of Jerusalem.' Predicting civil war, Arafat unveiled his intentions: 'The PLO will now concentrate on splitting Israel psychologically into two camps. Within five years, we will have six to seven million Arabs living on the West Bank and Jerusalem ... We will make life unbearable for Jews by psychological warfare and population explosion. Jews will not want to live among Arabs.' [116]

As demonstrated by the incident in Johannesburg nearly two years earlier, what Arafat communicates through the western media is inconsistent with what he communicates to the Arab world. Through the former he is portrayed as a man with a heart for peace who desires to live side by side with the Jewish nation. However, the evil intentions of his real heart are often revealed by what he says to the Arab world.

Barely three months later the western world was to fall prey to another deception by Yasser Arafat.

To the applause of Shimon Peres, Bill Clinton and other world leaders, he announced that he had finally succeeded in amending the PLO founding Charter, which calls for the destruction of the Jewish State. The announcement came on 24 April, which happened to be *Yom HaAtzma'ut* – Israel's Independence Day. The late Yitzhak Rabin had insisted on amendment to the Charter as part of the DOP signed in September 1993, and so far Yasser Arafat had apparently successfully stalled its implementation. Shimon Peres had threatened to suspend the 'peace' process only weeks earlier if Arafat did not comply. According to Arafat the Palestine National Council (PNC) had voted to amend the Charter – twenty-eight of its thirty-three articles call directly or indirectly for Israel's annihilation – by 504 votes to 54. This report was carried throughout the western media as fact. However, according to journalist David Dolan, there was one problem with what Arafat was saying:

> 'It was not true. In reality, the PNC only voted to establish a committee that will *propose* amendments to the Charter later this year. This was later confirmed by

PNC Chairman, Salim Zaanoun. He wrote on May 16 in *An-Nahar*, a leading Palestinian newspaper, that while the Charter "had been amended, there were no specific articles that were cancelled". A PLO think-tank in Ramallah wrote that the Charter had only been "frozen" by the PNC vote. "The text of the Palestine Charter remains as it was, and no changes were made to it." ' [117]

Only if and when the necessary amendments are actually approved by the PNC can it be said that Arafat has fulfilled his written pledge to rescind those parts of the Charter which call for Israel's destruction.

Then there is the matter of the PLO's 'Phased Plan'. Dolan continues:

'Arafat's true intentions were more clearly demonstrated in a speech he gave at the special PNC session, held in the Gaza Strip. He said amending the Charter would line up with the PNC's 1974 decision to enact the so-called Phased Plan, whose ten points call for Israel's obliteration in stages. "In 1974, the Palestine National Council endorsed the establishment of a National Authority on any part of the Palestinian territory we liberate, or from which the Israelis withdraw," he told the session, adding, "We have now established such an Authority."

All of the delegates got the drift of Arafat's apparent endorsement of the Phased Plan, knowing that the plan openly states that any established Palestinian Authority will go on "liberating" the land in stages until Israel is entirely wiped off the face of the mainly-Moslem Middle East.' [118]

The PLO Charter – Annulled or Not?

The opposition Likud Party, waiting in the wings for an election only a few weeks away, was not fooled by Arafat's double-talk. When he assumed power, Binyamin Netanyahu was to hold the issue of the annulment of the PNC Charter constantly before the PLO leader.

The Wye Memorandum of October 1998, which was supposed to resuscitate the faltering Oslo Accords, brought the Charter to the fore once again. This time Arafat was cornered. Or at least everyone thought he was.

In December 1998 US President Bill Clinton, aboard Air Force One, touched down at the brand new Gaza Airport, which the Palestinian Authority (the governing body of the PLO in the Palestinian autonomous regions) had just been allowed to open under the Wye agreement. Just minutes before he landed, the Judiciary Committee of the US House of Representatives had voted to impeach the President for lying over his involvement in a sex scandal that had dominated the American media for the whole of that year. The official reason for the Clinton visit to Gaza was to fulfil his promise at the Wye Plantation Summit to attend a Palestine National Council meeting and witness the annulment of the PLO's controversial founding Charter. David Dolan reported at the time:

> ' "I am proud to be the first American President to visit a Palestinian-governed city," Clinton told his enthusiastic audience in Gaza City. The comment came soon after Arafat spoke to the packed hall, insisting peace will not come until Israel "abandons its settlements and hands over control of all our occupied land, including holy Jerusalem".
>
> At the end of his speech, the PLO chief called for a show of hands in support of the Charter's annulment. Most of the one thousand or so people gathered in the hall (only about half of them actual PNC delegates) raised them high in the air. A beaming Clinton warmly hailed the move as courageous. Netanyahu and other officials later expressed satisfaction at the show of hands even though some questioned whether it was only a charade.' [119]

Their questioning may prove to be justified. The question as to whether or not the Charter has been legally annulled according to the PNC Constitution still remains.

David Bar-Illan, who is a former editor of the English-language daily *The Jerusalem Post* and was media advisor to

Binyamin Netanyahu when he was Prime Minister, believes the spirit of the Charter is 'alive and kicking'.

> 'As of now, the Palestinians are openly saying that if they reach independence, their aim is to liberate all of Palestine. For them that means all of the area between the Jordan River and the Mediterranean Sea, which includes, obviously, the State of Israel. Which means that the desire expressed in the Palestinian Charter, and now the Fatah Charter, which is the predominant party in the Palestinian Authority – that desire to obliterate the State of Israel and replace it with an Arab Palestinian State – still exists unfortunately.' [120]

The Question of Jerusalem

As negotiations for the blueprint of the Final Status talks of the Oslo Accords got under way in late 1999, another battle of rhetoric was raging over Jerusalem. Yasser Arafat made it clear once again that he would never compromise with Israel on his often repeated demands for control over the eastern part of Jerusalem, including the Old City with its holy places and shrines. In mid November the Palestinian Authority Cabinet, declaring there would be no peace unless their demands were met, issued a statement saying that there would be no Final Status agreement unless 'occupied East Jerusalem becomes the capital of a sovereign Palestinian State.'

On the other side, the fourth Israeli Prime Minister in as many years, Ehud Barak, was reiterating that Jerusalem would remain as an undivided city under Jewish sovereignty. Jerusalem's Mayor, Ehud Olmert, who at the time was the only member of the opposition Likud Party to hold an administrative position in public office, went one step further. Stating that he believed a fundamental error had been committed in even allowing the status of Jerusalem to go on the agenda for negotiation in the Final Status of the Oslo Accords, Olmert said:

> 'If we hadn't allowed [the idea that the status of Jerusalem might be negotiable] to develop, there

wouldn't be so much pressure on us, because deep down the international community knows the truth that no other people can claim Jerusalem but the Jews. That no other people have the right – an historical right – to consider Jerusalem as their capital but the Jewish people. And if there is one reason why the Palestinians want Jerusalem to be their capital – it's not because of its importance to the Palestinian history, which never existed in this city. It is not because they have a background in Jerusalem because of their Palestinian ethos. It is only because Jerusalem is so important to us that they want Jerusalem. And therefore if we will make sure that Jerusalem is not for sale, it will not be "for sale".' [121]

Chapter 7

Jerusalem Becomes
a Burdensome Stone

A Secret Deal with the Vatican

In 1993 the Vatican made overtures towards the Jewish State that had by then been in existence for forty-five years. Hitherto, the Holy See had not formally recognised the State of Israel, or the right of the Jewish people to dwell in their biblical homeland. During that year Israeli leaders visited the Vatican, and by December 1993, the Israeli government and the Church of Rome had concluded a formal treaty with full diplomatic relations on both sides. However, the Vatican chose to establish its diplomatic mission in Tel Aviv rather than in Jerusalem, thus sidestepping recognition of Jerusalem as Israel's capital.

Jewish reaction to this new relationship with the Vatican was optimistic, if somewhat guarded. After all, the Roman Catholic Church had been one of the major perpetrators of hatred against the Jews since the time of Christ. Furthermore, there were grave suspicions about the Vatican's complicity with Adolf Hitler during World War II.

While the establishment of diplomatic ties received a good deal of positive coverage in the world's media, another secret dialogue was in progress between Israel's Foreign Minister Shimon Peres and Pope John Paul II.

French intellectual Mark Halter, a close friend of Peres, told the weekly Israeli journal *Shishi* that in May 1993 he delivered a letter from Peres to the Pope, which outlined the

Foreign Minister's plans for Jerusalem. According to Halter, 'Peres offered to hand over Jerusalem's sovereignty to the Vatican.'

Ironically, this secret deal was taking place at the same time as leaders of every Jewish community were bringing their Jerusalem Covenant scrolls back to their beloved capital city, and they knew nothing of it. Halter elaborated on the plan:

> 'Jerusalem will stay the capital of Israel, but the Old City will be administered by the Vatican. The city will have an Israeli mayor and a Palestinian mayor, both under orders from the Holy See. The program was originally submitted to the Vatican by Peres [in 1993] just before the Oslo talks began.'[122]

When this plan was presented to the PLO during the Oslo negotiations and just before the signing of the Declaration of Principles, Arafat agreed not to oppose it. It also had the support of influential Palestinian intellectuals who had been consulted on the idea. However, the Jewish people – the people to whom Jerusalem belongs as their capital – were kept in the dark by their own leaders.

Much to his dismay, the Foreign Minister's plan was published in the Italian newspaper *La Stampa* on 10 September 1993, just three days before Prime Minister Yitzhak Rabin met Arafat in Washington for the 'Oslo' ceremony. At the time Peres ordered the Foreign Ministry to deny that such a policy existed. A few weeks later Rabin, who surely would have known what his Foreign Minister was doing, emphatically and emotionally declared to an audience of nearly five thousand pilgrims at the International Christian Embassy's Feast of Tabernacles celebrations: 'Jerusalem will remain as the undivided Capital of Israel forever!'[123]. A year later, Foreign Ministry workers were no longer issuing denials, but were privately confirming the existence of the Vaticanisation plan.

Further details of the plan revealed the Vatican's intention to have Jerusalem as the second seat of power for the Church of Rome. Furthermore, all three major religions would be represented under the authority of the Holy See. In the plan a Palestinian State would emerge in confederation with Jordan. Such a State would have its religious capital in Jerusalem, but its administrative capital situated elsewhere, possibly Nablus.[124]

Peres' secret 'sale' of Jerusalem, if he was able to implement it, would disinherit the Jewish people of their ancient capital which, according to the Abrahamic Covenant, is rightfully theirs and no one else's. For the time being, the plan seems to have been buried somewhere and forgotten. Whether it will ever be resurrected is anybody's guess. Such a move would have devastating ramifications for the Jewish people – it would be like tearing the heart and soul out of the nation once more. Not only would the Vaticanisation plan attract the ire of Jewish people all over the world, but the God of Israel is not silent on this matter either, for the prophet Zechariah records:

> ' "I am zealous for Jerusalem
> And for Zion with great jealousy.
> I am exceedingly angry with the nations at ease;
> For I was a little angry,
> And they helped – but with evil intent."
> Therefore thus says the LORD:
> "I am returning to Jerusalem with mercy;
> My house shall be built in it," says the LORD of hosts.'
>   (Zechariah 1:14–16)

Peace with Jordan

By mid-1994, following the Johannesburg incident, relations between the PLO and the Rabin government had turned sour, particularly over Jerusalem. Now a new player was at the forefront of the peace process: the late King Hussein of Jordan. For many years it had been rumoured that Israel had been conducting a secret dialogue across the Jordan River. The Hashemite King, whose country's population consists of a two to one majority of 'Palestinian' Arabs, had been running a political gauntlet which could have easily ended with an assassin's bullet. His grandfather, King Abdullah, was assassinated on the Temple Mount in 1951 following an attempt to make peace with Israel.

The historic handshake between King Hussein and Yitzhak Rabin on the lawns of the White House on 25 July 1994 could have been a rerun of the ceremony with Yasser Arafat ten months earlier, but for two things. Absent this time was the grimace on the Israeli Prime Minister's face, and the double-talk from his counterpart. This time there seems to have been a genuine warmth. Three months later, on 25 October, they met again in a strip of desert between their two countries and, in the presence of the American President, signed a formal Peace Treaty.

As with the PLO, however, there was a central bargaining chip: Jerusalem.

The Hidden Price Tag

King Hussein, who was widely regarded as the most moderate of Israel's neighbours, was given an offer he could not refuse. The United States offered to write off a huge debt, and Israel offered recognition that Jordan had 'some standing vis-à-vis the holy Islamic sites in Jerusalem', particularly on the Temple Mount.

The Israeli government was prepared to give this recognition because Jordan had financed the Moslem *Waqf*, and King Hussein had personally financed the renovating of the Dome of the Rock.

When Yasser Arafat heard of this concession by the Israeli government to the Jordanians, he was furious. Demanding that talks on the final status of Jerusalem begin immediately – and not wait until 1996 as stated in the Oslo Accords – he retorted, 'For us, it is a sovereignty issue as well as an issue of holy, sacred places for Christians and Moslems.' [125] The 'autonomy government' of the outraged Arafat, which had no legal authority in Jerusalem anyway, promptly established its own 'Islamic Trust' (*Waqf*) to rival the already existing *Waqf* under the authority of Jordan. The PLO Regional Minister, Sheik Mohammed Abu Sardeneh, stated that the purpose of this was to 'strengthen attempts by all sincere people to return Al-Quds [Jerusalem] to its true owners.'

The anger over the Rabin government's move, which was largely motivated by its atheistic humanist ideology, was not restricted to the PLO. Many Jews were outraged too. Ariel Sharon, who had been Defence Minister when Likud was in power, wrote in *The Jerusalem Post*:

> 'This government seems to respect all religions except its own. Jordan isn't the only country with standing on the Temple Mount. The King of Morocco is angling for influence, and the monarch of Saudi Arabia is lusting for a share. And what about Yasser Arafat?
>
> A vigorous argument is raging over who has the more right. Yet the only element not cited by the Jewish government of Israel is the Jewish people.
>
> Some clarification is in order: Only one people – the Jewish people – exercises sovereignty over Jerusalem in all its parts – especially our holy sites, and primarily the Temple Mount. The government's reasons for handing the Temple Mount to foreigners lie somewhere between ignorance and contempt. We cannot accept any foreign sovereignty over Jerusalem. Full rights of religious worship, yes; sovereign status – never.' [126]

Jerusalem 3000 Starts with a Bang and a Fizz

On the evening of 4 September 1995, the skies over the Holy City were filled with a spectacular light show at the commencement of the fifteen-month-long celebrations, commemorating the 3000th anniversary of Jerusalem's establishment as Israel's capital. The Israeli government and the organising committee of '*Jerusalem 3000*' had sent invitations to all the nations who had embassies in Israel to attend this spectacular opening.

But as the fireworks boomed and banged over the city, the opening of the celebrations had fizzled out. Led by the nations of the European Union, Jerusalem was the subject of an international boycott once again.

All of the major nations of the world – including the so-called Christian countries – declined to attend. They preferred to turn a blind eye to the fact that the Bible they use records the historical account of King David's move from Hebron to Jerusalem, and their churches refer to the Lord Jesus Christ as the Son of David. Rather than acknowledge the true facts of history, they decided to do the 'politically correct' thing and stay away from the event. Whether they knew it or not, their boycott supported the Moslem world and the PLO in their attempt, falsely, to rewrite the history of Jerusalem – a 'history' which has the sole intention of denying that the Jewish people had any historic presence in the Holy City.

The Three 'Cities of David'

As the *Jerusalem 3000* celebrations got under way, the immediate future of the Holy City began to look bleaker, its problems insurmountable.

On 28 September 1995, in another ceremony on the front lawn of the White House, the second phase of the Peace Accord – known as Oslo II – was signed between Israel and the Palestinian Authority.

Under the terms of the agreement eight towns and about 450 villages in Judea and Samaria were to be handed over to the Palestinian Authority, with varying degrees of control. The IDF (Israeli army) was to be redeployed in stages to agreed positions. Four of the eight towns – Ramah (Ram'Allah), Shechem (Nablus), Bethlehem and Hebron – have significant Jewish holy sites. The latter two – both 'cities of David' – are an indispensable part of Israel's heritage.

Bethlehem is the site of Rachel's tomb and the birthplace of both King David and his greater Son, Yeshua. Hebron, at one time Israel's capital, is where the patriarchs were buried and where David was crowned King of Judah. Because of this Hebron, as the oldest Jewish city in the world, is the most important city to the Jewish people after Jerusalem. Apart from a period in the Middle Ages and the thirty-nine years between 1929 and 1968, Hebron has had a continuous Jewish presence since the early days of the *Diaspora*.

As the other 'city of David', Jerusalem, began to celebrate the 3000th anniversary of her foundation as Israel's capital, sadly, Bethlehem and Hebron were in the process of being taken over by Israel's enemies. Just before Christmas, Yasser Arafat made a historic visit to Bethlehem. The world's media, broadcasting PLO propaganda, proclaimed that 'true peace' had come to the birthplace of Jesus, as tens of thousands of ecstatic Palestinian Arabs revelled and fired their guns into the air in Manger Square. Arafat, himself a Moslem, stood on the roof of the Church of the Nativity, and before the TV cameras of the world, declared: 'This is the birthplace of our Lord the Messiah, the Palestinian, the Palestinian.' The media and the Church establishment did nothing to challenge this brazen lie and blasphemy. Fortunately, the Roman Catholic Church did step in to prevent a laser beam show, which would have depicted Arafat and Jesus walking together in the sky over Bethlehem.

However, the future of Hebron continued to hang in the balance for another year. The handover of this 'city of David' was delayed as a result of a series of suicide bombings by HAMAS, which left sixty innocent Israelis dead in the space of eight days.

The capitulation of Bethlehem was a great tragedy for the 150,000 Jews living in towns and villages across Judea and Samaria – many of whom chose to live there because they believe in their right to do so according to the Abrahamic Covenant. For them, another step in the PLO's Phased Plan to liquidate Israel had been achieved. The question in the minds of many was: 'Would the "Capital City of David" suffer the same fate as the other two cities that bear his name?'

The immediate answer to that question was to come via the ballot-box several months later.

Throughout the Oslo II talks, Yitzhak Rabin had gone to great lengths to prevent the *YESHA* Communities [127] from exercising their democratic rights of public demonstration in support of what they believe. The world witnessed sad scenes as Jewish law enforcement officers forcibly, and sometimes violently, removed Jewish men, women and children as they demonstrated on the hilltops of their ancient homeland.

The World Mourns Yitzhak Rabin

Two months after the opening ceremony of *Jerusalem 3000*, the guests who had been invited but had boycotted that event arrived in Jerusalem for an entirely different reason – to attend the funeral of Yitzhak Rabin, who had been assassinated after speaking at a 'peace rally' in Tel Aviv two days earlier.

Rabin's assassination deeply shocked the entire nation, including those opposed to the so-called peace process. The funeral was attended by leaders of more than seventy nations, including US President Bill Clinton. Both King Hussein of Jordan and President Hosni Mubarak of Egypt made historic visits to Jerusalem for the occasion.

The grieving nation was comforted by the show of international support at the funeral, and especially by the speeches of Bill Clinton and King Hussein, who were themselves deeply grieved by what had happened.

But the most tragic aspect of the assassination was the fact that the perpetrator was not an Islamic fundamentalist, as one might have expected, but a 25-year-old Israeli by the name of Yigael Amir – an army reservist in the crack Golani regiment.

While most of the media reporting on the assassination was sympathetic towards Israel, it failed to relate the heart of the matter objectively. As horrible as Rabin's murder was, it was a direct consequence of the alienation and fear of the future felt by the *YESHA* communities in Judea, Samaria and the Golan Heights – even though the overwhelming majority of them would never condone such an act, and were deeply shocked by it. It was also the consequence of the Government's savage vilification against those who held any belief in the Abrahamic Covenant, which accounts for a significant proportion of the population. In the eyes of many, this highly dubious 'peace accord' had been pursued in contravention of the Government's pre-election promises in 1992, and without proper reference to the democratic principles that normally operate in Israel.

With Rabin gone, the man who was one of the real architects of the Oslo Peace Accord – Shimon Peres – took the helm. By some strange coincidence – or perhaps by divine destiny – his name in Hebrew means 'to divide'.

Despite the media's initial fears that the Accord may have died with Rabin, Peres vowed to pursue it with even greater determination, and to put as many 'facts on the ground' as possible before the nation went to the polls.

Another Change of Government

'I have a deep faith – and it resonates amongst most of the people of Israel – that the promise God gave to Abraham, and to Isaac, and to Jacob, this *brith* (covenant), is the most powerful force we have. It has guided us through millennia of struggle, strife, pogrom, degradation and holocaust. It has brought us back from the ashes of the dead. It has brought this country back to life, and I believe that with God's help we will prevail.

Generations of Jews and non-Jews waited for the day we would all celebrate the triumphant realisation of the great prophecies of Jeremiah, Isaiah, Ezekiel and others, who said that Zion would be rebuilt, and the fallen tabernacle of David would be raised up...

Zionism was always in the heart of the Jewish people; in our prayers, our dreams. But it did not become a real force until the late 19th century, with arrival of men like Theodore Herzl and Max Nordau. And it was fifty years before these great men, men of the Christian faith visited Palestine, saw the Land of Israel, and imagined in their mind's eye the return of the Jewish people who alone, they said, "Could bring this barren land back to life." These Christians and Jews believed that the great prophecies were something to be acted upon...

There is one land for one people, and that land is the Land of Israel for the People of Israel.' [128]

These words were spoken by the leader of the then opposition Likud party, Binyamin Netanyahu. The audience of about three thousand Christians he was addressing, at the Feast of Tabernacles in Jerusalem, were encouraged to see a ray of hope for the nation of Israel.

Just seven and a half months after he gave this particular speech, which was greeted with a thunderous standing ovation by the Christians, he was elected as Israel's new Prime Minister. For many God-fearing Jews and Christian intercessors, the election result was an answer to prayer. Many thought it was no coincidence that his name, Binyamin Netanyahu, in Hebrew means 'Son of My right hand – given by God'.

Even though Netanyahu was fundamentally opposed to the 'Oslo' blueprint for peace, he had said in his election campaign that he would continue to make peace with Israel's 'Palestinian' neighbours, but it would be a 'peace with security'. The new Prime Minister also made it plain that he was not prepared to trust the fate of his nation to the likes of Yasser Arafat – or those who supported him. Unlike his predecessors in government, he expected Arafat to honour in practice every commitment he had made either verbally, or in writing, before Israel would move ahead with the next phase in the 'Oslo' process. This was what Netanyahu referred to as 'reciprocity'.

Consequently, there was a distinct slowing of the 'Oslo' process. The international media wasted no time in painting Binyamin Netanyahu as a warmonger. Even the Israeli media, particularly the electronic media, which is dominated by mainly left-wing journalists, did everything they could to undermine Netanyahu. It would not be an exaggeration to say that no Prime Minister of Israel ever faced the defamation in the media that Netanyahu faced. As a true Zionist, they hated him. In the eyes of the media, being a Zionist was no longer 'politically correct'. Zionism was now passé.

However, even as a Zionist, Netanyahu had one major weakness – he was also a pragmatist. During his three years as Prime Minister, Netanyahu came under the most intense pressure imaginable – from all sides. From the left who, along with certain sectors of the media, were determined to depose him by any means possible. From the PLO, who were determined to get what they wanted in return for as little as possible. From the international community – especially the American administration – which was determined to see the 'Oslo' process succeed, whatever the cost to Israel. And from his own multi-faction, multi-party coalition government, which was deeply divided over the 'peace' process. In many ways, the latter was possibly the most difficult for him to live with.

In the coalition on the one hand there were the 'doves' like his Foreign Minister, David Levy, and Defence Minister, Yitzhak Mordechai – both members of Likud to begin with (but both later defected from the party) – who were wanting to accelerate the 'Oslo' process. On the other hand there were the 'hawks' like Ze'ev (Benny) Begin (son of former Prime Minister Menachem Begin) who were opposed to any transfer of land to the PLO under any circumstances. (Ze'ev Begin also quit the Likud Party over the ceding of Hebron.) So even without the pressures from outside, Netanyahu was walking a tightrope to maintain the confidence of his own government, which often he did not have. In many ways, it was surprising that he lasted as long as he did in government, but perhaps the prayers of the saints had something to do with that.

However, it was Binyamin Netanyahu's pragmatism that was to be his undoing. That pragmatism led him to cave in to the enormous pressure from the Clinton administration on two occasions. The first occasion was in January 1997, over Hebron.

Hebron

The handover of Hebron to the Palestinian Authority had been delayed by the Labour government nearly twelve months earlier because of a spate of atrocious bus-bombings. And so the problem of what to do about Hebron now fell into Netanyahu's lap. After much wrangling and bitter debate within his Cabinet and the coalition government parties, Netanyahu announced that four-fifths of Hebron would be ceded to Arafat. However, there would be strict conditions attached to the handover. The PLO chief was required to sign an undertaking – later known as the Hebron Accord – that he would abide by agreements he had already signed under 'Oslo II'. Among the things that Arafat agreed to do was to annul the PLO founding Charter, curb terrorism, hand over a number of known terrorists to Israel, reduce the armed PA 'police' force to the agreed levels, and stop incitement to violence. It is questionable whether Arafat honoured any of these commitments, although there was a show of co-operating with Israel over curbing terrorism when it suited him.

Politically speaking, the handover of Hebron proved almost disastrous for Netanyahu. The Prime Minister lost the confidence of the *YESHA* communities, as well as the right-wing element of his coalition. A major scandal known as the 'Bar-On Affair' erupted as a direct consequence of the Hebron deal. The anti-Netanyahu media alleged that the Prime Minister had promised the position of Attorney General to lawyer Roni Bar-On in return for the Shas Party's support in the Knesset vote over Hebron. A police investigation followed in which Netanyahu narrowly escaped indictment for alleged corruption. In any case, even if Netanyahu had been behind such an offer (which was never proved), Bar-On never took up the position anyway. The fall-out from the Hebron deal nearly destroyed the Prime Minister, and he never regained the confidence he lost.

Thousands of Christian intercessors upheld Binyamin Netanyahu through this very difficult time, many of whom believed that the whole affair was a spiritual assault by the powers of darkness upon the Prime Minister whom the Lord had raised up. No doubt this was true, but there were some who believed that there was also an element of chastisement from God for handing over a portion of His Land, which is not 'for sale', to an enemy of Israel.

The Wye Memorandum

Despite many heated verbal exchanges between the Palestinian Authority and the Israeli government during the next eighteen months or so, the Oslo Accords made virtually no progress at all. As usual, Israel was blamed for the lack of progress. The left wing and the media vociferously blamed Binyamin Netanyahu for being intransigent over the 'peace' process. In reality Arafat was up to his old tricks in not carrying out the agreements he had signed in 'Oslo I', 'Oslo II' and the 'Hebron Accord'. The Prime Minister was simply sticking to his policy of 'reciprocity' – in other words if Israel was to keep her side of the bargain in handing over 'land in exchange for peace', then Arafat had to carry out his side of the bargain too.

By the second half of 1998, the Clinton administration was becoming exasperated with the lack of progress with the Oslo Accords. The US President had been publicly humiliated into apologising to the American people for his indiscretions with a White House intern by the name of Monica Lewinsky, and faced the possibility of impeachment by the Congress for lying under oath about the affair. His credibility was in tatters. Desperate for his name to go down in history as one of the greatest American presidents, what better opportunity to restore his credibility than by resurrecting the faltering Oslo Accords?

Whether or not that was the motivation behind calling the parties in the Oslo Accords to the October 1998 summit at the Wye River Plantation in Maryland USA, only the Lord knows. Clinton appeared like a conjuror, desperate to 'pull a rabbit out of the hat'. To encourage the parties, particularly Israel, to move ahead with his agenda, Clinton 'dangled' a huge financial 'carrot'. Netanyahu was driven into making concessions which, under different circumstances, would have been against his better judgement. At one stage the Israeli delegation came very close to walking out of the summit, and had they done so, Binyamin Netanyahu may well have survived another year in office as Prime Minister. But the disgraced Clinton had a trump card up his sleeve – the gaunt King Hussein, who had only a few months to live, rose from his hospital bed in Minnesota and was flown to the Wye River Plantation where his presence clinched the deal for the President.

Essentially, Israel agreed to pull back in three stages from a further 13 per cent of Judea and Samaria. In return Arafat agreed, yet again, to abide by earlier commitments he had made and failed to keep. Among them, as already mentioned, was the promise to delete the phrases in the

Palestinian National Covenant – the PLO's founding Charter – which call for the liquidation of the State of Israel. Because the destruction of the Jewish State is the basic theme of the document, it effectively meant annulling the entire Charter. Arafat was also required to desist from his often-repeated threats to make a unilateral declaration of a Palestinian State with Jerusalem as its capital.

In November, after at least one delay, the Israelis made a withdrawal from 200 square miles of northern Samaria. However Arafat – apart from making a show of annulling the Charter in the presence of the US President – as before, did not reciprocate. He not only continued to threaten that he would declare Palestinian independence the following year, on 4 May 1999 – originally the scheduled date for the completion of the Oslo Accords – but he also threatened, once again, that he might order an armed *jihad* to conquer Jerusalem. This flagrant violation of both the Oslo and Wye Accords, together with a dramatic upsurge of violence in Judea and Samaria, and another terrorist attack in the heart of Jerusalem, resulted in the suspension of any further withdrawals by the IDF.

The signing of the Wye Memorandum, and the fall-out that followed it, left the Prime Minister in a politically impossible position. A substantial number of his coalition partners, including members of his Cabinet, turned against him. Labour leader, Ehud Barak, made it plain he would not be part of a national unity government, which may have been Netanyahu's only hope of remaining in office. On 21 December, the Knesset voted to go to the polls. The election was held on 17 May the following year, and after a long and bitter campaign, Netanyahu was convincingly defeated.

It seems that the Lord removed Netanyahu's mantle following this second cave-in to outside pressure to cede a portion of the Lord's Land to the PLO. At least for the time being. However, there is little doubt that Netanyahu was raised up by God to lead Israel through this very difficult time, and many positive things were achieved in the three years that he was Prime Minister.

Netanyahu's Legacy

Apart from a revitalisation of Israel's economy, Netanyahu postponed the conclusion of the Oslo Accords, and the consequences they will bring upon Israel, by at least two years. Another very tangible result of Netanyahu's policy of 'peace with security' which, because of Arafat's lack of 'reciprocity' meant little progress was made, was a marked drop in the number of fatal terrorist attacks. In fact, in the three years of the Netanyahu government, the death toll dropped to one-third of the level it had been in the three years of the Rabin/Peres-led government.

Notwithstanding Netanyahu's pragmatism towards some areas of the 'Oslo' blueprint of 'land-for-peace', which he was fundamentally opposed to, there were other areas where the former Prime Minister was steadfast. One of them was that the *YESHA* communities would not only be maintained, but strengthened. He saw this as especially necessary as Arafat and his regime continued to send out hostile signals over the State of Israel's existence. Netanyahu's policy regarding the *YESHA* communities – which, contrary to popular belief, was not contravening the Oslo Accords – was a continuing thorn in the side of the Palestinian Authority. Even though, for the most part, Netanyahu operated within the letter of the Oslo Accords, his allowing 'natural expansion' of the communities frequently drew the ire of Bill Clinton and his Secretary of State, Madeleine Albright. Then there was always the matter of what was technically a 'settlement'. Both sides had different interpretations of what Arafat's phrase 'settlement activity' actually meant, and usually the American administration and the European Union sided with Arafat. This was especially true when it came to Jerusalem. If there was one thing about which Binyamin Netanyahu was steadfast and immovable, it was Jerusalem. One dramatic illustration of this was the development at Har Homa.

Har Homa

The furore over Har Homa broke out in the United Nations and the international media in early 1997 as the Netanyahu government began preparing the area for development into a new suburb to house both Jews and Arabs. At that time Har Homa was a tree-covered hill within the municipal boundaries of Jerusalem about five kilometres due south of the Old City and two or three kilometres north-east of Bethlehem. This hill was 75 per cent Jewish-owned prior to its seizure by Jordan in 1948. After 1967 it was returned to its original owners until it was resumed and paid for by the Rabin government in the early 1990s.

As the bulldozers moved in to clear the trees, Israel was immediately accused of establishing a 'new settlement' in 'Arab East Jerusalem'. However, Netanyahu stood against virtually the entire world and nearly half of the Knesset in his determination to break ground and build on Har Homa. He was determined that nobody was going to tell the Israelis that they could not build in their own capital. 'We're not building a settlement,' he said, 'we're building a neighbourhood in the municipal boundaries of Jerusalem, which is done every day in Amman, in Gaza, in Cairo and in Moscow.'[129]

Har Homa quickly became the political battleground on which the issue of sovereignty over Jerusalem was being fought. For the Palestinian Authority, Jabal Abu Ghneim (Har Homa) was a test of their power to call at least some shots over Jerusalem. Had they managed to force Israel not to build on Har Homa, it would have assisted their cause in making future claims on Jerusalem. More importantly, it would have given them a continuous strip of settlement from Bethlehem, via Silwan, to the Old City and on to 'the West Bank'. However, a predominantly Israeli neighbourhood at Har Homa would complete a ring of Jewish neighbourhoods encircling Jerusalem as well as thwart Palestinian aspirations of continuity between Bethlehem and Jerusalem.

The controversy over Har Homa raged for months. During 1997 the General Assembly of the United Nations met no less than four times to condemn Israel over this suburban development in an uninhabited part of its capital city – and each time when there were real emergencies elsewhere in the world which urgently needed their attention. One political cartoonist aptly described the situation thus: 'The AIDS plague, genocide in Africa, global warming, the crushing of Tibet, persecution of Copts in Egypt, the Balkans, the nuclear threat of crumbling reactors in Russia, the hole in the ozone layer will all have to take a back seat! The Jews are building homes in Jerusalem!' [130]

Perhaps there was more than meets the eye to this rather bizarre furore over the development of a Jewish suburb in Jerusalem. Could Har Homa be the spiritual battleground on which the issue of Jewish sovereignty over Jerusalem was being fought? If it is, then the Lord's protection is assured, for it is written:

> *'As the mountains surround Jerusalem,*
> *So the* Lord *surrounds His people*
> *From this time forth and forever.'*   (Psalm 125:2)

As is often the case in Israel, the name of a person or place can have a significant or prophetic meaning. Har Homa seems to be no exception. *Har* means 'mount' or 'mountain' and *Homa* means 'defensive wall' or 'rampart'! [131]

Indeed, as one considers where events are leading, we can clearly see one of the great end-time prophecies of Zechariah concerning Jerusalem being fulfilled before our eyes:

> *' "Behold, I will make Jerusalem a cup of drunkenness to all*
> *the surrounding peoples ... in that day I will make Jerusalem*
> *a very heavy stone for all peoples; all who would heave it*
> *away will surely be cut in pieces, though all nations of the*
> *earth are gathered against it." '*   (Zechariah 12:2, 3)

Resolution 181 Revisited

As the final year of the twentieth century unfolded, it brought with it a couple of ominous developments which could have serious ramifications for Israel's future. The first development had been going on behind the scenes as Israel focused on its election campaign and the possibility of the unilateral declaration of a Palestinian State threatened by Yasser Arafat. While on a visit to Moscow the PLO leader announced: 'The right for a Palestinian State to exist is based on Resolution 181 and not on the Oslo agreements.' During the spring of 1999 Arafat embarked on a diplomatic campaign to revive the United Nation's Partition Plan of November 1947. As noted in Chapter 4, the 1947 Partition Plan – UN Resolution 181 – called for the establishment of both a Jewish and an Arab State in what was then known as Palestine. The Arabs (who, incidentally, refused to be known as 'Palestinians' in those days) rejected Resolution 181 out of hand, while the Jewish Palestinians (as they were then known) accepted it. Israel's UN Ambassador, Dore Gold, declared in a letter sent to UN Secretary-General Kofi Annan in April 1999, that by rejecting Resolution 181 in 1947, and subsequently attacking the fledgling Jewish State in 1948, the Arab parties had nullified it.[132] Furthermore, Resolution 181 had been superseded by countless other resolutions, including Resolution 242 after the Six-Day War and Resolution 338 after the Yom Kippur War – neither of which conflicts Israel started.

Arafat called for a Palestinian State on Resolution 181 boundaries rather than Resolution 242 boundaries because it would give him much more territory (see Appendix F, maps 3 and 4). Not only would it give him a considerably enlarged Gaza and 'West Bank', which would be linked together, but it would also give him an enclave in western Galilee taking in Acre and the areas close to the Lebanese border, also linked to the 'West Bank'. This would effectively carve Israel into three separate areas, making her militarily indefensible. Furthermore, Jerusalem itself would be completely surrounded by a Palestinian State, and even more vulnerable than it was in 1948.

However, the most alarming aspect of Arafat's 'Resolution 181' campaign was that the UN Human Rights Commission in Geneva passed a resolution, with European Union support, calling for a division of the land based on UN Resolution 181. The resolution also demanded the right of return for all 'Palestinian' refugees based on UN Resolution 194, which Israel has always rejected on the grounds that she did not create the refugee problem. Not only that, but there was no specific mention of the 'Oslo' process, or its foundation in UN Security Council Resolutions 242 and 338. Thus the Geneva resolution stands in direct opposition to any agreements made between Israel and the Palestinian Authority under 'Oslo'. Israel's lobbying efforts to modify it failed, and the United States was the only country among the fifty-three in attendance that opposed it.[133]

It is well known that the European Union nations, including Britain, have always refused to acknowledge Israel's sovereignty over any part of Jerusalem, even though Jordan illegally annexed East Jerusalem following the War of Independence. Arafat and the European Union turned a blind eye to the fact that Resolution 181 stated that Jerusalem would have international status. And yet Arafat persistently continued to declare Jerusalem would be 'the capital of Palestine' with their support.

The Kosovars and the Palestinians

Another ominous event in 1999 was the military conflict in the Balkans, as the NATO nations bombed into submission the Serbian regime of Slobodan Milosevic over the ethnic cleansing of Moslem Kosovars of Albanian descent, who made up 90 per cent of Kosovo's population. The world, quite rightly, was outraged by Milosevic's brutality. This ethnic cleansing was also condemned by the Jewish State. However Israel, apart from supplying humanitarian aid to the displaced Moslems, was reluctant to become embroiled in the conflict, mainly because the Serbs had offered Jews protection from the Nazis during World War II. There was also some concern by Israel that the full story behind the conflict had not been properly told.

As far as Israel was concerned, the most alarming development to come out of the Balkan war was largely ignored by the international media. As the NATO bombardment of the Serbs wound down, Yasser Arafat demanded that the world community liberate 'occupied Arab lands' for 'the Palestinians' in the same way that they liberated Kosovo for the Moslem ethnic Albanians. This chilling demand by Arafat raises four crucial questions:

(1) Is Arafat seriously interested in either the negotiating table, or even living peaceably with Israel?

(2) Has the Kosovar war set a precedent for dealing with nations which do not conform to the will of the 'New World Order' (however justified the situation may or may not be)?
(3) Could that precedent be used in an attempt to disinherit Israel from the land and the city which God has covenanted to her as an everlasting possession?
(4) If so, have we witnessed another rehearsal for the last great conflict, prophesied by Zechariah, when the armies of the world will be gathered against Jerusalem?

Yet Another Change of Government

In mid-1999 Israel had a Labour government once again, only this time under a new banner called 'One Israel', which in practice was an alliance of centre-left parties. Arguably, the American administration played a direct part in having Binyamin Netanyahu ousted and Ehud Barak installed as Prime Minister. Clinton's election campaign advisors James Carville and Stanley Greenberg, who had also assisted in getting the leaders of Britain and Germany into power, contributed successfully to Barak's campaign as well.

Ehud Barak had always regarded Yitzhak Rabin as his mentor. Like Rabin, Barak had served as Chief of Staff of the Israel Defence Force (IDF) and was a highly decorated soldier – in fact the most decorated soldier in the IDF. Also, like Rabin, the mainspring of his ideology in government is secular humanism.

On assuming power, the 'Oslo' process quickly became one of Barak's priorities and things began to move again. After a flurry of shuttle diplomacy, the Wye Memorandum was revitalised in early September at a summit held at the Egyptian resort of Sharm E-Sheikh. Dubbed 'Wye II' or 'Sharm' by the media, the new agreement did not substantially differ from the original Wye agreement, other than it stipulated a timetable for the progress of the Final Status talks of the Oslo Accords. The deadline for the start of talks would be 13 September 1999, and the completion deadline would be 13 September 2000, exactly seven years after the original signing of the Declaration of Principles. However, the new Prime Minister had already laid down some 'red lines' over which he said he would not be moved.

These included:

(1) Jerusalem would remain as a unified city under Israeli sovereignty.

(2) There would be no return to the 1967 borders, as the borders between Israel and the 'West Bank' were not internationally recognised.

(3) There would be no return to Israel of refugees, or their descendants, who were displaced as a result of either the 1948 or the 1967 wars.

(4) There would be no foreign army (i.e. Palestinian army) west of the Jordan River.

At the time the Final Status talks began, the Israeli Prime Minister would not be drawn into stating whether or not he supported the formation of a State of Palestine. He said he did not think about it, not 'even in the shower'.[134]

The Ultimate Fate of the 'Peace' Process

If what Yasser Arafat says to both the western media and the media in the Arab world is anything to go by, then he intends to cross all the 'red lines' set by Barak. Furthermore, he ultimately intends to eradicate the State of Israel. And there are certainly enough Moslem nations in the Middle East who would be only too glad to assist him. As far as Yasser Arafat is concerned, only when Israel is wiped off the map, will there be peace. With the enormous gap between the aspirations of what Ehud Barak and Yasser Arafat are expecting from the 'peace' process, it is not difficult to perceive that the prospects of achieving lasting peace in the Middle East are pretty slim, if not impossible. And yet there are many Israelis on the left side of politics, including Barak, who predict that the Oslo Accords will bring lasting peace to the war-weary State of Israel. Moreover, they believe in the good faith of Yasser Arafat and his cohorts. Speaking in a television interview about the difficulties posed by the 'peace' process, the Israeli Prime Minister said:

'It will not be solved by Heaven, but by human beings who happen to be leaders, especially a man like Arafat who is the founding father of his national movement: these are the only people who will have the political and moral authority to put an end to this conflict.'[135]

Unfortunately, the ancient Israeli prophets do not endorse the Prime Minister's optimism. Many Christian intercessors, who pray regularly for the 'peace of Jerusalem', fear that the Oslo Accords will eventually bring disaster to Israel.[136] Many God-fearing Jews living in *Eretz Yisrael* believe the same. The prophetic Scriptures indicate that lasting peace will not come by human endeavour at all, but only from heaven through the 'Prince of Peace' (Isaiah 9:6), the returning *Mashiach*. The prophet Ezekiel warns:

> ' *"The Lord GOD says: My hand shall be against you, and you shall be cut off from among the leaders of Israel. For these evil men deceive My people by saying, 'God will send peace,' when that is not My plan at all! My people build a flimsy wall and these prophets praise them for it – and cover it with whitewash! Tell these evil builders that their wall will fall. ... I will break down your whitewashed wall, and it will fall on you and crush you, and you shall know I am the Lord. Then at last My wrath against the wall will be completed. I will say: The wall and its builders both are gone. For they were lying prophets, claiming Jerusalem will have peace when there is no peace, says the Lord GOD."* '
>
> (Quoted in part from Ezekiel 13:8–11,
> 14–16, Living Bible)

It is a chilling thought that the assassination of Yitzhak Rabin may have been a partial fulfilment of this prophecy. Jeremiah has another warning:

> 'Thus says the LORD of hosts:
> "Do not listen to the words of the prophets who prophesy to
>   you. ...
> They speak a vision of their own heart,
> Not from the mouth of the LORD.

> *They continually say to those who despise Me,*
> *'The LORD has said, "You shall have peace" ';*
> *And to everyone who walks according to the imagination of*
>   *his own heart,*
> *'No evil shall come upon you." '*
> *For who has stood in the counsel of the LORD,*
> *And perceived and heard His word? . . .*
> *The anger of the LORD will not turn back*
> *Until He has executed it and performed the thoughts of His*
>   *heart.*
> *In the latter days you will understand it perfectly.'*
>   (Jeremiah 23:16–18, 20 in part)

Whether or not Jeremiah and Ezekiel were speaking specifically of the Oslo Accords is not yet certain – no doubt time will tell. But these prophecies do address leaders of Israel who attempt to make 'peace' with – or appease – corrupt godless enemies, without reference to the God of Israel and His will in the matter. This especially applies when the bargaining chips are the Lord's Land and His Holy City – Israel's inheritance. Jeremiah puts the context of the above warning 'in the latter days' – the days in which we live. This warning, therefore, needs to be heeded in the present situation. Rather than the peace that the leaders of the 'New World Order' predict, and are trying to impose on Israel, the prophetic Scriptures clearly indicate that there will be an ultimate global conflict that will centre on Jerusalem. There are also indications that there could be other major wars fought over Israel before then.

The Spiritual Conflict over Jerusalem

The conflict surrounding Jerusalem cannot and will not ultimately be resolved by compromise or political settlement. This is because the conflict is not merely a human, or even a religious conflict – even though that may appear to be the case. As previously noted, in the Scriptures the God of Israel has declared the Holy City to be His dwelling place for ever, and He has promised that He will return to Jerusalem in the person of the Messiah and will rule the world from there. The

Lord has also stated that the Jewish nation, her possession of the Land of Israel and the Holy City is central to His plan.

Furthermore, He has promised to fulfil *all* the prophecies and the covenants recorded in the *Tanakh*. Yeshua confirmed this in the Sermon on the Mount:

> ' "Don't think that I have come to abolish the Torah or the Prophets. I have come not to abolish but to complete. I tell you that until heaven and earth pass away, not so much as a yud or a stroke will pass from the Torah – not until everything that must happen has happened." '
>
> (Matthew 5:17–18, Jewish New Testament)

This being the case, then the conflict over Jerusalem is essentially a spiritual conflict, as the spiritual forces of darkness try to thwart the purposes of the God of Israel. This invisible spiritual conflict is being made manifest in the human arena. At present it is being played out in the political and religious arenas. Later it will be in the military arena, and it will involve the whole world.

The Prince of Persia and the Prince of Greece

The spiritual conflict over the Holy City, *Eretz Yisrael* and the Jewish people can be illustrated through an encounter between Daniel and a heavenly messenger. This particular encounter happened after Daniel had been fasting and praying for three weeks. It is described in Daniel 10. The heavenly messenger, who is not actually named, tells Daniel that he has been delayed by the *'prince of the kingdom of Persia'* for twenty-one days and that *'Michael, one of the chief princes'* came to his aid (v. 13). It is widely believed that the Archangel Michael is the guardian angel of the nation of Israel and the Jewish people (cf. Daniel 10:21, 12:1 and Revelation 12:7). Before the heavenly messenger departed from Daniel, he told him that he was returning *'to fight with the prince of Persia'* and *'then the prince of Greece will come'* (Daniel 10:20).

What can we glean from this? Well, firstly, like the Archangel Michael, the Prince of Greece and the Prince of Persia are angelic or spiritual beings. Secondly, unlike the Archangel Michael, they are not part of the Kingdom of God, but part of the kingdom of darkness – otherwise why would they oppose the heavenly messenger and Michael? Some Christians believe the Princes of Persia and Greece are demonic 'principalities' (Ephesians 6:12). Thirdly, because they are like angelic beings, their life spans millennia, if not all of time. Some Christians believe that such beings often dominate particular territories, cultures and thought patterns in the world.

If this is the case, it is not unreasonable to suggest that the two spiritual 'princes' mentioned in Daniel 10 are alive and well today – and still actively influencing the course of history.

Let us consider the sphere of influence of each of them in turn.[137] Firstly, the Prince of Persia.

The Prince of Persia

Daniel was told this 'prince' would be the main spiritual power influencing the Persian Empire. In chapter 11 verse 2, Daniel was informed that there would be three more Persian kings after the one reigning at that time, Darius. History reveals that this came to pass. It was during the reign of the successor to Darius I, King Ahasuerus, that Haman plotted to murder all the Jews living within the Persian Empire, which covered most of the civilised world at that time. Could it be that the demonic 'prince' which dominated Persia was the real mastermind behind Haman's *jihad* against the Jewish race? Of course, the God of Israel, through Esther and Mordecai, delivered the Jews from Haman's plot as is recorded in the Book of Esther. This miraculous deliverance is still celebrated today in the Jewish Feast of *Purim*.

But what happened to the 'Prince of Persia' whose territory included modern-day Afghanistan, Iran, Iraq and possibly Saudi Arabia? Could this be the demonic principality which has masterminded Islam?

Could this evil spirit, which tried to wipe out God's chosen people in ancient Persia, be the main antagonist in the continuing conflict between the sons of Isaac and the sons of Ishmael?

Is it this ancient 'Prince of Persia' – working through the forces of Islam – which is attempting to disinherit the Jewish people from the land and the city which God has covenanted to them? Is it not the demonic principality behind Islam which is attempting to heave the Temple Mount – God's holy mountain – away from the Jewish people so that the Lord can never literally dwell there among His people?

And the other nations of the world, knowingly or not, are aiding and abetting this tug of war against the Jewish people. They are being deceived, willingly or not, into denying Israel's incontrovertible historic and religious claim to Jerusalem and the site of their ancient Temple, which dates back more than three thousand years. And at the same time they legitimise the false claims of the PLO and the Islamic world, whose historic claims only go back one thousand three hundred years, and whose religious claims are based entirely on myth and theological argument.[138]

Invasion from the North

As far as Jerusalem is concerned, the most prominent enemy against the purposes of God in the world today is the very powerful and dangerous satanic spirit behind Islam. It is this spirit which has worked millions of fundamentalist Moslems into a frenzy of 'holy war' or *jihad* against what they call the 'Zionist infidel'. It is this spirit that is the *real* enemy of Israel, rather than the Moslem people themselves, whom God also loves. This brutal spirit has imprisoned millions of Arabs, as well as other peoples all over the world, and deceived them into thinking they can liquidate Israel and conquer the world. A final Islamic *jihad* against the Jewish nation is inevitable. Many of Islam's captives will be set free, but sadly many will perish. The possible scenario for this great *jihad* is found in Ezekiel 38 and 39.

This important prophecy occupies two entire chapters of the Bible and describes the invasion of the armies of 'Gog and Magog' from the North. While Jerusalem itself is not directly mentioned in the prophecy, the action will take place in fairly close proximity and therefore will affect the Holy City. Chronologically it is set between the prophecies concerning the restoration of Israel (Ezekiel 36 and 37) and the restoration of the Temple in the Messianic Age (Ezekiel 40–48, which will be discussed further in Chapters 8 and 11). Its placing, therefore, gives some idea of the time in history when it is likely to be fulfilled.[139] If these assumptions are correct, then this invasion of Israel is probably imminent. It is recommended that the reader take time to study Ezekiel 38 and 39 at this point.

The prophecy is very detailed, especially in its outcome. God says that the very purpose of the prophecy and its fulfilment is that *'the house of Israel shall know that I am the* LORD *from that day forward'* (39:22).

A little knowledge of biblical geography at the time of Abraham will help the reader to understand who are the main players. Translating these names into the present-day world map, it is not difficult to identify the leading attacker who comes from *'the far north'* (38:15). Geographically, Moscow is due north of Jerusalem. This means it is likely to be Russia who will lead an alliance that includes some of the former Soviet Republics as well as Iran, Ethiopia, Sudan and Libya. It seems that Germany and/or some Eastern European countries and Turkey may be part of the alliance too. They will attack and invade an apparently secure and peaceful Israel. The reader will recognise that many of these countries have Islamic regimes in power today, some of them very radical. In all of them anti-Semitism is either running at fever pitch or on the rise. Syria, Jordan and Egypt seem to be notably absent from the attacking horde. But there will be a number of countries (and perhaps even the UN) who will stand by and shrug their shoulders when the invasion takes place.

Israel, it seems, will face annihilation at that time, but the outcome for the attackers is clearly predicted in 38:18–22 and 39:1–8. The invading forces will incur the swift and devastating judgement of God as a great earthquake takes place and 85 per cent of their armies perish on the mountains of Israel.[140] The length of time it takes Israel to bury the dead gives us some idea of the scale of the carnage and destruction. The countries from whence they came will not remain untouched either. If the Islamic shrines are still standing on the Temple Mount at that time, what will happen to them? As a result of the intervention of the Lord, the nations will recognise the sovereignty of the God of Abraham, Isaac and Jacob and His purposes for the nation of Israel.

If this prophecy does in fact portray the last great Islamic *jihad*, then clearly Islam will suffer a final and devastating defeat. But unless it coincides with the prophecies concerning the last great conflict (known as Armageddon) and the advent of the Messiah, which are described by other prophets – particularly Isaiah, Jeremiah, Joel, Zechariah and John in the Book of Revelation – then the spiritual battle over Jerusalem will not have been finalised. It seems that another great spiritual force, which has been active in the world for thousands of years, is still at work and attacking the nation of Israel in the closing moments of this age. This spiritual principality may be even more dangerous to Israel, because it appears as an 'angel of light'.

The Prince of Greece

While the Persian Empire still dominated the ancient world, the next great empire was in its embryonic stages under the influence of the other demonic principality mentioned to Daniel – the 'Prince of Greece'. The empire's forefathers were the prominent Hellenic philosophers such as Socrates, Plato and Aristotle. The latter was mentor to Alexander the Great, who displaced the Persians and conquered the then-known world – just as Daniel had prophesied some two hundred years earlier.

The Greeks brought their Hellenic culture and philosophy to Israel. Some Jews welcomed it with open arms, while the more orthodox God-fearing Jews resisted it strongly – and thus the Jewish nation was divided. As far as Israel was concerned, the most devastating of the Greek rulers was Antiochus Epiphanes. Author Bruce Reekie describes him thus:

'Antiochus was a fervent believer in Hellenic (Greek) culture and civilisation, and possessed an extraordinary love of art. He was a man of great ingenuity, and a master of dissimulation and deceit. His vision was to unite the nations of the Eastern Mediterranean basin in a pan-Hellenic "common market" – a revived Alexandrian Empire. Under the pretence of treaties, leagues and alliances, Antiochus encroached on people's sovereign rights, and tricked them into subjection. The keynote of his policy was "unity", and to this end he sought to impose Greek culture, thought and customs under his dominion, and to eradicate "parochialism", whether culture, language or religion.

Interestingly enough, a "progressive party" emerged in Israel at about the same time which sought to throw off the shackles of "medieval religion" and help the nation take its place in the rapidly developing "New World Order".

Antiochus was obsessed with the design of reducing the Jews to a conformity of manners and religion with other nations; or, in other words, of abolishing those distinctive features which made the Jews a peculiar people, socially separated from all others. This design was odious to the great body of the people, although there were many among the higher classes who regarded it with favour.' [141]

Israel was deceived by Antiochus and the worst bloodbath of the inter-Testament period followed (see Chapter 9). As the Second Book of Maccabees records:

> *'They disdained all their ancestors had esteemed, and set the highest value on hellenic honours. But all this brought its own retribution; the very people whose way of life they envied, whom they sought to resemble in everything, proved to be their enemies and executioners.'*
>
> (2 Maccabees 4:15–16, The Jerusalem Bible)

Despite the fact that the political and military supremacy of the Hellenists was relatively short-lived, their spirit was to continue to dominate the empire that followed – the Roman Empire – which also embraced the teaching of the Greek philosophers. And so, it appears, the 'Prince of Greece' lived on through the Roman Empire. Later, the teachings of Socrates, Plato, Aristotle and others began to infiltrate and corrupt the Christian Church establishment as Christianity became the State religion of Rome and the official religion in the nations of Eastern Europe and Western Asia. Then, a thousand years later, the legacy of the Greek philosophers emerged again as a driving force in the Renaissance of Western Europe, and a modern form of Hellenism was born – humanism.

It is not necessary to document the influence of humanism on western culture today. But it is notable that within the nation of Israel secular humanism has become the philosophical mainspring of roughly half the population, as the 1992, 1996 and 1999 elections revealed.

In reality, the division in Israeli society, which has become so bitter in recent years, is not so much along political lines as spiritual lines. The basic division is between those, on the one hand, who believe that *Eretz Yisrael* is the God-given inheritance of the Jewish people according to the Abrahamic Covenant; and on the other hand, those who believe that the Land of Israel is just like any other piece of 'real estate' on the face of the earth which can be negotiated to appease one's neighbours. Coincidentally, the former are generally those inclined to be politically to the right, and the latter are more politically inclined to the left.

Again, as in the days of Antiochus Epiphanes, on the one hand there are those who want to preserve Israel's unique identity as a nation set apart for God; and on the other there are those who believe that Israel should be a nation like any other. There are those who believe that the destiny of the nation is in the hands of the God of Israel, and those who believe that Israel's destiny is in her own hands.

In a spiritual sense, one could describe the division as being between 'the sons of Zion' and the 'sons of Greece'.

However, the 'Prince of Greece' is not simply attacking the nation of Israel from within, but also from without. Political leaders of the nations of the western world – aware that the Middle East is like a nuclear bomb ready to explode – are trying to impose a humanist solution on what is basically a spiritual conflict. These 'sons of Greece', who account for many of the nations in the United Nations Assembly, appear to regard Israel as nothing more than a nuisance that needs to be conformed to their concept of a 'New World Order'. Many of them also regard Zionism as something that must be eradicated.

As far as can be ascertained, Israel's previous Prime Minister, Binyamin Netanyahu, is a true Zionist. The external pressures upon him and his government to capitulate to the 'Prince of Greece', and consequently to the 'Prince of Persia', were enormous. Under Prime Minister Ehud Barak, who is a humanist, Israel faces exactly the same pressures, but with greater vulnerability. For those who are 'watchmen on the walls of Jerusalem', this is a matter for intercession.

However, the God of Israel, who neither slumbers nor sleeps, has promised to stand by the 'sons of Zion':

> ' *"As for you also,*
> *Because of the blood of your covenant,*
> *I will set your prisoners free from the waterless pit.*
> *Return to the stronghold,*
> *You prisoners of hope.*
> *Even today I declare*
> *That I will restore double to you.*
> *For I have bent Judah, My bow,*
> *Fitted the bow with Ephraim,*
> *And raised up your sons, O Zion,*
> *Against your sons, O Greece,*
> *And made you like the sword of a mighty man."* '
>
> (Zechariah 9:11–13)

This is a promise that was fulfilled through the Maccabees when they liberated the Holy City and the Sanctuary from the forces of Antiochus Epiphanes in the second century BCE.

If, as I believe, the demonic principality which was revealed to Daniel as the 'Prince of Greece' is alive and well today, then the ancient promise of God to 'the sons of Zion' – i.e. those whose faith is in the God of Israel – still stands.

As discussed, it seems that there are some remarkable similarities between Israel during the second century BCE and Israel today. This raises an awesome question: Are we about to see those horrific events of history repeated as the prophecies of Daniel relating to the end of the age (which will be considered in more detail in Chapter 9) are fulfilled?

There seem to be only two major elements missing for this to happen: firstly, a modern-day 'Antiochus Epiphanes', and secondly, a Jewish Temple standing on the Temple Mount.

Chapter 8

Jerusalem and the
Rebuilding of the Temple

Aspirations to Rebuild the Temple

The subject of rebuilding the Temple is perhaps the most sensitive issue one can talk about in Jerusalem, for Moslems, for Christians – and even for Jews.

To see the Temple standing on the Temple Mount once again has been one of the fondest dreams in the heart of many God-fearing Jews. By implication this aspiration is enshrined in The Jerusalem Covenant, through quotations from the *Tanakh* which make up much of the Covenant's text. However, at the time of the writing of this book, the realisation of another Temple is as far away as ever, mainly because of a number of Moslem structures standing in the way – particularly the Dome of the Rock and the Al-Aqsa Mosque, which dominate the Temple Mount.

Added to that, there is a good deal of controversy among religious Jews as to how and when the rebuilding of the Temple might take place. While some say another Temple is unnecessary, many Orthodox Jews believe that the Messiah Himself will cause the Temple to be built when He comes.

However, there are other religious groups who believe that the Messiah will not come until the Temple is rebuilt. We have already mentioned one group, the Temple Mount Faithful, who intended to lay the cornerstone of the third Temple [142] at *Sukkot* in 1989 and again in 1990. Under the leadership of Gershon Salamon, who one would have to describe as one of the 'sons of Zion', they have continued to go through with the same ceremony every year since, in the sincere belief that the Lord will one day soon grant them the desire of their hearts. Another group is the Society for the Preparation of the Temple, who publish a bimonthly journal *Yivneh Ha-miqdash* ('Let the Temple Be Built!'). Its aim is to focus Jewish thought on the Temple.

Yet another establishment is the Temple Institute, founded in 1988 by Rabbi Israel Ariel who also was among the first paratroopers to reach the Western Wall in the Six-Day War. Ironically, his first army assignment after the war was to guard the Dome of the Rock – the very object standing in the way of the Temple being rebuilt! [143]

The Temple Institute has re-created most of the articles used in the ancient Temple as described in the Bible. Among these are the golden crown of the high priest, the priestly garments, the laver for the purification of the priests, implements for sacrificial service and silver trumpets for calling worshippers to the Temple. In addition, a six-foot-high gold-plated Menorah, containing 94.6 lbs of gold and costing $10 million, has been completed. These articles are not intended simply as replicas, but as usable vessels destined for future service in the third Temple. [144]

Other groups are preparing men to serve as priests in the Temple, and another is breeding red heifers. Without ceremonial purification, it is believed nobody is able to enter the Temple precincts to rebuild the Temple, let alone to perform the services of the priesthood. The only remedy for this state of impurity is the ceremony of purification, which requires the ashes of sacrifice from a particular type of *parah adumah*, or red heifer (Numbers 19).

The proliferation of individuals and groups who are supporting and working towards the building of the third Temple has increased, and new industries have sprung up as a result.

One such industry is *Beged Ivri*, meaning 'Hebrew Clothing', which produces garments for Levitical function designed from biblical and historical sources, and another is that of making ancient-style musical instruments. After a two-thousand-year absence, the sounds of the biblical harp have returned to Jerusalem.[145]

Pinpointing the Site of the Temple on the Temple Mount

There are three main theories regarding the precise location of the ancient Temple. The most widely recognised theory is that the Temple stood where the Dome of the Rock now stands. The rock inside the mosque was probably the summit of Mount Moriah, and traditionally marks the site where Abraham offered Isaac (Genesis 22). The Moslems claim that Abraham offered Ishmael on this site. They say this is also the site from which their prophet Mohammed rose into heaven on a winged horse. The 'Dome of the Rock' theory of the precise location of the Temple has two variations. Some Jewish archaeologists believe the rock is the site of the Holy of Holies in the Temple. Others believe it is the site of the altar on which the sacrifices were offered, placing the location of the Holy of Holies a few yards to the west of the Dome of the Rock.

The second main theory is that the Temple stood to the south of where the Dome of the Rock currently stands – between it and the Al-Aqsa Mosque. This theory is supported by an orthodox Jewish architect by the name of Tuvia Sagiv. The Holy of Holies, according to Sagiv, would have been approximately fifty feet underneath where the Al-Kas foot-washing pool is today – roughly on the same level as the present-day Western Wall Plaza. He says that the ruins of the second Temple are buried behind today's Western Wall, somewhere beneath the Al-Kas. Furthermore, Sagiv believes that the Moslems used the ruins of the Roman temple as the foundations for both the Al-Aqsa Mosque and the Dome of the Rock.

The third theory, put forward by physicist Dr Asher Kaufmann, is that the Holy of Holies stood where the Dome of the Tablets now stands, about a hundred yards to the north-west of the Dome of the Rock.[146]

Both Tuvia Sagiv's and Asher Kaufmann's theories have an impressive body of research behind them – however both theories have both been rejected by the archaeological community in Israel. Almost all Jewish archaeologists and rabbis believe the Temple stood where the Dome of the Rock now stands. The problem facing all who attempt to investigate the original location of the Temple is lack of accessible archaeological evidence. Dame Kathleen Kenyon, a British archaeologist who excavated extensively in the Temple area several decades ago, concluded: 'Absolutely nothing survives of the Temple built by Herod.'[147] It seems that, unless further documentary evidence comes to light, the exact location of the Temple and the Holy of Holies can only be conclusively pinpointed after extensive archaeological digging under the Mount to trace any possible subterranean remains of the foundations.

Apart from the lack of structural remains, there are two other significant problems. Firstly, as noted earlier, Jewish religious law forbids any Jew from stepping on the *'azarah'*, the sacred precinct of the ancient Temple. Since today all Jews are ceremonially impure, to do so would defile the entire Temple Mount. Secondly, the Israeli Protection of Holy Places Law supports the Moslem position and makes it a crime to desecrate a holy place in any way, which the Moslems say would certainly occur if the site were to be excavated.[148]

Dr Kaufmann's theory has particularly caught the attention of Evangelical Christians who have an interest in biblical prophecy, because it would appear that a northern location would remove a major obstacle for the rebuilding of the Temple today. If, they say, the Temple could be built alongside and to the north of the Dome of the Rock, then the only thing standing in the way of Temple construction is a negotiated settlement with the Arabs to share the Temple Mount.

However, this would not resolve the problem of rebuilding the Temple. As far as Orthodox Jewry is concerned, the very presence of an Islamic shrine on the Temple Mount defiles the area and makes access for construction impossible. In fact, those in the Temple movements in Israel are emphatic that not only must the Dome of the Rock be removed, but also the Al-Aqsa Mosque, which would be within the Temple precinct.[149]

The Controversy Surrounding the Building of the Third Temple

As noted, the subject of the third Temple is highly controversial. The Moslem *Waqf* says that because a Jewish Temple has never existed, Israel has no right to build one. If the Moslems are preventing Jewish archaeologists from going on, or even under, the Temple Mount to excavate in order to find subterranean foundations of the first and second Temples, then they will certainly do everything they can to prevent a third Temple being erected. The riots of 1990 and 1996 are unquestionably an indication of that.

I have already also referred to the differing views among Jewish people about the rebuilding of the Temple. It would be true to say that the overwhelming majority of Jews, both in Israel and the *Diaspora*, would not sanction the rebuilding of the Temple, given the tensions that exist at the present time. Those involved in preparations to rebuild the Temple, however far advanced they may be, are a small minority.

There is also considerable disagreement among Christians as to whether another Temple should be built, or indeed ever will be built. As most of the church establishment believes that modern Israel is an accident of history and has no place in the purposes of God, they are opposed to the idea.

Then there are the theological problems which the rebuilding of the Temple and the re-introduction of the sacrificial system would pose for Christians. The New Testament, and particularly the Book of Hebrews, teaches us that the death of the Messiah and the shedding of His blood has atoned for all sin for all time for those who put their faith in Him. What then would be the point of reintroducing the offerings and sacrifices? For Christians, this is perhaps the most important – and controversial – question of all. Even among Evangelical Christians, who believe that the whole Bible is the inspired Word of the God of Israel, there is a diversity of opinion as to whether the Temple either should or will be rebuilt.[150]

However, if one takes the view that the prophetic Scriptures concerning Israel will be literally fulfilled – and we have already considered many which have – it is difficult not to come to the conclusion that a Temple will be standing on the

Temple Mount again one day. Many of the Old Testament prophets speak of attributes of a future Temple which have never yet been fulfilled.

The prophet Haggai tells us that the glory of the latter Temple shall be greater than the glory of the former Temple. He also declares that the nations will come to 'the Desire of All Nations' – that is the Messiah – and that the Lord will fill the Temple with His glory and that there will be peace (Haggai 2:7–9).

The prophets Isaiah and Micah both speak of the nations beating their swords into ploughshares and their spears into pruning hooks. They also prophesy that the nations will come to the House of the Lord, to learn His ways (Isaiah 2:2–4 and Micah 4:1–3).

Ezekiel describes the glory of the Lord residing in the Temple once again, and a river of 'living water' flowing out from it. Furthermore, he envisages a Temple whose overall dimensions are as large – if not larger – than the whole of the present-day Old City of Jerusalem (Ezekiel 43:4, 47:1 and 42:15–19).

The prophet Zechariah even tells us who will build this Temple:

> *"'Behold, the Man whose name is the BRANCH!* [151]
> *Yes, He shall build the Temple of the LORD."'*
> (Zechariah 6:12–13 in part)

These prophecies all refer to the Temple that will dominate Jerusalem in the Messianic Era, when the Lord dwells in the midst of His people, and we will look at them in more detail in Chapter 11.

However, both the Old and New Testaments suggest the existence of a Temple in Jerusalem immediately prior to Messiah's return, which raises the probability that we will see not only a third Temple, but even a fourth Temple – the one to be built by the Messiah. This is the Temple described in the final chapters of the Book of Ezekiel.

As we shall see in the next chapter, the prophetic Scriptures indicate that if a third Temple is built, like the first and second Temples, someone energised by Satan will defile it. In fact, we may well see a repeat of history as a 'modern-day Antiochus Epiphanes' deceives and seeks to destroy the nation of Israel.

The fulfilment of these prophecies will be a sure sign that the return of the Messiah in all His glory is very close, which is one reason why some Evangelical Christians are excited about the prospect of the Temple being rebuilt. However, it is not my intention to speculate as to how or when the Temple might be rebuilt, or what form it might take.[152] Time will tell. But I do believe that the prophecy which Yeshua and Paul were referring to in Matthew 24:15 and 2 Thessalonians 2:4 will have a literal fulfilment. This means there will have to be a physical structure of some description, where the biblical offerings and sacrifices take place, standing on the site of the first and second Temples. The Book of Revelation, which was written more than twenty years after the destruction of the second Temple by the Romans, describes such a Temple (in chapter 11). Notwithstanding the symbolic nature of the language in this passage, it is difficult to imagine that the prophetic vision that the Apostle John saw was the spiritual Temple of God – the Church. The mere fact that he was told to measure the Temple of God, the worshippers and the altar, but leave out the Court of the Gentiles, suggests what he saw was a physical structure with people in it (vv. 1 and 2).

The Significance of the Third Temple for the Jewish People

'This is the time to rebuild the House of God. Actually, I would say that in the Six Day War, when the God of Israel brought the people of Israel back to Mount Moriah, in this moment God expected from the people of Israel to rebuild His House, the third Temple. Unfortunately we missed this great moment – our leadership missed it.'

These words were spoken by Gershon Salamon, leader of the Temple Mount and Land of Israel Faithful, the group who have been attempting to lay a cornerstone to the third Temple for several years at *Sukkot*.[153] He continued:

> 'We are living in the time of the redemption of the people of Israel and the Land of Israel. And until the Temple is rebuilt there will never be peace – not in Israel, not in the Middle East, and not all over the world. Because when we rebuild the House of God we shall show God that we want Him again to be in the middle of our life. We want to bring the God of Israel in the midst of the life of this nation – exactly as it was in the biblical time in Jerusalem. On Mount Moriah.'

Indeed Gershon Salamon's desire to rebuild the House of the Lord is reminiscent of the desire and purpose of the Lord Himself, for He said to King Solomon when the Temple was first commissioned:

> ' *"For now I have chosen and sanctified this House, that My name may be there forever; and My eyes and My heart will be there perpetually."* '   (2 Chronicles 7:16)

If one is to take this Scripture literally, then the Lord's name, His eyes and His heart are still residing on Mount Moriah today – despite the appearance to the contrary. Many Evangelical Christians and many observant God-fearing Jews, like Gershon Salamon, are in agreement on this point. Both sides would also agree that the Temple will play a major part in the spiritual restoration of Israel – in bringing the God of Israel back into the centre of the life of the nation – and the coming of Mashiach. However, it should be pointed out that Gershon Salamon and his colleagues do not agree with the Christian view concerning the identity of the Messiah, and therefore, like the majority of Jewish people at this time, would probably not concur with all that follows.

Rev. Malcolm Hedding, who is Chairman of the South African based ministry 'Christian Action for Israel' also believes the third Temple will have a central role in the spiritual recovery of Israel. He bases his belief on his under-standing of Zechariah 4 and Revelation 11:

'Firstly, I want to say that salvation is by faith alone in the work of Jesus Christ. This has been so for all eternity – there is no other way to be right with God other than the finished work of our Lord Jesus. The Bible says that the Lord Jesus died before the foundation of the earth (Revelation 13:8). In other words, if anybody ever got saved and was brought into right standing with God from the beginning of time to the present day, it is only by the finished work of our Lord Jesus.

Secondly, the Temple is a symbol of Messiah's work. It is a basic instructive medium by which the work of Messiah is pictured in all its aspects. It is a symbol, a picture of Messiah's finished work on the cross. It is this symbol, according to the Bible, that operated before Messiah comes, and even after Messiah comes. And, of course, the Temple is the seat of Messiah's reign. Thus we have the exhaustive description in the Bible of Ezekiel's Messianic Temple.

The Bible teaches that Israel's restoration in the latter days will have two phases. It teaches that Israel's restoration in the first place would be a physical restoration, in other words she would come back in unbelief generally and largely. Then, the Bible teaches, once she is in the land, there will be a spiritual recovery of the nation of Israel (Ezekiel 36:24–27). The Bible also teaches that Israel's spiritual recovery will bring the second coming of the Mashiach. For Jesus to return to the planet, there has to be an invitation from Israel (Matthew 23:39 and Acts 3:17–21). Hidden in this small nation is the secret of world peace. Not only the secret of world peace, but also the destruction of the devil. That is why this nation is going to come under greater attack as the days now pass. But God Himself will defend her, and spiritually recover her.

How will Israel be spiritually recovered? This is the issue. We need to know that for nearly 2,000 years Judaism has gone through a mutation. After the destruction of the Temple in AD 70, Rabbi Yochanan re-codified Judaism, and vicarious or substitutionary sacrifice as the way of redemption was excluded from the rabbinical canon of theology. From that time onwards "a good life" became the means of "eternal life". This has been the theological foundation of Rabbinical Judaism to the present day.

The Bible teaches in the Old and New Testaments that Israel will be spiritually recovered, among other things, by the Third Temple. If we turn to Zechariah chapter 4, we find that the context of this chapter is the building of the second Temple. But the Word of God teaches that this particular passage also applies to the building of the third Temple, and I will demonstrate that from the Word of God in a moment. In this chapter, Israel's spiritual recovery is contrasted with the building of the third Temple. And it is in that context that the prophet says: " '*Not by might nor by power, but by My Spirit,' says the LORD of hosts*" (verse 6). The context of Zechariah 4 is the third Temple being raised up on Mount Moriah "not by might, not by power, but by the supernatural working of 'My Holy Spirit'!" And Zechariah contrasts the work of "the two anointed ones" (verse 14) with the building of the Temple. What the prophet sees is "two anointed ones" in the form of "two olive trees" standing on either side of a menorah. The menorah is the symbol of Israel – even to this present day. The two olive trees are a symbol of the anointing of the Holy Spirit. So they are two men filled with the Holy Spirit. They are "the two anointed ones who stand before the Lord of the whole earth" (verse 14). And from them are pipes that go into the menorah (verse 2). In other words they feed the oil of the Holy Spirit into the nation of Israel, and they ignite her with the fire of God. Their ministry is discharged within the Temple, so their ministry in Zechariah 4 is contrasted with the construction of the Temple, which according to the prophet will have to be a supernatural thing by the power of the Holy Spirit, because nobody will believe it is possible!

Moreover, the Word of God says when these "two anointed ones" discharge their ministry in the Temple, then Israel will know that the Messiah has been to them (verse 9): *"The hands of Zerubbabel have laid the foundations of this Temple. Then you will know that the LORD of hosts has sent Me"* – the Messiah – *"to you".* So the ministry of the "two anointed ones who stand before the Lord of the whole earth", in the Temple, is going to recover Israel spiritually.

Now, what does the New Testament have to say about this? Let us turn to Revelation chapter 11. This is why we can demonstrate that Zechariah 4 can be applied to the third Temple. When the Apostle John penned the Book of Revelation, it was well after the destruction of the Temple in AD 70, and there was no Temple standing on Mount Moriah at the time. And yet he is saying that the Temple will come back to Mount Moriah in which "the two anointed ones" or "two witnesses" will minister (Revelation 11:3 and 4) and they will concentrate on their ministry to Israel. Who are these two witnesses? Verse 4 reads: *"These are the two olive trees and the two lampstands standing before the God of the earth."* In other words, John is calling upon the reader to go back to Zechariah 4, and look at the whole chapter to see what they do, because these "two witnesses" are the "two anointed ones" of Zechariah *"who stand before the Lord of the whole earth."*

To prophesy, according to the Bible, is to preach. Their ministry will concentrate on the Altar and those who worship there (Revelation 11:2). They will preach under the power of the Holy Spirit at the Altar, because the Altar is a symbol of the cross. It brings Israel back to vicarious or substitutionary suffering. And the two witnesses will preach about the sacrificial death of the Messiah, once for all.

The Bible, therefore, teaches that the Temple Mount and the third Temple will be one of the major media by which God recovers Israel spiritually. The Bible also says that "His eyes and His name is upon the Temple Mount forever." If the Temple is the mechanism that God uses to bring Israel back to the Messiah, then surely every single one of us should be praying for its rebuilding. **Praying.**' [154]

If what Malcolm Hedding says comes to pass – that the third Temple will be one of the major factors in the spiritual rebirth of Israel – then the rebuilding of the Temple will also herald the coming of the Messiah. And the coming of the Messiah, as we shall see in the next chapter, will bring an end to Satan's time on earth. This is why the Temple Mount is the most coveted piece of real estate on the face of the earth. It is also the reason why Satan and the demonic principality behind Islam have a stranglehold on it. However, the day will come when the Almighty, the Lord God of Israel, will take it away from them.

In view of the significance of the third Temple for the nation of Israel, Malcolm Hedding has challenged Christians to *pray* for its rebuilding. However, it needs to be said, that is *all* he is suggesting that we do. In his address at the Feast of Tabernacles, Malcolm Hedding emphatically warned against Christians becoming engaged in activities on the Temple Mount itself – in any way whatsoever. It is too dangerous and could cause unnecessary risk physically or spiritually.

Having considered the probable consequences of the rebuilding of the physical Temple in Jerusalem, let us now consider another area: the rebuilding of the spiritual Temple in Israel.

The Rebuilding of the Spiritual Temple

Since the Six-Day War of 1967, the Lord has been performing another significant miracle in the Land of Israel. This miracle has gone virtually unnoticed in the Church around the world. In a spiritual sense the Lord has been 'rebuilding the tabernacle of David' which had all but disappeared from the Lord's land. Even though it has had small beginnings, this rebuilding of the 'spiritual tabernacle' is also a vital part of the spiritual rebirth of the nation, and the return of the nation to the God of Abraham, Isaac and Jacob, and His Messiah.

For the first time since the first century CE – the heyday of the Jewish Body of Messiah in Israel – there is an indigenous Church in the land. This Church is not an extension or an offshoot of what has become the Gentile church establishment, rather it is a growing movement – a living organism – which the Lord Himself is planting among His ancient covenant people Israel, as they discover that Yeshua is their living Messiah. To use the Apostle Paul's image of 'the olive tree' found in the Letter to the Romans, chapter 11 (to be discussed further in Chapter 10), the *natural branches* are being grafted back into the tree – as he predicted they would be. Ofer Amitai, who is pastor of one of the Hebrew Messianic congregations in Jerusalem, gives a brief history of this spiritual rebirth:

> 'Since the late sixties there was an outpouring of the Holy Spirit on the workers – the expatriate workers here – but also some local believers. It seems like that was the time more people came to the Lord and you could say probably that the modern Messianic movement got its "push" at that time. Since then we have grown from a handful of people and congregations. Some now estimate the Body at about 5,000 people, some at an even higher number. Of course, this does not include the secret believers at all. There are between eighty and a hundred or so congregations, home groups, independent home groups, depending on how you count them. In world terms that is not a very large growth. But for Israel it is phenomenal, since it comes after two thousand years of history of almost nothing.' [155]

There are two significant characteristics of the Messianic movement which bear the fruit of the Holy Spirit.

Firstly, in this indigenous Body of Messiah there are few of the pagan influences which came about as the result of the Gentile church establishment deliberately severing the Hebrew roots of its faith. For the most part, the Messianic Jewish Congregations in Israel have grown from the roots of the same Hebrew Scriptures as the New Testament Church described in the Book of Acts (which was completely Jewish in its earliest days). Consequently, they are much closer to the practices and theology of the Early Church than has been witnessed in Christendom for many centuries. Amitai continues:

'Our identity as both Jews, and even Israeli Jews – in the sense that we're back in our land – is very significant, because the Church has always seen itself as a spiritual body. Here we are also in a physical entity called Israel. The spiritual may be even more interesting to some because we have come back to our biblical source. To us the Bible is one book, it is not a separate thing. Most congregations – if not all – celebrate the Feasts, for instance. We are still groping with things like "Christmas or not" – what is the significance of it? This may sound strange to someone who so identifies Christmas with Christianity. For us it's not an emotional issue so much. We are examining it.' [156]

Secondly, a true spirit of reconciliation and brotherhood between Jewish and Arab followers of Yeshua has a chance to grow. Although most on both sides would admit it is not easy, where there was mistrust, hatred and unforgiveness, bonds of trust, love and forgiveness are now beginning to be established – and Arabs and Jewish believers in Messiah are meeting and fellowshipping together. This is the real miracle of the gospel of Yeshua HaMashiach in action – *'so as to create in Himself one new man from the two ... making peace ... that He might reconcile them both to God in one body through the cross, thereby putting to death the enmity ...'* (Ephesians 2:15b–16).

Ultimately it is this sort of peace – built on truth, generosity and love, not deception, greed and hatred, and truly found only in Yeshua – which will bring about a real and lasting reconciliation between Jew and Arab. This is the 'peace process' that the Christian Church should be recognising and supporting by prayer and fasting.

It is also this 'temple' – the spiritual temple of the living God in *Eretz Yisrael* – that the Gentile Church should be supporting, both spiritually and financially. The Apostle Paul gave the following encouragement to the Gentile Church:

'Now I am going to Jerusalem to minister to the saints. For it pleased those from Macedonia and Achaia to make a certain contribution for the poor among the saints who are in Jerusalem. It pleased them indeed, and they are their debtors.

> For if the Gentiles have been partakers of their spiritual
> things, their duty is also to minister to them in material
> things.'   (Romans 15:25–27)

Actually, this is more than an encouragement to assist the
'saints in Jerusalem'. It is a biblical mandate. It is a fact that
many of the believers in Yeshua in Jerusalem, and other parts
of Israel, suffer hardship. Sadly, because of their faith in
Yeshua as the Messiah, they are regarded by some as
'traitors', and no longer Jews. As a result they are often
discriminated against, especially in the area of employment.
Many have been refused residency or citizenship when they
make *aliyah*. Some have even been refused entry into Israel.

However, they still belong to the 'natural seed' of Abraham, Isaac and Jacob. And they belong to the 'spiritual seed'
as well.[157] They are the true 'remnant of Israel' at this present
time (Romans 11:5).

The Messianic Jews, as nearly all other Israelis who are
eligible, serve in the Defence Forces. Like other Israelis in the
IDF they will make the ultimate sacrifice for their country if it
is required of them. In every sense of the word, they are truly
Israel.

They are the first fruits of the regathered 'house of Israel
and house of Judah' – who now have the freedom to live in
the reunified Covenant City – to enter into the New Covenant (Jeremiah 31:31–34). 'We ourselves consider ourselves
as "first fruits",' says Ofer Amitai.

> 'We consider ourselves as an earnest of something. We
> are seen as a minority, and perhaps even "out of the
> stream" kind of Israelis. And yet those of us who read
> the Bible are convinced in our hearts that [these first
> fruits] are just the beginning of what we believe, hope,
> pray and wait for – to turn into a massive tidal wave of
> our people coming back to God.'

Indeed, as the spiritual temple of the Lord in Israel, the
Messianic Body sees its main role to be like the 'two
witnesses', and to share their faith in Yeshua with their
brethren who are also the 'seed of Abraham'.

The 'Messianics', like many ultra-Orthodox, Orthodox, Conservative and Reform Jews, long for – and pray for – the coming of the Messiah.

The main difference is that the Messianic Jews have found eternal life and peace through their Messiah, and in the final words of *HaB'rit Chadashah* (the New Testament), they pray: *'Amen! Come, Lord Yeshua!'* (Revelation 22:20, Jewish New Testament)

Chapter 9

Jerusalem and the Coming of the Messiah

Jewish Expectancy of the Coming Messiah

Across the Land of Israel there has been a growing anticipation of the approaching Messianic Age. This expectation is shared by nearly all branches of Judaism from Liberal to ultra-Orthodox. However, there is a considerable difference of opinion among Jews as to exactly what the Messianic Age might constitute and, in particular, who or what the Messiah might be.

There is universal agreement, though, that the Messianic Age will be an unprecedented time of peace and prosperity for the nation of Israel, which will be reflected throughout the world. In this sense, the Jerusalem Covenant is a Messianic document.

Some branches of Judaism are more specific about the identity of the Messiah than others. For instance, in the view of the ultra-Orthodox Lubavitcher sect, the Messiah will be a great sage and a descendant of King David. He will, they believe, be largely responsible for an unprecedented *aliyah* to *Eretz Yisrael* from all over the world, and will accomplish the rebuilding of the Temple and the reintroduction of offerings and sacrifices. These achievements will establish the Messiah's credentials.

It was the Lubavitchers who placed banners stating 'The Messiah Is Coming!' all over Jerusalem and other parts of Israel in the early 1990s. The man they were proclaiming to

be the Messiah was their leader, Lubavitcher Rebbe Menahem Mendel Schneerson, a resident of Brooklyn who never
actually set foot in Israel.[158] He died in 1994 at the age of
ninety-two.

Two events have encouraged belief among religious Jews
that the Messiah's advent is near: one is the rebirth of the
nation in *Eretz Yisrael*, and the other is the reunification of
Jerusalem under Jewish sovereignty.[159]

Gentile Aspirations of a Messianic Era

Aspirations of a 'Messianic Era' – or 'New Age' as some would
prefer to call it – are not confined to the Jewish people, or even
Christians, for that matter. Nearly all the religions of the
world have an expectation of an imminent 'Golden Era' in
which there would be worldwide peace and harmony. Indeed,
this expectation reflects the deep-seated desire of most human
beings on the face of the planet. The New Age Movement
would call this 'the Age of Aquarius'. It is important to note,
however, that the concept of 'the Age of Aquarius' is very
different from the Messianic Age which the Bible predicts. The
philosophy of the former is rooted in humanism and eastern
religion, the ultimate goal of which is self-realisation for the
individual, as well as the human race. The Bible, on the other
hand, tells us that the hallmark of the Messianic Age will be
the presence and absolute rule of the Kingdom of God on
earth. Its main characteristics will be righteousness and
justice, from which peace and prosperity will flow.

Moreover, it is worth noting that these two divergent
aspirations for a 'New Age' have their origins in different
and opposing spiritual kingdoms. It is the conflict between
these spiritual kingdoms – the kingdom of *Light*[160] versus the
kingdom of darkness (Satan and his minions, which include
the demonic principalities we have already considered) – that
will cause the greatest holocaust the world has ever seen,
prior to the Kingdom of the God of Israel and His Anointed
One, Yeshua, being victoriously established on earth.

The geographic centre of this conflict on earth will be the
place that the God of Israel has declared to be His dwelling
place and the throne of His Anointed One – Jerusalem.

The Last Days

There are numerous prophecies in the Old and New Testaments which the Bible specifically says will be fulfilled in 'the last days'. Many centre around Jerusalem and the Land of Israel, and most will have ramifications for the entire world. The majority of the prophecies dealing with the period before Messiah's return paint a picture of unprecedented horror and tribulation. They tell of the impending judgement of God on an unbelieving, loveless and lawless generation.

The Apostle Peter painted a vivid prophetic picture about attitudes that would characterise the last days:

> *'First, I want to remind you that in the last days there will come scoffers who will do every wrong they can think of, and laugh at the truth. This will be their line of argument: "So Jesus promised to come back, did He? Then where is He? He'll never come! Why, as far back as anyone can remember everything has remained exactly as it was since the first day of creation."*
>
> *They deliberately forget this fact: that God did destroy the world with a mighty flood, long after He had made the heavens by the word of His command, and had used the waters to form the earth and surround it. And God has commanded that the earth and the heavens be stored up for a great bonfire at the judgement day, when all ungodly men will perish.*
>
> *But don't forget this, dear friends, that a day or a thousand years from now is like tomorrow to the Lord. He isn't really being slow about His promised return, even though it sometimes seems that way. But He is waiting, for the good reason that He is not willing that any should perish, and He is giving more time for sinners to repent. The day of the Lord is surely coming, as unexpectedly as a thief ... and the earth and everything on it will be burned up.'*
>
> (2 Peter 3:3–10, Living Bible)

Since Peter's time, nineteen-and-a-half centuries ago, there has never been as much evidence of the truth of Scripture as there is in the present day: the fulfilment of biblical prophecy is unfolding before our eyes. The generation in which we live has witnessed one of the great events foretold by the ancient prophets of Israel – the regathering and rebirth of the nation of Israel in the land of their forefathers. Even with this evidence, people today scoff at the Word of God more than they have ever done before. In his introduction to the passage just quoted, Peter exhorts us to *'be mindful of the words which were spoken before by the holy prophets'* (v. 2). His endorsement of Old Testament prophecy, the only Scriptures available in his day, is plainly stated earlier in the letter:

> *'We also have the prophetic word made more sure, which you do well to heed as a light that shines in a dark place, until the day dawns and the morning star rises in your hearts; knowing this first, that no prophecy of Scripture is of any private interpretation, for prophecy never came by the will of man, but holy men of God spoke as they were moved by the Holy Spirit.'*   (2 Peter 1:19–21)

In this section of the book we will examine some of the prophecies of the Bible that relate to what the Old Testament often refers to as 'the latter days' or 'the time of the end'.

The Book of Daniel

The Book of Daniel is sometimes referred to as the 'Apocalypse of the Old Testament'. It gives us a detailed and comprehensive prophetic sweep of history, and includes a global prophetic plan for the Gentiles as well as a prophetic plan for the Jewish nation and their capital, Jerusalem. The time span of the realisation of the visions given to Daniel extends from his day to this current generation and beyond. It should be of great interest to those living in these present times, who have experienced an increase in mobility and knowledge unknown to any previous generation, to know that Daniel was told to *'shut up the words, and seal the book until the time of the end; many shall run to and fro, and knowledge shall increase'* (Daniel 12:4).

The Vision of the Great Image

Chapter 2 of the Book of Daniel records a dream given to King Nebuchadnezzar of Babylon, who had previously ransacked Jerusalem and taken its people captive. Nebuchadnezzar concealed the content of the dream from those who sought to interpret it, believing that the person with the correct interpretation would be able to tell him both the content of the dream and its true meaning from God. Indeed, the Spirit of the Lord revealed not only the content of the dream to Daniel, but also its message.

In his dream, the King was given a vision of a great image, or statue. Its head of gold represented Nebuchadnezzar's own kingdom, its chest and arms of silver represented the Medes and Persians who later defeated the Babylonians. They, in turn, were defeated by the next kingdom, Greece, pictured by the statue's belly of bronze. The image had legs of iron, and its feet and toes were made partly of iron and partly of clay. They represented a kingdom that would be *'as strong as iron, inasmuch as iron breaks in pieces and shatters all things; and like iron that crushes, that kingdom will break in pieces and crush all the others'* (Daniel 2:40). This kingdom has been widely recognised as the imperial empire of Rome.

Daniel then went on to prophesy that the feet and toes of iron and clay would *'mingle with the seed of men; but they will not adhere to one another, just as iron does not mix with clay'* (Daniel 2:43).

The climax of the vision came when *'a stone [that] was cut out without hands ... struck the image on its feet of iron and clay, and broke them in pieces'* (Daniel 2:34).

There are differing theories among teachers of eschatology regarding which kingdoms are represented by the feet and toes of the image. The most popular theory is that they represent the modern European Union, which at the time of writing, has a membership of fifteen nations with others proposing to enter. Another theory is that they could represent the Club of Rome world order which divides the entire world into ten regions or 'kingdoms', of which the European Union is one. Yet another theory is that they represent an Islamic or Arab confederacy which surrounds Jerusalem as previous empires have done. It remains to be seen which, if any, of these theories is correct. But it can be said with reasonable certainty that the feet and toes in the vision represent the dominant world order at the time of the Lord's return. The *'stone cut without hands'* represents the judgement of God upon that world system in the form of the coming Jewish Messiah. Daniel goes on to tell us:

> ' "In the days of these kings the God of heaven will set up a kingdom which shall never be destroyed ... it shall stand for ever." '   (Daniel 2:44)

And so here we have a glimpse of the Messianic Era to come – the Kingdom of God on earth.

The Visions of the Four Beasts and the Ram and the Male Goat

The fulfilment of the prophecies contained in chapters 7, 8 and 11 of the Book of Daniel spans from Daniel's epoch to some time in the future, seen from our standpoint in history. The prophecies predict the rise of the Medes and Persians, their subsequent overthrow by the kingdom of Greece and the ensuing upheaval as that kingdom was split. As discussed earlier, they were graphically fulfilled in the few hundred years after Daniel's lifetime. During this period, Jerusalem was controlled by the Greeks under Alexander the Great (Daniel 8:21 and 11:3), the Ptolemites, who were Egyptian Greeks (Daniel 11:5), and the Seleucids, who were Syrian Greeks (Daniel 11:7). Bible commentators tell us that over one hundred specific prophecies of historical events contained in the Book of Daniel literally came to pass in that era. It appears, then, that both the visions of the Four Beasts (Daniel 7) and the vision of the Ram and the Male Goat (Daniel 8) have been at least partially fulfilled in history.

It also appears that both visions have a common element to be fulfilled in the future – the rise of 'the Little Horn' (Daniel 7 and 8) or 'Wilful King' (Daniel 11). In the second century BCE these characters were typified by the Seleucid ruler Antiochus Epiphanes, mentioned in Chapter 7. Author

Bruce Reekie gives the following account of Antiochus' horrific desecration of the Covenant City and the Covenant People:

'[Antiochus] sent his chief collector of tribute, Apollinius, with a detachment of 22,000 men to destroy Jerusalem. Addressing the people with what appeared to be peaceful words, Apollinius gained their confidence, and then suddenly fell on the city, dealing it a terrible blow. He pillaged the city and set it on fire, tore down its houses and encircling wall, took the women and children captive and put thousands of people to the sword. Using the stones of the wall, Apollinius built a citadel commanding the Temple Mount, from whence his soldiers fell on and slew the worshippers, so that the Temple service was discontinued.

On December 8th, 167 BC, Antiochus erected the abomination of desolation in the Temple – a statue of Olympian Zeus – and at its dedication, sprinkled the blood of a pig in the Holy of Holies. During the next three years (167 to 164 BC), it was almost impossible to stay alive and remain uncompromised. Jerusalem was deserted by priests and people, and the daily sacrifice at the altar was entirely discontinued, being replaced by the daily sacrifice of a pig.

The enemies of the Covenant People took advantage of the Sabbath to slay them on the day when they would not fight. Some were roasted alive in caves where they retired to keep the Sabbath; women were put to death for having their children circumcised, and their infants were hanged about their necks; and the land fairly ran with the blood of the faithful. Antiochus went near to extirpating the worship of Yahweh.' [161]

In the year 164 BCE the Temple was cleansed and rededicated by Judas Maccabee after a successful revolt against the Seleucids. His victory is commemorated at the Jewish Feast of *Chanukkah*. This eight-day festival is referred to as the Feast of Dedication in the New Testament. Many teachers of eschatology believe that Antiochus was possibly the closest type of the one to come in the latter days – the Antichrist [162] – who, as we shall see, will defile the Temple and attempt to exalt himself against the Messiah (Daniel 8:25), but who will be crushed *'without human hand'* by the Kingdom of God.

The visions in the Book of Daniel show both diversity and unity. Although they differ, there are common threads running through them, especially concerning the end-times. Indeed, Daniel was specifically told that these prophecies would be sealed up for the end-times (Daniel 8:26, 10:14, 12:4 and 12:9). We will shortly consider these more closely.

Let us first look at a key prophetic passage contained in the New Testament referring to 'the last days'.

The Olivet Discourse

The scene is set two hundred years after Antiochus Epiphanes had desecrated Jerusalem and the House of the Lord. Herod's Temple, which was one of the wonders of the world at that time, dominates the Jerusalem skyline. Yeshua was having a private moment with His disciples on the Mount of Olives, overlooking the magnificent Temple, just a few days before He was crucified. Although the disciples seemed to be ignorant of what was about to happen to Yeshua (even though He had told them), they believed He was the Son of God, and they were questioning Him about the future – and particularly about His return to earth at the end of the age. The Gospel of Matthew devotes two whole chapters (24 and 25) to this meeting in which Yeshua gave His followers the clearest picture of the last days found in the New Testament. Parallel passages are found in the Gospel of Mark, chapter 13, and the Gospel of Luke, chapter 21. Included in the answers to the disciples' questions, particularly in Luke's account, is Yeshua's prophecy of the destruction of Jerusalem and the Temple by the Romans, which, as we have already seen, was fulfilled in the finest detail about forty years later. Most of what the Messiah had to say in these passages – often referred to as the Olivet Discourse – was in relation to His own promised return, and the period leading up to it.

My intention is not to make a detailed study of this prophetic passage but simply to highlight some aspects of it. Rather, I will concentrate on specific parallel prophecies in other parts of the Bible, particularly those which affect the destiny of Jerusalem. However, the Olivet Discourse is essential reading if what follows is going to be understood, and for the benefit of those who do not have easy access to a copy of the New Testament, most of Matthew chapter 24 and part of chapter 25 is reproduced in Appendix C.

The reader of the Olivet Discourse will be amazed at the number of global disasters that Yeshua talked about two thousand years ago, which are now daily headlines in our newspapers and television news bulletins. Famines, earthquakes and wars are at an unprecedented level in the history of humankind. Yeshua said:

> *'All these* [things] *are the beginning of sorrows.'*
> (Matthew 24:8, Mark 13:8)

One of Yeshua's most emphatic warnings was concerning false messiahs. As discussed earlier, false messiahs have been evident in every era, but none more so than the last century. One common characteristic, especially of the political messiahs, has been tyranny. Of the names that come to mind, the most obvious is Adolf Hitler, who in the early days of his dictatorship was regarded as the saviour of the German nation. One characteristic of every false messiah, whether political or religious, has been deception.

Yeshua's warning to His followers was emphatic:

> *'For false messiahs and false prophets will arise and show great signs and wonders, so as to deceive, if possible, even the elect. See, I have told you beforehand.'*
> (Matthew 24:24–25, also Mark 13:22–23)

There is one particular false messiah about whom the Scriptures have much to say. Yeshua and the apostles warned us about him, as did the ancient prophets of Israel, including Daniel.

This false messiah will rise to dominate and desecrate the world. Like Hitler, to begin with he will be seen as a saviour. But again, in marked similarity to Hitler, his most deadly assignment will be against the Jewish people – to deceive them and, if he were able, to destroy them. He is often referred to as 'the Antichrist'.

The Antichrist

The Bible indicates that the Antichrist will be a man possessed and empowered by Satan like no other individual in history. The Apostle Paul refers to him as 'the man of sin' or 'the son of perdition'.[163] Other designations include: 'the lawless one', 'the beast' and 'the little horn'.

His spiritual heritage is fairly easy to trace. The prophet Isaiah predicts a time when Satan, the arch-enemy of the God of Israel, will exalt himself as God.

> ' "How you are fallen from heaven,
> O Lucifer, son of the morning!
> How you are cut down to the ground,
> You who weakened the nations!
> For you have said in your heart:
> 'I will ascend into heaven,
> I will exalt my throne above the stars of God;
> I will also sit on the mount of the congregation
> On the farthest sides of the north;
> I will ascend above the heights of the clouds,
> I will be like the Most High.' " '   (Isaiah 14:12–14)

It is believed that Lucifer was once the most glorious of all the angels in heaven but he led a rebellion against the Lord and, after being defeated, was cast down to the earth with his cohorts. The reference to the *'mount of the congregation'* given here in Isaiah 14:13, together with the description of Mount Zion given in Psalm 48:2 as being on *'the sides of the north'*, indicates this to mean the Temple Mount. This is the very place the Lord has declared to be **His** dwelling place forever.

Isaiah goes on to tell of Satan's ultimate fate:

> ' "Yet you shall be brought down to Sheol,
> To the lowest depths of the Pit." '   (Isaiah 14:15)

The Antichrist's ultimate fate is endorsed by other Scriptures, which we shall shortly consider.

The human origin of the Antichrist has been a subject of much debate among Bible scholars. The most popular view is that he will be a descendant of the Roman Empire. The basis for this belief is found in Daniel 9:26–27, where the person or 'prince' who many believe will make and break a covenant with Israel is from the same 'people' who destroyed Jerusalem and the Temple in 70 CE. (This belief assumes that the 'Seventieth Week of Daniel' has yet to be fulfilled – see later in the chapter.) Some believe the Antichrist to be 'the Assyrian' (Isaiah 14:25). Others think he could be a descendant of the Greek Empire (Daniel 8:21–23) which seems to have shared its spiritual heritage with the Roman Empire. Yet another view is that he will be either a Jew (Daniel 11:37 and John 5:43) or a pseudo-Jew (i.e. an impostor). Only time will reveal which of these theories is correct.

The Revelation of the Antichrist

There have been many persons throughout the centuries whom Christians, in their time, have believed to be the Antichrist – and with some justification. The Apostle John believed the end was near nineteen hundred years ago when he wrote in his first letter:

> *'It is the last hour; and as you have heard that the Antichrist is coming, even now many antichrists have come, by which we know that it is the last hour.'* (1 John 2:18)

It is interesting that it was revealed to the Apostle John that he was living in the *'last hour'*. By comparison, then, we must surely now be in the last minutes, even seconds! While reading John's statement, however, we need to keep Peter's words in mind:

> *'But don't forget this, dear friends, that a day or a thousand years from now is like tomorrow to the Lord. He isn't really being slow about His promised return, even though it sometimes seems that way.'* (2 Peter 3:8, The Living Bible)

The point John is making is that the spirit of Antichrist has been in the world for a long time, and there have been many who have had this evil spirit in them.[164]

One of the characteristics of these Antichrist types, e.g. Antiochus Epiphanes, Adolf Hitler and Josef Stalin, was rampant anti-Semitism. They all engaged themselves in persecution of both the Jews and the true Church. And so will the Antichrist yet to be revealed. The Apostle Paul tells us:

> *'And now you know what is holding* [the man of lawlessness] *back, so that he may be revealed at the proper time. For the secret power of lawlessness is already at work; but the one who holds it back will continue to do so till he is taken out of the way. And then the lawless one will be revealed, whom the Lord Jesus will overthrow with the breath of his mouth and destroy by the splendour of his coming. The coming of the lawless one will be in accordance with the work of Satan displayed in all kinds of counterfeit miracles, signs and wonders, and in every sort of evil that deceives those who are perishing. They perish because they refused to love the truth and so be saved.'*
>
> (2 Thessalonians 2:6–10, NIV)

This is one of the more difficult passages in the New Testament to understand fully, because there is an apparent ambiguity in verse 7. It is not certain what or who is doing the restraining that will be taken out of the way, thus allowing the Antichrist to be revealed. Paul had probably given the congregation in Thessalonica his interpretation of the restraining power while he was with them, but, unfortunately for us, he did not repeat the explanation in this letter.[165]

In recent times, the identity of the Antichrist has been the subject of much speculation among some Christians, and names of various world political leaders and power-brokers have been mentioned, sometimes publicly. The main point to be made here is that there is an appointed time in God's timetable for the Antichrist to be revealed. Deuteronomy 29:29 tells us:

' "The secret things belong to the LORD our God, but those things which are revealed belong to us..." '

The Scriptures give certain revelations about the Antichrist so that we will recognise him at the appointed time, and not be deceived by him. However, as his personal identity has not been revealed yet, we will not speculate as to who he might be, or if indeed he is alive today.

We might now consider the questions: how and when will the Antichrist be revealed? The Book of Daniel and the Book of Revelation both contain prophetic visions of his rise to supremacy in the affairs of the world. The visions of the Four Beasts and the Ram, the Male Goat and the Little Horn in Daniel 7 and 8 have already been noted. In chapter 13 the Book of Revelation describes the vision of the Beast from the Sea (which may tie in with the Little Horn in Daniel) and the False Prophet.[166]

The Antichrist's sphere of influence and destruction will be worldwide during the final few years before the return of Yeshua. However, since the purpose of this book is to explore the destiny of Jerusalem, the study of the Antichrist and his activities will be confined to their impact upon the Holy City and the Jewish people.

Speaking to the disciples, Yeshua was very clear about the identity of the Antichrist, pointing out that, like a number of his preceding 'types', he too will defile the Temple.

'Therefore when you see the "abomination of desolation", spoken of by Daniel the prophet, standing in the holy place, then let those who are in Judea flee to the mountains.'
(Matthew 24:15–16)

It is important to understand the context of this verse. Yeshua is specifically talking about the end-times (see Matthew 24:14) and the future fulfilment of a prophecy by Daniel concerning the defiling of the 'holy place' which is in the Temple:

'[The little horn] *even exalted himself as high as the Prince of the host* [the Messiah]; *and by him the daily sacrifices were taken away, and the place of His sanctuary* [the Temple of the Lord] *was cast down. Because of transgression, an army was given over to the horn to oppose the daily sacrifices; and he cast truth down to the ground. He did all this and prospered.'* (Daniel 8:11–12)

To ensure there is no doubt as to when this prophecy will be fulfilled, Daniel was then told by the angel Gabriel:

'Understand, son of man, that the vision refers to the time of the end.' (Daniel 8:17)

The Apostle Paul also understood its fulfilment would be in the period immediately prior to the Lord's return. He refers to this event in his second letter to the church at Thessalonica, written almost twenty years before the destruction of the Temple in 70 CE. He was writing to the believers in the Church, telling them of the events which will precede 'the Day of the Lord'. He says:

'Now, brethren, concerning the coming of our Lord Jesus Christ and our gathering together to Him ... Let no one deceive you by any means; for that Day will not come unless the falling away comes first, and the man of sin is revealed, the son of perdition, who opposes and exalts himself above all that is called God or that is worshiped, so that he sits as God in the temple of God, showing himself that he is God.' (2 Thessalonians 2:1, 3–4)

As discussed in the previous chapter, if these prophecies are to be fulfilled literally, it is a crucial observation that some time between now and then the Temple will be rebuilt in one form or another, and *Torah* (the Law of Moses, which includes the sacrificial system) will be re-instituted.[167]

The 'Seventieth Week' of Daniel

For most Evangelical Christians of a 'pre-millennial' persuasion – as I am – the prophecy of the 'Seventy Weeks of Daniel' is one of the most interesting prophetic passages of the Old

Testament. It would not be an exaggeration to say that, among those interested in Bible prophecy concerning the 'Last Days', it is one of the pillars of eschatology. However, in consideration of prophecies to be fulfilled in the lead-up to the Lord's return, I have refrained so far from referring to the 'Seventieth Week' mentioned in Daniel 9:27 for a very good reason. As I explained towards the end of Chapter 2, there are a number of Hebrew-speaking Messianic Jews, and also some Gentile Christians, of a 'pre-millennial' Evangelical persuasion who seriously question whether the fulfilment of the 'Seventieth Week' lies in the future.

As I have already noted, their belief that the 'Seventieth Week of Daniel' was fulfilled by the death of the Messiah and the ratification of the New Covenant is based purely on what the original Hebrew text actually says. I am not conversant with the Hebrew language myself, and therefore I am reliant on those who are. However, I am told two things about this prophecy, and particularly in relation to verse 27. Firstly, the Hebrew text itself is somewhat ambiguous, which makes it difficult to translate and make clear sense out of it. Secondly, the translation in all the English versions of the Bible does not truly reflect what the Hebrew text says.

If our Hebrew-speaking friends are correct in what they say – and I truly do not know whether or not they are – then there is a need to re-examine some of the predictions made concerning the future fulfilment of the 'Seventieth Week of Daniel'. Appendix A contains an explanation of this alternative position, and Appendix D provides notes on some of the eschatological implications of a past fulfilment of the 'Seventieth Week of Daniel'.

I have an open mind on whether the fulfilment of Daniel 9:27 has already taken place, or whether it lies in the future. However, I think it is unwise, given the uncertainty of the meaning of the text, to make dogmatic predictions as to how this particular prophecy may be fulfilled in the future. If, however, the fulfilment of the 'Seventieth Week of Daniel' does lie in the future, then it will only serve to endorse these other prophecies we are considering.

'The Time of Jacob's Trouble'

I find the subject of suffering particularly hard to write about,
especially in view of what the Jewish people in Europe went
through at the hands of Adolf Hitler during World War II. The
thought of further suffering for the Jewish people is appalling
to any decent human being. What is to come is not confined
to the Jews, but will be endured by all true followers of the God
of Israel and His Anointed One. I feel, though, I would be
blameworthy if I did not warn my readers of what lies ahead,
according to my understanding of the prophetic Scriptures.[168]

It is absolutely true that beyond the holocaust that is to
come upon the earth – and particularly the Middle East –
there is a glorious future for the nation of Israel. This will be
when the Messiah is reigning on David's throne and the
covenants of promise, which the Almighty God made with
the descendants of Abraham, Isaac and Jacob, have been
finally consummated. We will consider the Messianic Age
more fully in Chapters 10 and 11, but first we need to
continue to examine some of the prophetic Scriptures which
I believe must be fulfilled before then.

For those Jewish people who do not recognise that Yeshua
is the Messiah, I would implore you to heed the warning He
gives regarding the time when the Antichrist will stop the
offering and sacrifices in the Temple. This will offer a way of
escape for you. Yeshua warned:

> *'Therefore when you see the "abomination of desolation"
> spoken of by Daniel the prophet, standing in the holy place
> (whoever reads, let him understand), then let those who are
> in Judea flee to the mountains. Let him who is on the
> housetop not come down to take anything out of his house.
> And let him who is in the field not go back to get his clothes.'*
>
> (Matthew 24:15–18)

Yeshua gave a similar warning to His contemporaries,
urging them, when they saw the Roman armies surrounding
Jerusalem, to flee into the mountains (Luke 21:20). A
substantial number heeded the warning in 67 CE and
escaped the siege, its ensuing slaughter and enslavement.

Of the time ahead, the prophet Jeremiah records:

> ' "*For behold, the days are coming,*" *says the* LORD, "*that I will bring back from captivity My people Israel and Judah,*" *says the* LORD. "*And I will cause them to return to the land that I gave to their fathers, and they shall possess it.*"
>
> *Now these are the words that the* LORD *spoke concerning Israel and Judah.*
>
> "*For thus says the* LORD:
> '*We have heard a voice of trembling*
> *Of fear, and not of peace.*
> *Ask now, and see,*
> *Whether a man is ever in labour with child?*
> *So why do I see every man with his hands on his loins*
> *Like a woman in labour,*
> *And all faces turned pale?*
> *Alas! For that day is great,*
> *So that none is like it;*
> *And it is the time of Jacob's trouble,*
> *But he shall be saved out of it.*' " '   (Jeremiah 30:3–7)

This picture is reminiscent of the horror in the death camps of Europe during World War II. It is difficult to imagine that the Holocaust could ever be repeated, but the prophets suggest that it will. In his vision of the Ram, the Male Goat and the Little Horn, the prophet Daniel tells us that in the latter times:

> ' "*When the transgressors have reached their fullness,*
> *A king shall arise* [the Antichrist],
> *Having fierce features,*
> *Who understands sinister schemes.*
> *His power shall be mighty, but not by his own power,*
> *He shall destroy fearfully,*
> *And shall prosper and thrive;*
> *He shall destroy the mighty, and also the holy people.*
> *Through his cunning*
> *He shall cause deceit to prosper under his hand;*
> *And he shall magnify himself in his heart.*
> *He shall destroy many in their prosperity.*

> *He shall even rise against the Prince of princes* [the
> Messiah]*;*
> *But he shall be broken without human hand."'*
>
> (Daniel 8:23–25)

The king in this passage is the same as 'the Little Horn'
referred to earlier. The 'holy people' and 'the saints' almost
certainly refer to the Jewish people. A further picture of the
devastation is given in Daniel's interpretation of the Fourth
Beast:

> '"The fourth beast ... shall devour the whole earth,
> Trample it and break it in pieces...
> He shall speak pompous words against the Most High,
> Shall persecute the saints of the Most High,
> And shall intend to change times and law.
> Then the saints shall be given into his hand
> For a time and times and half a time* [three-and-a-half
> years]*."'* (Daniel 7:23, 25)

The Lord went on to tell Daniel:

> *'And there shall be a time of trouble,
> Such as never was since there was a nation,
> Even to that time.
> And at that time your people shall be delivered,
> Everyone who is found written in the book.'* (Daniel 12:1)

In Daniel 7:25 the time span for this period, often called
the Great Tribulation, is given as three-and-a-half years. The
same time frame is also mentioned in 12:11:

> '"And from the time that the daily sacrifice is taken away,
> and the abomination of desolation is set up, there shall be
> one thousand two hundred and ninety days."'*

This final three-and-a-half-year period before the return of
Yeshua to Jerusalem, also mentioned in the Book of Revelation, will be a time of unprecedented tribulation in the
world's history. All life on earth will be threatened. Yeshua
confirmed this to His disciples in the Olivet Discourse:

> *'Therefore when you see the "abomination of desolation"*
> *spoken of by Daniel the prophet, standing in the holy place*
> *... then there will be great tribulation, such as has not been*
> *since the beginning of the world until this time, no, nor ever*
> *shall be. And unless those days were shortened, no flesh*
> *would be saved; but for the elect's sake those days will be*
> *shortened.'*   (Matthew 24:15, 21–22)

Who, we might ask, could have known, two thousand years ago, that one day humankind would be capable of such destruction that everyone on the planet could be wiped out? It is common knowledge that the nuclear arsenals that still exist could destroy every living thing in the world several times over. Yeshua foresaw that one day the world would be faced with a catastrophe of this magnitude.

Many of the prophecies found in Revelation 6–19 confirm the end-time prophecies in the *Tanakh*, and the imagery, symbolism and language are similar. The Apostle John was given a vision of a place of escape in the wilderness in the midst of the holocaust:

> *'Then the woman* [the remnant of Israel] *fled into the*
> *wilderness, where she has a place prepared by God, that they*
> *should feed her there one thousand two hundred and sixty*
> *days ... she is nourished for a time and times and half a*
> *time* [three and a half years], *from the presence of the*
> *serpent* [Satan].'   (Revelation 12:6, 14b)

Presumably this is the place of escape for those who have fled Jerusalem and Judea. The prophecy goes on:

> *'The dragon* [Satan] *was enraged with the woman, and he*
> *went to make war with the rest of her offspring, who keep the*
> *commandments of God and have the testimony of* Yeshua
> HaMashiach.'   (Revelation 12:17)

The last phrase of this prophecy identifies the object of Satan's fury as the nation of Israel, and the rest of her offspring who are followers of the Messiah.

However, the Lord is not going to leave those that are His to the merciless onslaught of the powers of darkness.

> *'For He himself has said, "I will never leave you nor forsake you." So we may boldly say:*
> *"The LORD is my helper;*
> *I will not fear.*
> *What can man do to me?"'*   (Hebrews 13:5b–6,
>   quoting Joshua 1:5 and Psalm 118:6)

Yeshua has promised His disciples throughout all generations:

> *'Lo, I am with you always, even to the end of the age.'*
>   (Matthew 28:20)

He also gives a promise to those who lay down their lives:

> *'For whoever desires to save his life will lose it, and whoever loses his life for My sake will find it.'*   (Matthew 16:25)

The ultimate victory belongs to the saints, whether in life or in death. In his vision, the Apostle John heard a prophetic voice in heaven saying:

> *'Now salvation, and strength, and the kingdom of our God, and the power of His Messiah have come, for the accuser [Satan] of our brethren, who accused them before our God day and night, has been cast down. And they overcame him by the blood of the Lamb and by the word of their testimony, and they did not love their lives to the death.'*
>   (Revelation 12:10–11)

Revelation 12 also gives a picture of the nature of the Middle East conflict. It tells of the fury of Satan against Israel and all true believers in Yeshua. For if Satan were able to annihilate either or both of these groups from the face of the earth, then not only would the earth be completely his, but he would have destroyed God's covenant promises. This will not happen.

> *'Thus says the* LORD,
> *Who gives the sun for a light by day,*
> *And the ordinances of the moon and*
> *   the stars for a light by night . . .*
> *"If those ordinances depart*
> *From before Me, says the* LORD,
> *Then the seed of Israel shall also cease*
> *From being a nation before Me forever." '*
>
> (Jeremiah 31:35, 36)

Therein lies the ultimate security for the descendants of Abraham, Isaac and Jacob.

The Two Witnesses

> *'Then I was given a reed like a measuring rod. And the angel stood, saying, "Rise and measure the Temple of God, the altar and those who worship there. But leave out the court which is outside the Temple, and do not measure it, for it has been given to the Gentiles. And they will tread the holy city underfoot for forty-two months. And I will give power to my two witnesses, and they will prophesy one thousand two hundred and sixty days, clothed in sackcloth." These are the two olive trees and the two lampstands standing before the God of the earth.'* (Revelation 11:1–4)

We looked at the probable ministry of these two witnesses in the previous chapter. Apart from their ministry to the nation of Israel, they will stand and bear witness to the God of Israel and His mighty power and, it would appear, prepare the world for the imminent Day of the Lord and the coming of His Anointed One.[169] In subsequent verses we see that they have been given extraordinary power by God, including power over the elements. In the *Tanakh*, the only other person anointed with the power to prevent rain was Elijah, whom Jews universally believe will return to earth to prepare the way for the coming of the Messiah. Every year, when they celebrate Passover, they leave an empty place at the head of the table for Elijah in case he should suddenly appear.

Apart from connecting them with 'the two olive trees' of

Zechariah 4, the Book of Revelation does not directly identify who the two witnesses are or where they came from, but teachers of eschatology are almost universally agreed that one of them will be Elijah. This would certainly tie in with a prophecy in Malachi:

> ' "Behold, I will send you Elijah the prophet before the coming of the great and dreadful day of the LORD." '   (Malachi 4:5)

As for the other of the two witnesses, some believe he could be Moses, who appeared with Yeshua on the Mount of Transfiguration (Matthew 17:1–13), while others believe he will be the only person in the *Tanakh*, apart from Elijah, who never tasted death – Enoch (see 2 Kings 2:11 and Genesis 5:24).[170]

It appears that after three-and-a-half years of prophesying, the two witnesses will be killed by the Antichrist in Jerusalem, much to the glee of most of the world's population. Their bodies will lie in the streets of Jerusalem for all to see, but after three-and-a-half days they will rise from the dead and be taken up to heaven, causing great fear among those loyal to the Antichrist. It would seem this sign, and the earthquake that follows, will be the last warning before the great and terrible day of the Lord finally dawns upon the earth.

Armageddon – The Final Siege of Jerusalem

> 'And I saw three unclean spirits like frogs coming out of the mouth of the dragon [Satan], out of the mouth of the beast [the Antichrist], and out of the mouth of the false prophet [the world religious leader]. For they are spirits of demons, performing signs, which go out to the kings of the earth and of the whole world, to gather them to the battle of that great day of God Almighty. And they gathered them together to the place called in Hebrew, Armageddon.'
>
> (Revelation 16:13–14, 16)

> 'Behold, the day of the LORD is coming,
> And your spoil will be divided in your midst.
> For I will gather all the nations to battle against Jerusalem.'
>
> (Zechariah 14:1, 2a)

> ' "Behold, I will make Jerusalem a cup of drunkenness to all the surrounding peoples, when they lay siege against Judah and Jerusalem. And it shall happen in that day I will make Jerusalem a very heavy stone for all peoples; all who would heave it away will surely be cut in pieces, though all nations of the earth are gathered against it." '
>
> (Zechariah 12:2–3)

> 'Multitudes, multitudes in the valley of decision!
> For the day of the LORD is near in the valley of decision.
> The sun and moon will grow dark,
> And the stars will diminish in their brightness.'
>
> (Joel 3:14–15)

The Scriptures indicate that the situation for Jerusalem will appear to be hopeless at that time. Only one thing will stand between the Jewish nation and total annihilation: the covenants of the Lord and His promise to keep Israel. At that point in history, the whole Jewish nation will cry out to their God, in repentance, as they have never cried out to Him before. And the prophet Zechariah tells us He will respond thus:

> 'Then the LORD will go forth
> And fight those nations,
> As He fights in the day of battle.'   (Zechariah 14:3)

> ' "It shall be in that day that I will seek to destroy all the nations that come against Jerusalem." '   (Zechariah 12:9)

> 'And this shall be the plague with which the LORD will strike all the people who fought against Jerusalem:
> "Their flesh shall dissolve while they stand on their feet,
> Their eyes shall dissolve in their sockets,
> And their tongues shall dissolve in their mouths." '
>
> (Zechariah 14:12)

The Repentance of Israel

> ' "And I will pour on the house of David and on the inhabitants of Jerusalem the Spirit of grace and supplication; then they will look on Me whom they have pierced; they will

mourn for Him as one mourns for his only son, and grieve for Him as one grieves for a firstborn. In that day there shall be great mourning in Jerusalem, like the mourning at Hadad Rimmon in the plain of Megiddo." ' (Zechariah 12:10–11)

' "They will call on My name,
And I will answer them.
I will say, 'This is My people';
And each one will say, 'The LORD is my God.' " '
(Zechariah 13:9b)

This mourning for 'the pierced One' will mark the most significant turning-point in the long and turbulent history of the Jewish people, for they will be finally reconciled to their Messiah – who has so longed to be united with His own kith and kin. Their union with Yeshua will complete their reconciliation with the Lord their God. It is this act of repentance as a nation that will enable God to pour out the blessings He has covenanted to the descendants of Abraham, Isaac and Jacob for the last four thousand years.

The desolation of the House of Israel will at last be ended, as Yeshua promised when He lamented over Jerusalem nearly two thousand years ago:

'I say to you, you shall see Me no more till you say:
"Baruch ha ba b'hashem adonai" –
"Blessed is He who comes in the name of the LORD!" '
(Matthew 23:39)

The Coming of the Messiah

' "I was watching in the night visions,
And behold, One like the Son of Man,
Coming with the clouds of heaven!" '　　(Daniel 7:13a)

'And in that day His feet will stand on the Mount of
　　Olives,
Which faces Jerusalem on the east.
And the Mount of Olives shall be split in two,
From east to west,
Making a very large valley;

> *Half of the mountain shall move towards the north*
> *And half of it towards the south. . . .*
> *Thus the LORD my God shall come,*
> *And all the saints with You.'*   (Zechariah 14:4, 5b)

> *'The LORD also will roar from Zion,*
> *And utter His voice from Jerusalem;*
> *The heavens and earth will shake;*
> *But the LORD will be a shelter for His people,*
> *And the strength of the children of Israel.'*   (Joel 3:16)

> *'Then the sky receded as a scroll when it is rolled up, and*
> *every mountain and island was moved out of its place. And*
> *the kings of the earth, the great men, the rich men, the*
> *commanders, the mighty men, every slave and every free*
> *man, hid themselves in the caves and in the rocks of the*
> *mountains, and said to the mountains and rocks, "Fall on us*
> *and hide us from Him who sits on the throne and from the*
> *wrath of the Lamb! For the great day of His wrath has come,*
> *and who is able to stand?"'*   (Revelation 6:14–17)

What did Yeshua Himself have to say about His own return
to earth? What He described endorses the words given to the
ancient prophets of Israel and the apocalyptic vision given to
the Apostle John.

> *'As the lightning comes from the east and flashes to the west,*
> *so will the coming of the Son of Man be. . . . Immediately*
> *after the tribulation of those days the sun will be darkened,*
> *and the moon will not give its light; the stars will fall from*
> *heaven, and the powers of the heavens shall be shaken. Then*
> *the sign of the Son of Man will appear in heaven, and then*
> *all the tribes of the earth will mourn, and they will see the*
> *Son of Man coming on the clouds of heaven with power and*
> *great glory.'*   (Matthew 24:27, 29–30)

The Demise of the Antichrist

The prophetic visions of Daniel all finish on a common
theme: the overthrow of the Antichrist followed by the
establishment of the Lord's everlasting heavenly Kingdom

of righteousness on earth. The demise of Lucifer (Satan) and the one he empowers (the Antichrist) is prophesied by Isaiah:

> ' "*You shall be brought down to Sheol,*
> *To the lowest depths of the Pit.*
> *Those who see you will gaze at you*
> *And consider you saying:*
> '*Is this the man who made the earth tremble,*
> *Who shook the kingdoms,*
> *Who made the world as a wilderness*
> *And destroyed its cities?*' " '   (Isaiah 14:15–17)

The Apostle Paul confirms the fate of the Antichrist: '*whom the Lord will consume with the breath of His mouth and destroy with the brightness of His coming*' (2 Thessalonians 2:8).

Perhaps the most explicit account of what will happen is found in the prophetic vision of the Apostle John in the Book of Revelation:

> '*The beast was captured, and with him the false prophet who worked signs in his presence, by which he deceived those who received the mark of the beast and those who worshipped his image. These two were cast alive into the lake of fire burning with brimstone.*
>
> *Then I saw an angel coming down from heaven, having the key to the bottomless pit and a great chain in his hand. He laid hold of the dragon, that serpent of old, who is the Devil and Satan, and bound him for a thousand years; and he cast him into the bottomless pit, and shut him up, and set a seal on him, so that he should deceive the nations no more till the thousand years were finished. . . .*
>
> *And I saw the souls of those who had been beheaded for their witness to Yeshua and for the word of God, who had not worshipped the beast or his image, and had not received his mark on their foreheads or on their hands. And they lived and reigned with Messiah for a thousand years.*'
>
> (Revelation 19:20; 20:1–3a, 4b)

The prophet Daniel also graphically foretells the setting up of the Messianic Kingdom:

' *"Then to Him was given dominion and glory and a*
   kingdom,
That all peoples, nations, and languages should serve Him.
His dominion is an everlasting dominion,
Which shall not pass away,
And His kingdom the one
Which shall not be destroyed." '   (Daniel 7:14)

The days that the Jewish nation and their spiritual offspring have longed for – ever since the time when Jerusalem was established as Israel's capital just over three thousand years ago – will be ushered in by the One who is the Son of David.

> 'The LORD *will be king over the whole earth. On that day there will be one* LORD, *And His name the only name.'*
>   (Zechariah 14:9, NIV)

Chapter 10

Jerusalem and the Consummation of the Covenants and Promises

The New Covenant

> ' "Thus says the Lord GOD to Jerusalem...
> 'I will remember My covenant with you in the days of your youth, and I will establish an everlasting covenant with you.' " '
> (Ezekiel 16:3, 60)

At the beginning of this book we considered the earthly Zion as a divinely ordained unity – the city, the land and the people. In this context, we also looked at a prophecy which occupies the whole of Ezekiel 16 in which the Lord enters into a covenant with Jerusalem. We came to the conclusion that it was made with the people to whom the city of Jerusalem has been covenanted – the Jewish people. Ezekiel finishes the chapter with the promise that God would establish an everlasting covenant with Israel.

What is this everlasting covenant? It is referred to in a number of places in the *Tanakh*, but principally in Jeremiah 31:31–34.

> ' "Behold, the days are coming, says the LORD, when I will make a new covenant with the house of Israel and with the house of Judah – not according to the covenant that I made with their fathers in the day that I took them by the hand to bring them out of the land of Egypt, My covenant which they broke, though I was a husband to them, says the LORD. But

> *this is the covenant that I will make with the house of Israel*
> *after those days, says the LORD: I will put My law in their*
> *minds, and write it on their hearts; and I will be their God,*
> *and they shall be My people. No more shall every man teach*
> *his neighbour, and every man his brother, saying, 'Know the*
> *LORD,' for they shall all know Me, from the least of them to*
> *the greatest of them, says the LORD. For I will forgive their*
> *iniquity, and their sin I will remember no more.'' '*

It is no coincidence that this covenant, which could be described as the foundation stone of the New Testament, immediately precedes the Lord's declaration that He would never cast off the nation of Israel, quoted on page 213.

Let us examine, briefly, what the New Covenant says.

Firstly, the Lord specifically identifies those with whom He is making the covenant – the house of Israel and the house of Judah. Bearing in mind that the former kingdom of Israel had split into two at the time of Jeremiah, then it is addressed to all the citizens of the nation of Israel, whether they are descended from the ten northern tribes or the two southern tribes.

Secondly, the covenant would be made and fulfilled at some time in the future (from Jeremiah's time). We will shortly examine how and when.

Thirdly, *Torah*, or the Lord's Law or teaching, will be written in their minds and on their hearts. There will be no need for the ways of the Lord to be taught by one person to the next. Just as a migrating bird knows where to go by instinct, so will the people know His ways instinctively. The covenant goes on to say that all the people will know the Lord, from the least of them to the greatest of them. The implication here is that every single Jewish person could one day have an intimate knowledge of the Lord and His ways.

Fourthly, the Lord says He will forgive and forget all their sins. *Torah* specifically says that in order for there to be atonement for sin, then there has to be the shedding of blood (Leviticus 17:11). The sacrificial system, by which the sins of Israel were seen to be forgiven, ended with the destruction of the Temple in 70 CE. So how could this New Covenant possibly come into effect?

The Ratification of the New Covenant

The answer is in *HaB'rit Chadashah* – the New Testament, or as it is sometimes, and more accurately, called – the New Covenant.

The night before His death, Yeshua celebrated Passover with His disciples. When it came to the third cup – the Cup of Redemption – He took it and gave it to His disciples and told them all to drink from it. Then He said something which they probably did not fully understand until later. He said:

> '*This is My blood of the new covenant, which is shed for many for the remission of sins.*'   (Matthew 26:28)

What the Lord *Yeshua HaMashiach* was saying here was that He was ratifying the New Covenant by His death on the cross. Just as the Abrahamic Covenant was ratified by the shed blood of the heifer, and the Mosaic Covenant by the shed blood in the offerings and sacrifices, so the New Covenant has been ratified by the shed blood of Israel's Messiah.

That is exactly what John the Baptist meant when he prophetically uttered:

> '*Behold, the Lamb of God who takes away the sin of the world!*'   (John 1:29) [171]

The Fulfilment of the New Covenant in the Church

Just seven weeks later, at the Jewish Feast of Shavu'ot, Jews from all over the Roman Empire were gathered in Jerusalem, in accordance with *Torah*. Something remarkable happened during this time which was the fulfilment of a prophecy by Joel, at least in part. The event is recorded in Acts 2. The Holy Spirit was poured out on the disciples with accompanying signs and wonders. The New Covenant was initiated and the Church was born.

The believers were 'baptised in the Holy Spirit'. From that time, belief and salvation were often accompanied by signs – particularly speaking in 'other tongues'. More importantly, those who were filled with the Holy Spirit in this way found that they had God's Law written on their minds and in their hearts as the Spirit of the Lord revealed the truth to them. They knew God in a special way. What they experienced was what Yeshua referred to as 'being born of the Spirit' (John 3). And this gift of salvation and of the Holy Spirit was given to all who repented and believed in Yeshua. What happened to them totally and radically transformed their lives.

At the outset the Church was totally Jewish. Because of this it could be said that, in its truest form, Christianity was a development of biblical Judaism. Christianity is not a new religion as such, but an outworking of the New Covenant which the Lord made with the Jewish people. Furthermore, the New Testament Church was a living organism (the New Testament calls it 'the Body of Christ') – not an institution or establishment.

However, the Lord never intended that the blessings of the New Covenant would be exclusively for the physical seed of Abraham, Isaac and Jacob: indeed they would be universal. This is reflected in the Abrahamic Covenant in which the Lord told the great patriarch that through him *'all the families of the earth shall be blessed'* (Genesis 12:3).

In two of the great Messianic prophecies of Isaiah, the Lord spoke prophetically to the One who would be the Messiah, saying:

> *'I will keep You* [Yeshua] *and give You as a covenant to*
> *the people,*
> *As a light to the Gentiles.'*   (Isaiah 42:6)

> *'It is too small a thing that You* [Yeshua] *should be My*
> *Servant,*
> *To raise up the tribes of Jacob,*
> *And to restore the preserved ones of Israel;*
> *I will also give You as a light to the Gentiles,*
> *That You should be My salvation to the ends of the earth.'*
>   (Isaiah 49:6)

Shortly after His birth, the baby Yeshua was taken to the Temple for dedication in accordance with *Torah*. There He was held in the arms of an elderly man who had been told by the Holy Spirit that he would see Israel's Messiah before his death.

The old man, Simeon, blessed the Lord saying:

> '... *my eyes have seen Your salvation,*
> *Which You have prepared before the face of all peoples,*
> *A light to bring revelation to the Gentiles,*
> *And the glory of Your people Israel.'*   (Luke 2:30–32)

Clearly then the Jewish Messiah, Yeshua, was to be the salvation of the Gentiles as well as of the nation of Israel. In his letter to the Gentile church in Ephesus, the Apostle Paul explained how the covenants, which the Lord made with the nation of Israel, can now be applied to the Gentiles as well. He said:

> '[Before] *you were without Christ, being aliens from the commonwealth of Israel and strangers from the covenants of promise, having no hope and without God in the world. But now in Christ Jesus you who once were far off have been made near by the blood of Christ. ... For through Him we both* [Jew and Gentile] *have access by one Spirit to the Father. Now, therefore, you are no longer strangers and foreigners, but fellow citizens with the saints and members of the household of God, having been built on the foundation of the apostles and prophets, Christ Jesus Himself being the chief cornerstone.'*   (Ephesians 2:12–13, 18–20)

The Apostle Paul himself was a Pharisee trained by the prominent Rabbi Gamaliel. Yet his calling from the Lord was to take the gospel to the Gentiles. What started in Jerusalem quickly spread throughout the then-known world. In the course of time, the Church, which had started as a vital 'living organism' in its first century, evolved into an established system with a powerful hierarchy. And with power came corruption.

The Misappropriation of the New Covenant – 'Replacement Theology'

Salvation, it was soon taught, was something that could only be obtained through the church establishment, and on its terms. The Jews, it was maintained, had murdered the Messiah, the Son of God, and were therefore beyond any hope of salvation. With the corruption of the gospel which the Apostles had taught came the erosion of the Jewish roots of the Christian faith. At the Council of Nicea in 325 CE a deliberate decision was made to sever the Church from its Jewish heritage – for instance Passover was replaced with the pagan festival of Easter, and the birth of Christ was celebrated at another pagan festival which became known as Christmas.

The New Covenant, it was held, belonged to the Church – and the Old Covenant, which was seen as having been abolished, belonged to Israel. The Church had effectively replaced the nation of Israel as far as God's promises were concerned. It was taught (and still is by some) that where the Old Testament speaks of the promises and blessings of God for Israel, 'Israel' should be taken to mean 'the Church'; and where it speaks of judgement and curses, then 'Israel' should be taken to mean 'Israel' – hardly a consistent method of scriptural exegesis! This is what we often hear referred to as 'Replacement Theology'.

Not only is this theological position contrary to the teaching of the *Tanakh*, but it is contrary to the teaching of the New Testament as well. In his letter to the Ephesians, the Apostle Paul says the Gentile followers of Yeshua have become 'fellow-citizens' with Israel as far as the covenants are concerned (Ephesians 3:6). Some translations use the word 'partakers'. In a letter to another Gentile church, this time to the one at Rome, he makes the relationship of the Gentile Church to Israel very plain. He gives an illustration in which he likens the Gentile believers to 'wild olive branches' and the nation of Israel to the 'natural olive branches'; he warns of the possibility of the Gentiles being 'cut off':

> *'If some of the* [natural] *branches were broken off, and you, being a wild olive tree, were grafted in among them, and with them became a partaker of the root and fatness of the olive tree, do not boast against the branches. But if you boast, remember that you do not support the root, but the root supports you. You will say then, "Branches were broken off that I might be grafted in." Well said. Because of unbelief*

they were broken off, and you stand by faith. Do not be haughty, but fear. For if God did not spare the natural branches, He may not spare you either. Therefore consider the goodness and severity of God: on those who fell, severity; but toward you, goodness, if you continue in His goodness. Otherwise you also will be cut off. And they also, if they do not continue in unbelief, will be grafted in, for God is able to graft them in again. For if you were cut out of the olive tree which is wild by nature, and were grafted contrary to nature into a good olive tree, how much more will these, who are the natural branches, be grafted into their own olive tree?

For I do not desire, brethren, that you should be ignorant of this mystery, lest you should be wise in your own opinion, that hardening in part has happened to Israel until the fullness of the Gentiles has come in. And so all Israel will be saved, as it is written:

"The Deliverer will come out of Zion
And He will turn away ungodliness from Jacob;
For this is My covenant with them
When I take away their sins." '   (Romans 11:17–27)

This is the substance of Paul's teaching on the future of the nation of Israel. At the end of this passage he is citing the conclusion of Isaiah 59, which is referring to the same New Covenant we looked at in Jeremiah 31.

The writer to the Hebrews in the New Testament gives an exposition of the New Covenant in chapters 8 and 9 of his letter. He quotes the 'Jeremiah covenant' exactly as it was originally written, reiterating that it is a covenant with *'the house of Israel and the house of Judah'*. Clearly the New Testament writer to the Hebrews understood who was to be the prime beneficiary of the New Covenant.

With its Replacement Theology, the church establishment over the centuries has misappropriated the New Covenant in that it has attempted to rob the nation of Israel of the covenant which has been unconditionally promised to her by God. This gross theological distortion is nothing short of anti-Semitism. It has been the excuse for much of the devastation the Jewish people have suffered at the hands of so-called Christians.

It is by the grace of God and by the freely shed blood of the Jewish Messiah, the Lord Jesus Christ, that we Gentile Christians have been grafted into 'the olive tree', which Paul speaks of, and become partakers of the New Covenant.

It is time for the church establishment to repent openly for the horrendous crimes it has committed against the Jewish people, in the name of the Jewish Messiah, over the centuries.[172]

It is time for the church establishment as a whole to recognise that God has a destiny for the nation of Israel – which is further demonstrated by their miraculous return to the land of their forefathers, in our generation, in fulfilment of the prophetic Scriptures.

There are many in the church establishment, with their warped theology on Israel, who are aiding and abetting the nations of the world in trying to disinherit the Jewish people from their ancient homeland and their capital city, Jerusalem. Their actions may be inadvertent, or they may not be. The fact is that the Holy Scriptures clearly teach that the Holy Land and the Holy City were promised by God to the descendants of Abraham, Isaac and Jacob as an everlasting possession. As we saw earlier, the prophet Joel predicts severe judgement on those who seek to partition the Lord's Land (Joel 3:2).

If the words of the Apostle Paul are anything to go by, unless large sections of the Christian Church repent of their attitude towards Israel, those who practise anti-Semitism, deliberately or not, may well find they have no part in the New Covenant they have wrongly claimed to be exclusively their own.

One day we will all have to give an account for what we have done here on earth. The Lord Jesus, in His Sermon on the Mount, had a stern warning for those who refuse to do His will:

> *'Not everyone who says to Me, "Lord, Lord," shall enter the kingdom of heaven, but he who does the will of My Father in heaven. Many will say to Me in that day, "Lord, Lord, have we not prophesied in Your name, cast out demons in Your name, and done many wonders in Your name?" And then I will declare to them, "I never knew you; depart from Me, you who practice lawlessness."'* (Matthew 7:21–23)

There is ample evidence, therefore, in Scripture to indicate that anyone who harbours anti-Semitism in any shape or form, or anyone who stands against God's purposes to restore Israel both physically to the land and spiritually to Himself, in fulfilment of the covenants and promises, is standing on a very slippery slope indeed.

The Reality of the New Covenant

The fulfilment of the New Covenant began at Pentecost in Jerusalem nearly two thousand years ago. Despite its mis-appropriation by large sections of Christendom, there are millions of Gentiles and Jews alike for whom the New Covenant has been a vital living experience. Throughout the centuries, just as the Lord has kept a remnant for Himself within the Jewish nation, so He has within the church establishment. The New Testament refers to this remnant both as 'the Body of Christ', of which He is the Head, and the 'Bride of Christ'.

These people have discovered that Christianity is not a religion, but a dynamic living and loving relationship with Israel's God and Messiah, and consequently with their fellow human beings as well. Because of the death of the Messiah on the cross they have discovered that the middle wall of division between Jew and Gentile – and indeed anyone of a different nationality or race – has been broken down and they have been reconciled one to another (Ephesians 2:14–16). The miracles that are happening rarely get reported in the media, but the Spirit of God is moving across the face of the earth in the lives of millions of people in fulfilment of the New Covenant.

The Final Consummation of the New Covenant

The major prophecies of the Old Testament which deal with the restoration of Israel, speak first of the physical return of the Jews to their ancient homeland and then the spiritual restoration of the nation.

One of the best-known passages concerning the restoration of Israel is found in Ezekiel 36 and 37.

' "For I will take you from among the nations, gather you out of all countries, and bring you into your own land. Then I will sprinkle clean water on you, and you shall be clean; I will cleanse you from all your filthiness and from all your idols. I will give you a new heart and put a new spirit within you; I will take the heart of stone out of your flesh and give you a heart of flesh. I will put My Spirit within you and cause you to walk in My statutes, and you will keep My judgements and do them. Then you shall dwell in the land that I gave to your fathers; you shall be My people and I will be your God." '
(Ezekiel 36:24–28)

The next chapter, which contains the vision of the Valley of Dry Bones, confirms this restoration:

' "Thus says the Lord GOD: 'Behold, O My people, I will open your graves [of exile] and cause you to come up from your graves, and bring you into the land of Israel. ... I will put My Spirit in you and you shall live.' " '
(Ezekiel 37:12 and 14a)

Here, firstly, we have a picture of the physical rebirth of the nation of Israel which actually happened in 1948 with the Declaration of Independence. But the 'conception' took place with Theodore Herzl fifty years earlier and the physical growth of the nation continues today. Secondly, we have a picture of the spiritual rebirth of the nation, which has already begun with the birth of the first indigenous Church in the land since the apostolic days. This spiritual rebirth will be fully realised at a future time appointed by the Lord. In fact, just as the actual physical rebirth of the nation took place in a day, it seems that this will be true too of its spiritual rebirth, in fulfilment of Isaiah's prophecy:

' "Who has ever heard of such a thing?
Who has ever seen such things?
Can a country be born in a day,
Or a nation be brought forth in a moment?
Yet no sooner is Zion in labour
Than she gives birth to her children." ' (Isaiah 66:8, NIV)

Towards the end of Chapter 9 we considered the prophecy in Zechariah which pinpoints the actual event which will trigger this national turning back to God:

> ' *"And I* [the LORD] *will pour out on the house of David and on the inhabitants of Jerusalem the Spirit of grace and supplication; then they will look on Me whom they have pierced; they will mourn for Him as one mourns for his only son, and grieve for Him as one grieves for a firstborn."* '   (Zechariah 12:10)

This prophecy speaks of the nation's total repentance as they recognise the One who was crucified – *Yeshua HaMashiach*. It will be then, at the invitation of the Jewish people, that He shall return to earth.

Isaiah takes up the story in the prophetic word which Paul quoted at the end of his discourse and which we considered earlier in the chapter:

> ' *"The Redeemer will come to Zion,*
> *And to those who turn from transgression in Jacob,"*
> *Says the* LORD.
> *"As for Me," says the* LORD, *"this is My covenant with them: My Spirit who is upon you, and My words which I have put in your mouth, shall not depart from your mouth, nor from the mouth of your descendants, nor from the mouth of your descendants' descendants," says the* LORD, *"from this time and forevermore."* '   (Isaiah 59:20–21)

It will be then that the New Covenant will be consummated in its entirety.

At that time *'the house of Israel'* and *'the house of Judah'* will be baptised in the Holy Spirit. The Jewish race will be totally and permanently transformed, *'from the least of them to the greatest of them'* as Jeremiah wrote, faithfully recording the heart and intention of God.

And the nation of Israel will know the blessings and prosperity that God has promised without reservation.

> ' *"Behold, the days are coming," says the* LORD, *"that I will perform that good thing which I have promised to the house of Israel and the house of Judah:*

> *In those days and at that time*
> *I will cause to grow up to David*
> *A Branch of righteousness;*
> *He shall execute judgement and righteousness in the*
>   *earth.*
> *In those days Judah will be saved,*
> *And Jerusalem will dwell safely.*
> *And this is the name by which she will be called:*
> *THE LORD OUR RIGHTEOUSNESS.''*
>
> (Jeremiah 33:14–16)

The establishment of the kingdom of the Messiah will bring about the consummation of all the covenants of promise which the Lord has made with the nation of Israel throughout the course of history.

The One through whom they will be fulfilled will be none other than the Messiah Himself.

The Final Consummation of the Abrahamic Covenant

In a spiritual sense, the Abrahamic Covenant has been fulfilled through the course of history. In a literal sense, too, it has had a substantial degree of fulfilment. Nevertheless, in order for the covenant to be fully fulfilled, every element has yet to be realised in a greater degree.

In this covenant the Lord promised Abraham that his offspring would become a great nation. There has never been a time when the Jewish nation was numerically great. At her historical zenith during the time of David and Solomon, Israel was an extremely wealthy and powerful nation and, for a while, she was certainly great in that sense. Today, the estimated number of Jews in the world ranges from twelve to more than thirty million, of which about five million currently live in the Land of Israel. This is but a tiny fraction of the estimated world population of just over 6,000 million (6 billion) people. It could be said that Abraham's spiritual seed through Yeshua is indeed an innumerable number and perhaps could be likened to *'the stars of heaven'* (cf. Revelation 7:9). But will there ever come a time when Abraham's physical seed could be likened to *'the sand on the seashore'* (Genesis 22:17)? Could it be that this element of the Abrahamic Covenant is yet to be completed?

Next, the Lord promised Abraham that through him all nations would be blessed. The world has enjoyed many blessings through the Jewish people, including the Bible. But the greatest blessing is the gift of salvation through God's Son, *Yeshua HaMashiach*. However, there are greater blessings yet to come, when Yeshua is King over all the earth and *'of the increase of His government and peace there will be no end'*. Without doubt, all the nations of the earth will be blessed under the reign of Israel's Messiah from Jerusalem.

Then there is the component of the covenant which relates to the Land of Israel. While it is true that Israel has received her inheritance in the land, and we have witnessed the dramatic return of many of her people in our generation, the Jewish people have never occupied the Promised Land to its full extent, as defined in Genesis 15. To the north and north-east this would include most of Lebanon, most of Syria and part of Iraq. To the east it would include nearly all of Jordan and perhaps a piece of Saudi Arabia. To the south it would include Gaza, the Sinai desert and the northern part of Egypt east of the River Nile.[173]

In the era of the Messianic Kingdom there will be no *Diaspora*. The prophet Ezekiel indicates that when the nation of Israel is fully restored every Jewish person will be living in the Land of Israel:

> ' " 'When I have brought them back from the peoples and gathered them out of their enemies' lands ... then they shall know that I am the LORD their God, who ... left none of them captive any longer. And I will not hide My face from them anymore; for I shall have poured out My Spirit on the house of Israel,' says the Lord GOD.' '
>
> (Ezekiel 39:27a, 28, 29)

With a dramatically increased population, arising from both the *aliyah* foretold by the prophets and from natural multiplication, could it be that Israel may need the full inheritance of land promised to her forefather Abraham?

The Consummation of the Land Covenant

With the consummation of the New Covenant, the Land Covenant will have run its course. The direction of Israel's history has been charted by their lining up with the conditions of either the blessings or the curses which are found in this covenant (Leviticus 26 and Deuteronomy 28–30). Reconciled to her God and Messiah, she will have arrived at her destination – at last.

The Consummation of the Davidic Covenant

As mentioned in Chapter 2, the Lord made a covenant with King David promising him that his dynasty would be everlasting (2 Samuel 7:4–17 and 1 Chronicles 17:3–15).

The Lord, speaking through the prophet Jeremiah, endorses the Davidic Covenant in the strongest possible terms.

> ' "For thus says the LORD: 'David shall never lack a man to sit on the throne of the house of Israel; nor shall the priests, the Levites, lack a man to offer burnt offerings before Me, to kindle grain offerings, and to sacrifice continually.' " And the word of the LORD came to Jeremiah, saying, "Thus says the LORD: 'If you can break My covenant with the day and My covenant with the night, so that there will not be day and night in their season, then My covenant may also be broken with David My servant, so that he shall not have a son to reign on his throne, and with the Levites, the priests, My ministers.' " '* (Jeremiah 33:17–21)

Because day and night have followed one another consistently to this day, we must assume that this covenant is still in force.

Yet, some apparent difficulties seem to challenge the validity of this covenant for two reasons. Firstly, there are no visible descendants alive today who can prove their lineage back to King David; this is because all ancestral records were destroyed with the Temple in 70 CE. Secondly, there appear to be contradictions within the prophetic

Scriptures. Let us examine the latter difficulty by turning initially to an apparently contradictory prophecy found in the Book of Hosea:

> 'For the children of Israel shall abide many days without king or prince, without sacrifice or sacred pillar, without ephod or teraphim.'   (Hosea 3:4)

This prophecy has undoubtedly been fulfilled, because the Jewish nation has been without a reigning monarch since the destruction of the first Temple in 586 BCE and without offerings and officiating priests since the destruction of the second Temple in 70 CE.

Furthermore, Jeremiah himself was given a prophecy which seems to contradict the Davidic Covenant. The prophecy concerns King Jeconiah (also known as Coniah and Jehoiachin), the penultimate king to reign over Judah. Speaking through the prophet Jeremiah, the Lord said of Jeconiah: *'none of your descendants shall prosper, sitting on the throne of David, and ruling in Judah'* (Jeremiah 22:30).

This prophecy, too, was graphically fulfilled when, after only three months on the throne, Jeconiah was taken captive to Babylon and his uncle Zedekiah was installed as king in his place, by King Nebuchadnezzar of Babylon. Eleven years later Zedekiah suffered a similar fate, signalling the end of the Judean monarchy.

However, Jeremiah's confirmation of the Davidic Covenant did not actually state that there would always be a reigning monarch as such. What the Lord said was: *'David shall never **lack a man** to sit on the throne of the house of Israel'* (Jeremiah 33:17, author's emphasis). In other words there would always be a legitimate heir to the throne of David.

But if there was never to be a descendant of Jeconiah on the throne of David, then how could the Davidic dynasty continue?

The answer is found in the genealogies of Yeshua in the New Testament. In the genealogy in Matthew's Gospel, which goes back through his earthly father, we find Jeconiah in the family tree. But Joseph was not His biological father – God is – so Yeshua is not a descendant of Jeconiah. The genealogy found in Luke's Gospel goes back through Yeshua's earthly mother, who was also His biological mother (and a virgin at the time of His conception – Isaiah 7:14). Her lineage goes back to King David through his son Nathan. Thus Yeshua's bloodline goes back to King David avoiding the curse put upon Jeconiah. Due to the destruction of the records of the ancient Jewish families with the Temple in 70 CE, as already mentioned, it is improbable that there is a Jewish person alive on earth today who can prove their lineage goes directly back to King David. But there is one Jewish person alive in heaven. As we considered in Chapter 2, Yeshua rose from the dead and, in fulfilment of the Davidic prophecy in Psalm 110, is seated at the right hand of His heavenly Father:

> *'The LORD said to my Lord,*
> *"Sit at My right hand,*
> *Till I make Your enemies Your footstool."*
> *The LORD shall send the rod of*
> *Your strength out of Zion.*
> *Rule in the midst of your enemies!'* (Psalm 110:1–2)

The Psalmist goes on to say:

> *'The LORD has sworn*
> *And will not relent,*
> *"You are a priest forever*
> *According to the order of Melchizedek."'* (Psalm 110:4)

Thus Yeshua's priestly role satisfies the Lord's undertaking that there would always be a qualified priest (Jeremiah 33:18) to serve Him.

The prophecy of Hosea we looked at a little earlier continues in the next verse with:

> *'Afterward the children of Israel shall return, seek the LORD their God and David their king, and fear the LORD and His goodness in the latter days.'* (Hosea 3:5)

The prophet Hosea clearly understood that Israel would one day be restored to the land and to the Lord, and that

'David their king' would rule over them.[174] And thus, the apparent inconsistencies in these prophecies which are concerned with the Davidic dynasty can be elucidated. Indeed, they all point to the One who existed before Abraham and who today is alive at the right hand of God the Father.

Yeshua is the fulfilment of the Davidic Covenant.

As yet Yeshua has never ruled as King in Israel, and so the covenant has still to be completed. When He returns to Jerusalem as the King of Kings, then the prophecies of Isaiah will be fulfilled:

> *'Of the increase of His government and peace*
> *There will be no end,*
> *Upon the throne of David and over His kingdom,*
> *To order it and establish it with judgment and justice*
> *From that time forward, even forever.'*   (Isaiah 9:7)

> *'"And in that day there shall be a Root of Jesse,*
> *Who shall stand as a banner to the people;*
> *For the Gentiles shall seek Him,*
> *And His resting place shall be glorious."'*   (Isaiah 11:10)

In that day the Davidic Covenant will have its final consummation with Yeshua HaMashiach reigning upon the throne of David. And His resting-place, Jerusalem, will indeed be glorious.

Chapter 11

Jerusalem, the City of
the Great King

The Establishment of Messiah's Kingdom on Earth

' "Thus says the Lord G*OD* to Jerusalem:
'I will remember My covenant with you in the days of your
    youth, and I will establish an everlasting covenant with
    you.' " '   (Ezekiel 16:3, 60)

' "Comfort, yes, comfort My people,"
Says your God.
"Speak comfort to Jerusalem, and cry out to her,
That her warfare is ended,
That her iniquity is pardoned;
For she has received from the L*ORD*'s hand
Double for all her sins....
And the glory of the L*ORD* shall be revealed,
And all flesh shall see it together,
For the mouth of the L*ORD* has spoken." '

          (Isaiah 40:1, 2, 5)

'Sing, O daughter of Zion!
Shout, O Israel!
Be glad and rejoice with all your heart,
O daughter of Jerusalem!
The L*ORD* has taken away your judgments,
He has cast out your enemy.
The King of Israel, the L*ORD*, is in your midst;
You shall see disaster no more.'   (Zephaniah 3:14–15)

'There shall come forth a Rod from the stem of Jesse,
And a Branch shall grow out of His roots.
The Spirit of the LORD shall rest upon Him,
The Spirit of wisdom and understanding,
The Spirit of counsel and might,
The Spirit of knowledge and the fear of the LORD.
His delight is in the fear of the LORD,
And He shall not judge by the sight of His eyes,
Nor decide by the hearing of His ears;
But with righteousness He shall judge the poor,
And decide with equity for the meek of the earth;
He shall strike the earth with the rod of His mouth,
And with the breath of His lips He shall slay the wicked.
Righteousness shall be the belt of His loins,
And faithfulness the belt of His waist.'   (Isaiah 11:1–5)

' "Yet have I set My King
On My holy hill of Zion.
I will declare the decree:
The LORD has said to Me,
'You are My Son,
Today I have begotten You.
Ask of Me and I will give You the nations for Your
    inheritance,
And the ends of the earth for Your possession.
You shall break them with a rod of iron;
You shall dash them in pieces like a potter's vessel.' . . .
Kiss the Son, lest He be angry,
And you perish in the way,
When His wrath is kindled but a little.
Blessed are all those who put their trust in Him." '
                                          (Psalm 2:6–9, 12)

The Judgement of the Nations

It appears that the first event in the Messianic Kingdom will be the judgement of the nations and the restoration of the earth. Anyone who has studied end-time prophecy and read the Book of Revelation will realise that the planet will have been all but destroyed by the time Yeshua returns.

The most vital aspect of the cleansing of the earth will be dealing with the evil and wickedness that has influenced the state of the world since the fall of Adam and Eve. As we considered at the end of Chapter 9, the spiritual forces of darkness will have been removed from the face of the earth at the time of the Messiah's return. The Lord Yeshua will judge those who are still alive. Speaking through the prophet Joel, the Lord says:

> '"For behold, in those days and at that time,
> When I bring back the captives of Judah and Jerusalem,
> I will also gather all nations,
> And bring them down to the Valley of Jehoshaphat;
> And I will enter into judgement with them there
> On account of My people, My heritage Israel,
> Whom they have scattered among the nations;
> They have also divided up My land."'   (Joel 3:1–2)

There are a number of prophecies in the Old Testament, including this one, which speak of the judgement of the nations. This particular prophecy tells us that one of the major transgressions for which the nations will be held accountable is their treatment both of the Jewish people, to whom the Lord refers as 'My people', and of *Eretz Yisrael*, to which the Lord refers as 'My land'. In the New Testament Yeshua described this judgement [175] in the Olivet Discourse (see Appendix C).

> *'When the Son of Man comes in His glory, and all the holy angels with Him, then He will sit on the throne of His glory. All the nations will be gathered before Him, and He will separate them one from another, as a shepherd divides his sheep from the goats. And He will set the sheep on His right hand, but the goats on the left.'*   (Matthew 25:31–33)

Again, the dividing line in judgement will be according to how a person has treated those to whom the Lord Yeshua refers as *'the least of these My brethren'*[176] (Matthew 25:40 and 45).

The 'sheep' inherit the Kingdom, while the 'goats' go to everlasting damnation. Thus the earth shall be cleansed from those who have spilled innocent blood.

The Establishment of Righteous Government

The coming of the Messiah will see the end of corrupt government in the world. The prophet Isaiah predicted:

> *'For unto us a Child is born,*
> *Unto us a Son is given;*
> *And the government will be upon His shoulder.*
> *And His name will be called*
> *Wonderful, Counsellor, Mighty God,*
> *Everlasting Father, Prince of Peace.*
> *Of the increase of His government and peace*
> *There will be no end,*
> *Upon the throne of David and over His kingdom,*
> *To order and establish it with judgment and justice*
> *From that time forward, even forever.'*   (Isaiah 9:6–7)

This is one of the key prophecies of the Messianic Kingdom found in the Book of Isaiah. The Messiah's divine nature is established here in the names He is given which include *'Mighty God'* and *'Everlasting Father'*. His humanity is identified in the words *'Child'* and *'Son'*, and, of course, the Christian Church believes that the child referred to is the One who was born in a stable in Bethlehem two thousand years ago, in fulfilment of Micah's prophecy:

> *' "But you, Bethlehem Ephrathah,*
> *Though you are little among the thousands of Judah,*
> *Yet out of you shall come forth to Me*
> *The One to be ruler in Israel,*
> *Whose goings forth have been from of old,*
> *From everlasting." '*   (Micah 5:2)

The prophet Micah not only predicts the location where the Messiah would be born about 700 years later, but also speaks of His Eternal and Divine nature.

Both Micah's prophecy and Isaiah's prophecy speak about the One who is to govern or rule. This aspect of both these prophecies has yet to be fulfilled since Yeshua has never yet actually *governed* from David's throne in Jerusalem.

Isaiah's prophecy speaks of the very thing that Christians and Jews alike have longed for, for so long: **universal and everlasting peace**. For true and permanent peace can only come to the earth when righteousness, judgement and justice are established – and that will be when the Prince of Peace, Yeshua, returns.

Despite the removal of the spiritual powers of darkness, including Satan, from the face of the earth, it does appear that there will still be people on the earth who have the propensity to rebel against righteous government, even as they do today. The Scriptures say in a number of places that Messiah the King will rule the nations with a 'rod of iron' or an 'iron sceptre'.[177]

Both the Books of Isaiah and Micah carry almost identical prophecies which confirm that there will be universal peace in the world under the reign of the Lord Yeshua:

> *'He shall judge between many peoples,*
> *And rebuke strong nations afar off;*
> *They shall beat their swords into plowshares,*
> *And their spears into pruning hooks;*
> *Nation shall not lift up sword against nation,*
> *Neither shall they learn war any more.'*
>
> (Micah 4:3 and Isaiah 2:4)

The Restoration of the Earth

One can hardly imagine the extent of the physical chaos that will exist when Yeshua returns to the earth. The environment will be suffering from a combination of thousands of years of humankind's abuse of the earth – especially in the last hundred years, the aftermath of the Great Tribulation (which could include nuclear fall-out). On top of that there will have been the judgement of the Lord in the form of massive cosmic disasters and geological catastrophes (e.g. earthquakes that cause mountains to be tossed into the sea). The prophet Isaiah paints a vivid picture of those final days before Yeshua's return to earth:

> *'The earth is violently broken,*
> *The earth is split open,*

> *The earth is shaken exceedingly.*
> *The earth shall reel to and fro like a drunkard...*
> *Its transgression shall be heavy upon it...'*

Then a couple of verses later he says:

> *'For the* Lord *of hosts will reign*
> *On Mount Zion and in Jerusalem*
> *And before His elders, gloriously.'*   (Isaiah 24:19, 20, 23)

The prophetic Scriptures suggest that the restoration of the earth will not simply be a physical one, but a spiritual one too.

Isaiah 11 – another key Messianic prophecy – gives us a picture which would be quite impossible to imagine in today's world:

> *' "The wolf also shall dwell with the lamb,*
> *The leopard shall lie down with the young goat,*
> *The calf and the young lion and the fatling together;*
> *And a little child shall lead them.*
> *The cow and the bear shall graze;*
> *Their young ones shall lie down together;*
> *And the lion shall eat straw like the ox.*
> *The nursing child shall play by the cobra's hole,*
> *And the weaned child shall put his hand in the viper's den.*
> *They shall not hurt nor destroy in all My holy mountain,*
> *For the earth shall be full of the knowledge of the* Lord
> *As the waters cover the sea." '*   (Isaiah 11:6–9)

This is one of the most explicit prophecies describing the restoration of creation to its state before the Fall.[178] Before Adam and Eve sinned there would have been no death on the earth and therefore, it would seem, that both humankind and the animal kingdom were all created vegetarian.[179] It was not until after the Great Flood that human beings were permitted to eat meat (Genesis 9:3) and it is interesting to note that when gathering animals for the ark, Noah was told to gather one male and one female of each kind so that they would be preserved. There is no record of him gathering animals as food for other animals or for his own family, suggesting that creation was still vegetarian up until that point in time. The restoration of the earth will possibly mean that the animal kingdom will be restored to its original state, and animals will not kill each other for food. A similar passage in Isaiah tells us that *'dust shall be the serpent's food'* (Isaiah 65:25).

These passages in Isaiah imply that there will be no fear in the creatures of the earth – both in humankind and the animal world – because the threat of harm and death will no longer exist. So the restoration of the earth will mean not simply a cleansing from destruction and pollution, but also from sin, decay and death.

In the New Testament, the Apostle Paul takes up this theme in his letter to the church in Rome:

> *'What we suffer now is nothing compared to the glory* [God] *will give us later. For all creation is waiting patiently and hopefully for that future day when God will resurrect His children. For on that day thorns and thistles, sin, death and decay – the things that overcame the world against its will at God's command* (as a result of sin) – *will all disappear, and the world around us will share in the glorious freedom from sin which God's children enjoy.*
>
> *For we know that even the things of nature, like animals and plants, suffer in sickness and death as they await this great event. And even we as Christians, although we have the Holy Spirit within us as a foretaste of future glory, also groan to be released from pain and suffering. We, too, wait anxiously for that day when God will give us our full rights as His children, including the new bodies He has promised us – bodies that will never be sick again and will never die.'*
>
> (Romans 8:18–23, Living Bible) [180]

The Restoration of Jerusalem's Glory

> *'You who call on the* LORD,
>   *give yourselves no rest,*
> *and give him no rest till he establishes Jerusalem*
>   *and makes her the praise of the earth.'*
>
> (Isaiah 62:6b-7, NIV)

This plea, coming from the Holy Spirit through the heart of the prophet Isaiah, urges intercessors to implore the God of Israel to fulfil His promise to restore the glory of Jerusalem to what it was in the days of King Solomon.

The Scriptures tell us that when Messiah establishes His Kingdom, the glory of Jerusalem will be far greater than it was in its heyday three thousand years ago.

The Psalmist describes the Lord's holy mountain – Mount Zion – in Jerusalem as being:

> *'Beautiful in elevation,*
> *The joy of the whole earth.'*　　　　　　　(Psalm 48:2)

If the comments made by the Queen of Sheba concerning the House of the Lord are anything to go by, then this psalm may reflect the glory of Jerusalem as it was in King Solomon's time.

However, the glory of Jerusalem then was clouded by the sin of the nation. Jerusalem's glory finally disappeared with the departure from the Temple of the *Shekinah* glory of the Lord, and the city's destruction by the Babylonians followed. Though the city has been rebuilt many times since, its former glory has never returned.

As we saw in Chapter 3, a little more than a century ago Jerusalem was nothing more than a disease-ridden town in the barren Judean hills – and of no consequence to the rest of the world. Oh, how that has changed!

When predicting the destruction of Jerusalem by the Romans, and the *Diaspora* which was to follow, Yeshua used the word 'until'. He said that Jerusalem would be *'trampled by the Gentiles until the times of the Gentiles are fulfilled.'* We noted in Chapter 5 that the Six-Day War of 1967 was a milestone in the fulfilment of this prophecy, but even today the Lord's holy mountain has two Moslem structures on it which dominate the Jerusalem skyline. And the Temple Mount itself, although a part of the sovereign State of Israel, is under the control of the Moslem *Waqf.* We also noted in Chapter 9 that the Antichrist will control it for a season.

Only the return of Israel's Messiah will finally end the Gentile domination of Jerusalem.

> ' *"Then you shall know at last that I am the* Lord *your God in Zion, My holy mountain. Jerusalem shall be mine forever; the time will come when no foreign armies will pass through her any more."* '
> (Joel 3:17, Living Bible)

Jerusalem then will be under His permanent sovereignty as Israel's King. However, it seems that those Gentiles born in Jerusalem and who have made the Holy City their home will be able to stay there, as it is written:

> *'And of Zion it will be said,*
> *"This one and that one were born in her."*
> *. . . The* Lord *will record,*
> *When He registers the peoples:*
> *"This one was born there."* '
> (Psalm 87:5, 6)

> *'And it shall come to pass that he who is left in Zion and he who remains in Jerusalem will be called holy – everyone who is recorded among the living in Jerusalem. When the Lord has washed away the filth of the daughters of Zion, and purged the blood of Jerusalem from her midst, by the spirit of judgment and by the spirit of burning, then the* Lord *will create above every dwelling place of Mount Zion, and above her assemblies, a cloud and smoke by day and the shining of a flaming fire by night. For over all the glory there will be a covering.'*
> (Isaiah 4:3–5)

No doubt these two prophecies will have their ultimate fulfilment in the spiritual and eternal Zion (see Hebrews 12:22–23) as well as the earthly Jerusalem. However, the restoration of the glory of the earthly Jerusalem is central to the prophecies of the Messianic Kingdom. The glory of Jerusalem will be the presence of the Lord and His Anointed One dwelling in her midst.

> ' *"Thus says the* Lord:
> *'I will return to Zion,*
> *And dwell in the midst of Jerusalem.*
> *Jerusalem shall be called the City of Truth,*
> *The Mountain of the* Lord *of Hosts,*
> *The Holy Mountain.'* " '
> (Zechariah 8:3)

The actual dwelling place of the Lord's Anointed One, it appears, will be the Temple. Later we will examine prophecies which describe the House of the Lord during the Messianic reign in Jerusalem. However, Isaiah indicates that His glory will not simply fill the Temple, but radiate across the Holy City and beyond. The violence and misery of the present age will have evaporated.

> ' "*The sun shall no longer be your light by day,*
> *Nor for brightness shall the moon give light to you;*
> *But the* Lord *will be to you an everlasting light,*
> *And your God your glory. . . .*
> *And the days of your mourning shall be ended.*
> *Also your people shall be all righteous;*
> *They shall inherit the land forever. . . .*
> *Violence shall no longer be heard in your land,*
> *Neither wasting nor destruction within your borders;*
> *But you shall call your walls Salvation,*
> *And your gates Praise.*" '   (Isaiah 60:19, 20b, 21a, 18)

> ' "*I will rejoice in Jerusalem,*
> *And joy in My people;*
> *The voice of weeping shall no longer be heard in her,*
> *Nor the voice of crying.*" '   (Isaiah 65:19) [181]

The Reproach of the Jewish People Removed

As had been foretold by Moses in the Land Covenant and by the other prophets of Israel, the Jewish people have been scattered among the nations and borne reproach for more than two-and-a-half millennia. According to the prophets of Israel, this judgement of the Lord has been brought about by their rejection of His Word. Even today, after more than half a century of being back in the Land of Israel as a nation, the Jewish people still bear the reproach of the nations. The anti-Israel bias in the media and continual condemnation in the United Nations forum demonstrate this. The boycott of most of the nations of the world of the opening of the *Jerusalem 3000* celebrations is just another example. As we enter the twenty-first century, anti-Semitism is again on the rise.

However, the prophets also predicted a time when this reproach – the scourge of anti-Semitism – will be removed. When bringing the obligations of the Land Covenant to the attention of the Children of Israel (their breaking of which has been the basis of Israel's turbulent history ever since) Moses predicted the following conclusion to the nation's wandering and persecution:

> ' "*Then the* LORD *your God will bring you to the land which your fathers possessed, and you shall possess it. He will prosper you and multiply you more than your fathers. And the* LORD *your God will circumcise your heart and the heart of your descendants, to love the* LORD *your God with all your heart and with all your soul that you may live. Also the* LORD *your God will put all these curses on your enemies and on those who hate you, who persecuted you.*" '
>
> (Deuteronomy 30:5–7)

The prophet Ezekiel, speaking of the return of Israel to the land and to their God, records these words from the Lord:

> ' "*Nor will I let you hear the taunts of the nations anymore, nor bear the reproach of the peoples anymore, nor shall you cause your nation to stumble anymore,*" *says the Lord* GOD.'
>
> (Ezekiel 36:15)

The removal of this curse coincides with the spiritual restoration of the nation of Israel, which we will examine shortly.

Moreover, the Scriptures actually go further. They speak of the exaltation of the Jewish people following their restoration. Zephaniah prophesies:

> ' "*At that time I will bring you back,*
> *Even at the time I gather you;*
> *For I will give you fame and praise*
> *Among all the peoples of the earth . . .*"
> *Says the* LORD.'
>
> (Zephaniah 3:20)

In one of his great prophecies concerning Jerusalem in the Messianic Age, the prophet Zechariah paints a most touching picture of the Lord's beloved ancient covenant people:

> ' "Thus says the Lord of hosts: 'In those days ten men from every language of the nations shall grasp the sleeve of a Jewish man, saying, "Let us go with you, for we have heard that God is with you." ' " '   (Zechariah 8:23)

The prophet Isaiah endorses this:

> ' "They shall walk behind you,
> They shall come over in chains;
> And they shall bow down to you.
> They will make supplication to you, saying,
>   'Surely God is in you,
> And there is no other;
> There is no other God.' " '   (Isaiah 45:14)

At no time in their history, except possibly in the days of David and Solomon, have the Jewish people been revered like this. And yet Isaiah, Zechariah and Zephaniah, who lived several hundred years after David and Solomon, have all said that one day it will happen. The Lord God of Israel will bring it about.

Jerusalem, the Spiritual Capital of the World

> 'The word that Isaiah the son of Amoz saw concerning Judah and Jerusalem.
>   Now it shall come to pass in the latter days
>   That the mountain of the Lord's house
>   Shall be established on the top of the mountains,
>   And shall be exalted above the hills;
>   And all nations shall flow to it.
>   Many people shall come and say,
>   "Come, and let us go up to the mountain of the Lord,
>   To the house of the God of Jacob;
>   He will teach us His ways,
>   And we shall walk in His paths."
>   For out of Zion shall go forth the law,
>   And the word of the Lord from Jerusalem.'   (Isaiah 2:1–3)

This prophecy, which is also found in chapter 4 of the Book of Micah, is included in The Jerusalem Covenant. It is one of the aspirations of Judaism, which will only be fulfilled when the New Covenant is fully consummated.

This prophecy gives a few indications about Jerusalem's role in the Messianic Kingdom, but principally it highlights that, as the spiritual capital of the world, it will be the place to which all Gentiles come to worship the Lord.

Zechariah confirms this in a prophecy concerning the last great conflict over Jerusalem and the coming of the Messiah:

> *'And it shall come to pass that everyone who is left of all the nations which came against Jerusalem shall go up from year to year to worship the King, the LORD of hosts, and to keep the Feast of Tabernacles. And it shall be that whichever of the families of the earth do not come up to Jerusalem to worship the King, the LORD of hosts, on them there will be no rain.'* (Zechariah 14:16–17)

The centrepiece of the spiritual capital of the world – the place where human beings meet with the Lord and where His Anointed One dwells – will be the House of the Lord.

The House of the Lord

Many of the prophecies concerning an ultimate House of the Lord were made during the Babylonian exile or immediately after. It is therefore quite difficult to determine whether these prophecies refer to the second Temple, which was built by Zerubbabel (and later reconstructed by Herod the Great), or a future glorious Temple. Often one can only distinguish the two by comparing which elements of a prophecy have already been fulfilled and which have not.

One such prophecy is found in the Book of Haggai:

> ' "For thus says the LORD of hosts: 'Once more (it is a little while) I will shake heaven and earth, the sea and dry land; and I will shake all nations, and they shall come to the Desire of All Nations, and I will fill this temple with glory,' says the LORD of hosts. ... 'The glory of this latter temple*

shall be greater than the former,' says the LORD *of hosts.*
'And in this place I will give peace,' says the LORD *of hosts."'*
(Haggai 2:6, 7, 9)

This passage contains a unique description of the Messiah: the Desire of All Nations. So we have a picture here of the Messiah in the Temple and the people coming to Him.

A popular view among Christian scholars is that this prophecy refers to Zerubbabel's Temple, which was under construction at that time. It is believed this structure was far inferior to Solomon's Temple, which preceded it. It is well documented that when Herod the Great reconstructed the second Temple during the lifetime of Yeshua, it became one of the wonders of the ancient world, so great was its outward glory. We know, too, that Yeshua often taught in the Temple and many, including the religious leaders of the day, were astonished by the brilliance of His teaching. So the Temple was filled with the glory of God incarnate every time He crossed its threshold.

But, we might ask, was Yeshua's presence in the second Temple, which had been enlarged and enriched by Herod the Great, in fact the complete fulfilment of this prophecy? The fact that there are other details in the prophecy which were not fulfilled at that time probably gives the answer.

Firstly, the prophecy foretells that there would be physical upheavals in the heavens and earth. While there was an earthquake at the time of the crucifixion, much more upheaval is prophesied immediately prior to Yeshua's future return to the planet.

Secondly, a shaking of all nations is prophesied. The only nation that was really shaken in recorded history at that time was Israel. Again, there are numerous prophecies concerning the shaking of the nations during 'the Day of the Lord', which we considered in Chapter 6.

Thirdly, the Lord says, *'And in this place I will give peace'* (Haggai 2:9). History shows us that the second Temple knew anything but peace – and ever since it was destroyed nations have fought over the land on which it stood.

Fourthly, notwithstanding what has been said about the incarnate glory of God (Yeshua), the Talmud indicates that the *Shekinah* glory of God was not present in the second Temple. Neither was the Ark of the Covenant, nor the Urim and Thummim.

So the conclusion drawn here is that the Temple Haggai is prophesying about is one that will exist at some time in the future – most probably during the reign of Messiah.

The prophet Zechariah, a contemporary of the prophet Haggai, was given another prophecy concerning the Temple:

> ' "Behold the Man whose name is the BRANCH!
> *From His place He shall branch out,*
> *And He shall build the Temple of the* LORD;
> *Yes, He shall build the Temple of the* LORD.
> *He shall bear the glory,*
> *And shall sit and rule on His throne;*
> *So He shall be a priest on His throne,*
> *And the counsel of peace shall be between them both." '*
> (Zechariah 6:12b–13)

The 'Branch' mentioned here is, of course, the same as that mentioned in Isaiah 11:1 and also Zechariah 3:8. It is a direct reference to the Messiah, and – as noted in Chapter 8 – clearly indicates that He will build the Temple.

If this is the case, then what will happen to the Temple which will be defiled by the Antichrist?

There does not seem to be a conclusive answer to this in the Scriptures. However, the prophet Zechariah speaks of a great earthquake when the Messiah returns to the Mount of Olives. As a result, it seems, the whole topography around Jerusalem will be dramatically changed (Zechariah 14:4, 8 and 10). Could it be that most of the city, including the Temple, will be destroyed by that earthquake?

As was said in Chapter 8, it seems then that we will not only see a third, but also a fourth Temple built on the Temple Mount in Jerusalem.

The Elevation of the Holy City

At the present time Mount Zion (the Temple Mount) is dwarfed by the surrounding hills. The Mount of Olives looks down on it from the west and Mount Scopus from the north-east. In the west, the Citadel on the western wall of the Old City stands slightly higher than the Temple Mount, and West Jerusalem stands even higher on a ridge across the Hinnom Valley. Several kilometres to the south, the Mount of Evil Counsel (where the United Nations building is situated) is also elevated above the Temple Mount.

The prophet Zechariah tells us that after the earthquake:

> *'All the land shall be turned into a plain from Geba to Rimmon south of Jerusalem. Jerusalem shall be raised up and inhabited in her place from Benjamin's Gate to the place of the First Gate and the Corner Gate, and from the Tower of Hananeel to the king's winepress.*
> *The people shall dwell in it;*
> *And no longer shall there be utter destruction,*
> *But Jerusalem shall be safely inhabited.'*
>
> (Zechariah 14:10–11)

The landmarks mentioned here were in existence prior to the Babylonian destruction, and while the precise location of all of them may not be known, collectively they were in close proximity to the Temple and surrounded it. The general message in this prophecy is that the Temple Mount will be elevated and the city securely inhabited.

In a passage that immediately follows the prophecy of the New Covenant in the Book of Jeremiah, we find another promise concerning the future security of Jerusalem:

> *' "Behold, the days are coming," says the LORD, "that the city shall be built for the LORD from the Tower of Hananeel to the Corner Gate. . . . And the whole valley of the dead bodies and of the ashes, and all the fields as far as the Brook Kidron, to the corner of the Horse Gate toward the east, shall be holy to the LORD. It shall not be plucked up or thrown down anymore forever." '*
>
> (Jeremiah 31:38, 40) [182]

One can see a parallel between this prophecy and the prophecy in Joel 3 which relates to the judgement at the time of the Lord's return. Once the judgement of the nations and the carnage has been dealt with, Jeremiah tells us, the Holy City will never be destroyed again. Indeed, the Temple Mount itself will be holy and will be elevated. As we saw in Isaiah:

'Now it shall come to pass in the latter days
That the mountain of the LORD's house
Shall be established on the top of the mountains,
And shall be exalted above the hills;
And all nations shall flow to it.'   (Isaiah 2:2)

Another Scripture which mentions the elevation of Mount Zion is found in Psalms:

'Great is the LORD, and greatly to be praised
In the city of our God,
In His holy mountain.
Beautiful in elevation,
The joy of the whole earth,
Is Mount Zion on the sides of the north,
The city of the great King.'   (Psalm 48:1–2)

So, in the Scriptures we can see a marvellous picture of Jerusalem as the spiritual capital of the world, inhabited by a restored nation who walk righteously, and with the King of Glory reigning in her midst. It also seems that the Lord's holy mountain will have a physical glory which it has never had before. In Messiah's reign it will be *'the joy of the whole earth'*, not *'the burdensome stone for all peoples'* that it is rapidly becoming today.

Ezekiel's Vision of the House of the Lord

It is worth considering one other major prophetic passage which details the future glory of Jerusalem, and particularly the House of the Lord. It is contained in the last nine chapters of the Book of Ezekiel and chronologically follows both the prophecies of the national and spiritual restoration of Israel found in chapters 36 and 37, and those of the invasion by the armies of Gog and Magog found in chapters 38 and 39.

As we have noted earlier, there has been much conjecture in the Christian Church about whether another Temple will ever be built.

Some believe Ezekiel's vision was of the Temple that would be built after the exiles returned from Babylon.[183] However, there are a few major details which have never been prophetically fulfilled – and we will briefly look at some of these.

Others take the view that the Church is the fulfilment of this prophecy. While there is a sense in which the Church has spiritually fulfilled the prophecy, the precise measurements for the Temple seem irrelevant if this is only way it will be fulfilled.

Yet others are convinced that the whole vision is nothing more than wishful thinking on Ezekiel's part!

I am of the opinion that one day these prophetic Scriptures will be literally fulfilled down to the last detail.

The Dimensions of the Temple

Chapters 40–42 are devoted entirely to detailed measurements of the outer court, the inner court and the Temple itself. One of the most striking differences between this Temple and any previous one is the size of the Court of the Gentiles. Perhaps this is indicative of the multitudes who will come to worship the Lord in Jerusalem. Ezekiel tells us that each of the outer walls will measure five hundred rods in length – about one mile. This means the dimensions of the Temple complex will be approximately one mile square, which is slightly larger than the whole of the Old City of Jerusalem as it is today!

The *Shekinah* Glory Returns to the Temple

In Chapter 2 we saw that the *Shekinah* glory of the Lord dwelt in the Temple which was built by King Solomon (2 Chronicles 7:1–2). We noted that Ezekiel saw the *Shekinah* glory depart from the Temple shortly before its destruction by the Babylonians (Ezekiel 10:4 and 11:23), and that it appears it has never returned to the Temple since then, except briefly in the form of the incarnate Son of God at the time of the Herods.

This prophecy of Ezekiel is significant, because it heralds the permanent return of the presence of the God of Israel to dwell among His ancient covenant people.

> *'Afterward he brought me to the gate, the gate which faces toward the east. And behold, the glory of the God of Israel came from the way of the east. His voice was like the sound of many waters; and the earth shone with His glory. . . . And the glory of the LORD came into the temple by way of the gate which faces toward the east.*
>
> *The Spirit lifted me up and brought me into the inner court; and behold, the glory of the LORD filled the temple. Then I heard Him speaking to me from the temple, while a man stood beside me. And He said to me, "Son of man, this is the place of My throne and the place of the soles of My feet, where I will dwell in the midst of the children of Israel forever." '* (Ezekiel 43:1–2, 4–7a)

The Hebrew word *Shekinah* means 'dwelling' or 'resting'. It was used to describe the Divine Presence which was manifested when He dwelt with the children of Israel in the Tabernacle and later in the first Temple. What is so significant about this prophecy is that it confirms that the stated desire of the Lord God, to dwell among His people in Mount Zion, will one day be fulfilled. This was the thrust of our study in Chapter 1. At last He will be inhabiting that part of the earth that He has declared to be His dwelling place, and the unity of Zion will be truly restored.

But the *Shekinah* glory of God is more than just an aura or presence. In verse 2 the glory of God speaks with a voice *'like the sound of many waters'*. This identifies Him as the One who spoke to the Apostle John in the Book of Revelation (1:15) when He said:

> *'Do not be afraid; I am the First and the Last. I am He who lives, and was dead, and behold, I am alive forevermore. Amen.'* (Revelation 1:17–18)

This, of course, is none other than the resurrected Son of God, Yeshua HaMashiach, the King of Israel. On the day the *Shekinah* glory of God returns to the Temple, the prophecy concerning the coronation of the Lord's Anointed One will be consummated:

> ' "Yet have I set My King
> On My holy hill of Zion.
> I will declare the decree:
> The LORD has said to Me,
> 'You are My Son,
> Today I have begotten You.
> Ask of Me and I will give You the nations for Your
>   inheritance,
> And the ends of the earth for Your possession.' " '
> (Psalm 2:6–8)

A River from the Temple

In the first half of Ezekiel 47 the prophet describes a unique feature of the Temple during Messiah's reign: a river will flow from the Temple.

> *'Then he brought me back to the door of the temple; and there was water flowing from under the threshold of the temple toward the east, for the front of the temple faced east; the water was flowing from under the right side of the temple, south of the altar.'*   (Ezekiel 47:1)

Ezekiel is not the only prophet to mention this, for Zechariah tells us:

> *'And in that day it shall be
> That living waters shall flow from Jerusalem,
> Half of them toward the eastern sea
> And half of them toward the western sea;
> In both summer and winter it shall occur.'* (Zechariah 14:8)

The two seas mentioned here are the Dead Sea and the Mediterranean Sea respectively. Zechariah gives no more detail than that, but the prophet Ezekiel continues:

'Then he said to me: "This water flows toward the eastern
region, goes down into the valley, and enters the sea. When it
reaches the sea its waters are healed. And it shall be that
every living thing that moves, wherever the two rivers go, will
live. There will be a very great multitude of fish, because
these waters go there; for they will be healed, and everything
will live wherever the river goes." '   (Ezekiel 47:8–9)

The prophecy goes on to tell of fishermen fishing in the
Dead Sea and catching fish as they do in the Mediterranean.
Not only will the waters have healing properties, but so will
the trees along its banks.

'"Along the bank of the river, on this side and that, will
grow all kinds of trees used for food; their leaves will not
whither, and their fruit will not fail. They will bear fruit
every month, because their water flows from the sanctuary.
Their fruit will be for food and their leaves for medicine." '

(Ezekiel 47:12)

This picture of healing and restoration, peace and justice
is inconceivable in the world we know today. And yet it is
prevalent throughout prophecy relating to the reign of
Yeshua HaMashiach on the earth.

The Name of the Holy City

The Book of Ezekiel finishes on a wonderful note. The final
words tell us:

'"And the name of the city from that day shall be:
YHWH Shammah, THE LORD IS THERE." '

(Ezekiel 48:35)

The prophet Zephaniah encourages us with an equally
beautiful thought:

'Sing, O daughter of Zion!
Shout, O Israel!
Be glad and rejoice with all your heart,
O daughter of Jerusalem!

> *"Do not fear;*
> *Zion, let not your hands be weak.*
> *The Lord your God in your midst,*
> *The Mighty One, will save;*
> *He will rejoice over you with gladness,*
> *He will quiet you in His love,*
> *He will rejoice over you with singing." '*
>
> (Zephaniah 3:14, 16–17)

It is very moving, indeed, to think of the Lord actually singing with tenderness and love to His ancient covenant people. Surely, it will be the most exquisite sound the human ear has ever been privileged to hear.

The Thousand-year Reign of Messiah in Jerusalem

The Book of Revelation tells us that this earthly reign of Messiah in Jerusalem will last a thousand years (20:4). As the only place in the Bible where a time limit is placed on the Messianic Age on planet earth, it seems to be at odds with most of the prophecies in the *Tanakh* concerning the Messianic Kingdom, which emphatically tell us that it will be an everlasting Kingdom. But so it will be. Only the theatre of the Messianic Kingdom will be moved from one stage to another – see Chapter 12. As the Book of Revelation makes clear, at this time there will still be some unfinished business.

Satan Is Released and Leads a Rebellion

> 'Now when the thousand years have expired, Satan will be released from his prison and will go out to deceive the nations which are in the four corners of the earth, Gog and Magog, to gather them together to battle, whose number is as the sand of the sea.' (Revelation 20:7–8)

This passage of Scripture has perplexed many Christians. Why should Satan be released to terrorise the earth again? I can only offer one answer to this question, for the reader to consider. It was noted earlier that even in the absence of

Satan and his hordes, the Messiah would still have to rule the earth 'with an iron sceptre' because of the inclination of human beings toward evil.

For instance, among those who will attend the Feast of Tabernacles to worship the Lord in Jerusalem (Zechariah 14:16–17), there will be many who do so begrudgingly. They will be like rebellious children who are compelled to attend the synagogue or church. On the other hand, there will be many who worship Him freely and with a glad heart.

As we also noted earlier, it seems there will be potential evil on the earth in the hearts of men, women and children – just as there has been ever since the Fall. However, during the rule of the Messiah this evil will be restrained from openly running its course, as it does today. In other words, it seems that an individual's freedom of choice to do evil will be severely restricted. One might ask the question: will such restraint be the ultimate solution to eradicating evil from the universe completely?

I think not. Perhaps, in His wisdom, the Lord has decided that the best way to deal with evil is ultimately to let it run its course by allowing it to come out into the open. Maybe this is the reason why He will let Satan loose – to 'help' the rebels in their cause. Perhaps too, this prophetic Scripture is recorded so that those who really love the Lord will not be taken by surprise, believe the lies of Satan, and consequently become disheartened and be tempted to join the rebellion.

The Final Judgement

The outcome is clearly predicted:

> *'They went up on the breadth of the earth and surrounded the camp of the saints and the beloved city. And fire came down from God out of heaven and devoured them.*
>
> *And the devil, who deceived them, was cast into the lake of fire and brimstone where the beast and false prophet are. And there they will be tormented day and night forever and ever.'* (Revelation 20:9–10)

The Apostle John continues with the apocalyptic vision of the final judgement:

> *'Then I saw a great white throne and Him who sat on it, from whose face the earth and heaven fled away. And there was found no place for them. And I saw the dead, small and great, standing before God, and the books were opened. And another book was opened which is the Book of Life. And the dead were judged according to their works, by the things which were written in the books. The sea gave up the dead who were in it, and Death and Hades delivered up the dead who were in them. And they were judged, each one according to his works. Then Death and Hades were cast into the lake of fire. This is the second death. And anyone not found written in the Book of Life was cast into the lake of fire.'*
>
> (Revelation 20:11–15)

The Lord's ultimate aim is to bring about righteousness and perfection. The Apostle Peter tells us what the final fate of the world, as we know it, will be.

> *'The heavens and the earth which now exist are kept in store ... reserved for fire, until the day of judgement and perdition of ungodly men ... in which the heavens will pass away with a great noise, and the elements will melt with fervent heat; both the earth and the works that are in it will be burned up.'*
>
> (2 Peter 3:7, 10b)

Speaking to Peter and the other disciples in what we call the Olivet Discourse, Yeshua assured them:

> *'Heaven and earth will pass away, but My words will by no means pass away.'*   (Matthew 24:35)

Neither will the Messianic Kingdom pass away. It will simply enter a new and everlasting era.

Chapter 12

The New Jerusalem

Isaiah's Foretelling of New Heavens and a New Earth

> ' "Behold, I create new heavens and a new earth;
> And the former shall not be remembered or come to mind.
> But be glad and rejoice forever in what I create;
> For behold, I create Jerusalem as a rejoicing,
> And her people a joy.
> I will rejoice in Jerusalem,
> And joy in My people;
> The voice of weeping shall no longer be heard in her,
> Nor the voice of crying." '   (Isaiah 65:17–19)

The hope expressed in this prophecy from Isaiah resides deep in the heart of every Jewish man, woman and child. Although the *Tanakh* does not directly mention the New Jerusalem, the *Talmud* does refer to it. The Jerusalem Covenant goes so far as to link the heavenly city with the earthly city. Isaiah tells us here that in the New Jerusalem there will be no memory of the horror surrounding or associated with the previous city and the world in which it existed. The new heavens and new earth will become the place of the eternal Messianic Kingdom. The earlier prophecy of Isaiah concerning the Messiah will then be fully realised:

> 'Of the increase of His government and peace
> There will be no end,

> *Upon the throne of David and over His kingdom,*
> *To order and establish it with judgement and justice*
> *From that time forward, even forever.'* (Isaiah 9:7)

The Book of Revelation gives us much more detail about this new and eternal world order, which is nothing short of a new creation by the living God.

The Apostle's Vision of the New Jerusalem

'And I saw a new heaven and a new earth, for the first heaven and the first earth had passed away. Also there was no more sea. Then I, John, saw the holy city, New Jerusalem, coming down out of heaven from God, prepared as a bride adorned for her husband. And I heard a loud voice from heaven saying, "Behold, the tabernacle of God is with men, and He will dwell with them, and they shall be His people, and God Himself will be with them and be their God. And God will wipe away every tear from their eyes; there shall be no more death, nor sorrow, nor crying; and there shall be no more pain, for the former things have passed away."

Then He who sat on the throne said, "Behold, I make all things new." And He said to me, "Write, for these words are true and faithful."

And He said to me, "It is done! I am the Alpha and the Omega, the Beginning and the End. I will give of the fountain of the water of life freely to him who thirsts. He who overcomes shall inherit all things, and I will be his God and he shall be My son. But the cowardly, unbelieving, abominable, murderers, sexually immoral, sorcerers, idolaters, and all liars shall have their part in the lake which burns with fire and brimstone, which is the second death."'

(Revelation 21:1–8)

As we have already considered, many have questioned throughout the ages why the Lord has allowed evil, with all its associated pain, suffering and death, to exist in this present world. This prophetic passage at the end of the Bible clearly spells out the fate of evildoers and makes it clear that there will be no evildoers at all in the world to come. The

Apostle John goes on to give us a fuller description of the New Jerusalem.

> 'Then one of the seven angels who had the seven bowls filled with the seven last plagues came to me and talked with me, saying, "Come, I will show you the bride, the Lamb's wife." And he carried me away in the Spirit to a great and high mountain, and showed me the great city, the holy Jerusalem, descending out of heaven from God, having the glory of God. And her light was like a most precious stone, like a jasper stone, clear as crystal. Also she had a great and high wall with twelve gates, and twelve angels at the gates, and names written on them, which are the names of the twelve tribes of the children of Israel: three gates on the east, three gates on the north, three gates on the south, and three gates on the west. Now the wall of the city had twelve foundations, and on them were the names of the twelve apostles of the Lamb.[184]
>
> And he who talked with me had a gold reed to measure the city, its gates, and its wall. And the city is laid out as a square, and its length is as great as its breadth. And he measured the city with the reed: twelve thousand furlongs [1,500 miles]. Its length, breadth, and height are equal. Then he measured its wall: one hundred and forty-four cubits [about 215 feet], according to the measure of a man, that is, of an angel. And the construction of its wall was of jasper; and the city was pure gold, like clear glass. And the foundations of the wall of the city were adorned with all kinds of precious stones: the first foundation was jasper, the second sapphire, the third chalcedony, the fourth emerald, the fifth sardonyx, the sixth sardius, the seventh chrysolite, the eighth beryl, the ninth topaz, the tenth chrysoprase, the eleventh jacinth, and the twelfth amethyst. And the twelve gates were twelve pearls: each individual gate was of one pearl. And the street of the city was pure gold, like transparent glass.'   (Revelation 21: 9–21)

The dimensions of the future Holy City are enormous. From the description given here, the New Jerusalem will be a giant cube, each side being fifteen hundred miles long (2,400 kilometres). The city will be constructed of the most precious

and beautiful materials imaginable. Its glory will be unsurpassed by anything that any human being has seen up to
that time. But the centre of the heavenly Jerusalem's glory
will be God Himself. Notably absent will be the Temple.

> *'But I saw no temple in it, for the Lord God Almighty and the
> Lamb are its temple. And the city had no need of the sun or
> of the moon to shine in it, for the glory of God illuminated it,
> and the Lamb is its light. And the nations of those who are
> saved shall walk in its light, and the kings of the earth bring
> their glory and honor into it. Its gates shall not be shut at all
> by day (there shall be no night there). And they shall bring
> the glory and the honor of the nations into it. But there shall
> by no means enter it anything that defiles, or causes an
> abomination or a lie, but only those who are written in the
> Lamb's Book of Life.'*   (Revelation 21:22–27)

This wonderful passage at the end of the New Testament
gives us a picture of the glorious future that awaits those
whose names are written in the Lamb's Book of Life. When
Yeshua was here nearly two thousand years ago He gave this
promise to all of His disciples:

> *'In My Father's house are many mansions; if it were not so, I
> would have told you. I go to prepare a place for you. And if I
> go and prepare a place for you, I will come again and receive
> you to Myself; that where I am, there you may be also.'*
> (John 14:2–3)

Just as the Abrahamic Covenant promises the Land of
Israel and the earthly Jerusalem as the inheritance for all
Jewish people for all time, whether they are living in the land
or in the *Diaspora*, the New Testament promises the heavenly
Jerusalem as the eternal inheritance for those whose names
are written in the Lamb's Book of Life. That means all those
who are partakers of the New Covenant, whether they are
Jew or Gentile. As noted in Chapter 1, the inhabitants of the
New Jerusalem are all the redeemed of the Lord:

> *'You have come to Mount Zion and to the city of the living
> God, the heavenly Jerusalem, to an innumerable company of*

angels, to the general assembly and church of the firstborn
who are registered in heaven, to God the Judge of all, to the
spirits of just men made perfect, [and] to Yeshua *the*
Mediator of the new covenant. For here we have no continu-
ing city, but we seek the one to come.'

(Hebrews 12:22–24a and 13:14)

The question is: How can we be sure that we are redeemed,
that our names are written in the Lamb's Book of Life –
and that we are partakers of the New Covenant?

The Lamb's Book of Life

The way to salvation is very simple.

Firstly, the Scriptures teach us that there is only **one** way,
for both Jew and Gentile. Following on from the promise
Yeshua gave His disciples (which was earlier quoted from
John's Gospel), He made one of the most controversial
statements found in the New Testament. He said:

'I am the way, the truth and the life. No one comes to the
Father except through Me.' (John 14:6)

Jesus, despite what large sections of the church establishment might say, is uncompromising on this issue. Not too
many months after Jesus spoke these words, when the Apostle
Peter was appearing before the Jewish Sanhedrin, together
with a blind man he had been instrumental in healing, he
reiterated Yeshua's statement in the strongest possible terms:

' . . . let it be known to you all, and to all the people of Israel,
that by the name of Yeshua HaMashiach *of Nazareth,*
whom you crucified, whom God raised from the dead, by
Him this man stands here before you whole. This is the
"stone which was rejected by you builders, which has become
the chief cornerstone." Nor is there salvation in any other, for
there is no other name under heaven given among men
whereby we must be saved.' (Acts 4:10–12) [185]

So, acknowledgement that Yeshua is the **only** way of
salvation is the first vital step.

Secondly, we need to acknowledge that we have been separated from God by our sin. Sin is not simply evil-doing, though doing evil is definitely sin. Sin is failing to meet God's standards of purity and holiness. Moreover, sin is a desire to be independent of God. One writer expressed sin as 'seeking self-identification and self-realisation without God'.

This in essence is what Satan was tempting Eve to do in the Garden of Eden. It was here that humanism had its beginnings.

Since that time the whole of the human race has been polluted by 'seeking self-identification and self-realisation without God' which has resulted in the oppression, suffering and evil we know in the world today. The penalty of sin is death and eternal separation from God. But death is also a sign of God's mercy, otherwise we would be condemned to live eternally with the evil and suffering we have in the world.

However, it was God who made the move to restore humankind to Himself, without compromising His holy standards. The Apostle John recorded the words of the Saviour in his Gospel:

> 'For God so loved the world that He gave His only begotten Son, that whoever believes in Him should not perish but have everlasting life. For God did not send His Son into the world to condemn the world, but that the world through Him might be saved. He who believes in Him is not condemned; but he who does not believe is condemned already, because he has not believed in the name of the only begotten Son of God.'
>
> (John 3:16–18)

The issue here is not whether we are able to believe, but whether we are willing to believe. Mark's Gospel tells the story of a man whose son needed deliverance from an evil spirit (Mark 9:14–29). He wasn't sure whether he could believe if Yeshua could perform the necessary miracle and he said to Him: *'Lord, I believe; help my unbelief!'* The Lord answered his prayer and his son was healed. The man exercised his will and committed himself to believe. This is the essence of faith – it is an act of the will.

We are not justified in God's sight by *mitzvot*, by *karma*, or by good deeds, but by faith (see Genesis 15:6, Habakkuk 2:4 and Romans 3:28).

The way of salvation has been prepared and completed by Yeshua. Whether or not our names are written in the Lamb's Book of Life is a matter for each one of us to determine. It may mean putting our presuppositions aside and exercising our own will to receive the free gift of salvation on God's terms.

Yeshua, in His famous Sermon on the Mount, said:

'Enter by the narrow gate; for wide is the gate and broad is the way that leads to destruction, and there are many who go in by it. Because narrow is the gate and difficult is the way which leads to life, and there are few who find it.'

(Matthew 7:13–14)

If you desire to partake in the New Covenant and have your name written in the Lamb's Book of Life, then you need to speak with the Lord about this in prayer. You will find a simple prayer in Appendix E which you may like to use as a guideline.

A Personal Note from the Author

If you are Jewish you may have found little problem with what has been presented in this book concerning your ancient and beloved Holy City. However, you may have great difficulty with some of the truths about your Messiah, and especially with the assertion that Yeshua of Nazareth *is* the Messiah. As a Gentile Christian, I acknowledge that the Christian Church has shockingly abused the Jewish people for centuries, and some sections of it continue to do so today. In so doing we are guilty of slandering the character of the Messiah who loves you. We can only ask you to forgive us for doing this. Nevertheless, Yeshua is the Anointed One He claimed to be, and there are a growing number of Jewish people across the world, including in Israel, who are discovering Him. Only the Spirit of the Lord God of Israel can reveal this truth to you. Any Jewish disciple of Yeshua will tell you that he or she came to faith as a result of divine revelation rather than any missionary activity. Examine the *Tanakh* (and even *HaB'rit Chadashah*, which is, after all, a Jewish book [186]) and ask God to reveal the truth to you. The God of Israel promised:

> *'I know the thoughts that I think toward you, says the LORD, thoughts of peace and not of evil, to give you a future and a hope. Then you will call upon Me and go and pray to Me, and I will listen to you. And you will seek Me and find Me, when you search for Me with all your heart.'*
>
> (Jeremiah 29:11–13)

You will not lose your Jewish identity by coming to faith in Yeshua, as some may claim, but you will come into your full identity as a son or daughter of Abraham, Isaac and Jacob through the New Covenant (Jeremiah 31:31–4).

If you are a non-Jew and already a committed Christian, then what you have read may be an entirely new way of presenting the gospel. Not only are the roots of our Christian faith deeply embedded in the Jewish Scriptures, but also we share a common heritage in Yeshua HaMashiach, and we need to recognise this. We owe a tremendous debt to the Jewish people, especially in view of the dreadful crimes which the institutional Church has committed against them. One of the best ways of making reparation for the past is to support and uphold the Lord's plan and purposes according to His Word and intercede on behalf of them. The Lord has covenanted to restore the nation of Israel spiritually and physically and He has called the Church, at the very least, to pray to this end. Isaiah entreats us:

> *'"Comfort, yes, comfort My people!"*
> *Says your God.*
> *Speak comfort to Jerusalem ... "'*   (Isaiah 40:1–2a)

It is the love of Yeshua, expressed through those that are His, that will heal the scars of rejection and persecution that have been inflicted upon His ancient covenant people.

If you are a Moslem, and you have read to this point in the book, it should be obvious that Israel is not your enemy, neither are Christians. Your real enemies are those who try to set you against the stated purposes of the God of Israel, which we have explored in this book. The prophet Isaiah predicts a time when

> '... *there will be a highway from Egypt to Assyria, and the Assyrian will come into Egypt and the Egyptian into Assyria, and the Egyptians will serve with the Assyrians. In that day Israel will be one of three with Egypt and Assyria, even a blessing in the midst of the land, whom the* LORD *of hosts shall bless, saying, "Blessed is Egypt My people, and Assyria the work of My hands, and Israel My inheritance."* '
>
> (Isaiah 19:23–25)

This prophecy is already starting to come to pass. There are thousands of former Moslems who have come to faith in Yeshua, have been reconciled to their Jewish brethren and become partakers of the New Covenant. I have had the privilege to be at gatherings where Arab and Jew were side by side praising the God of Israel.

If you are a Hindu, or have embraced New Age thinking, then you will have a very different idea of who or what God might be. You possibly believe in polytheism – that there is a multiplicity of gods. God has not only revealed who He is in the Scriptures, but He clearly asserts:

> ' "*Thus says the* LORD, *the King of Israel,
> And His Redeemer, the* LORD *of hosts:
> 'I am the First and I am the Last;
> Besides Me there is no God.'* " ' (Isaiah 44:6)

> ' "*I, even I am the* LORD,
> And besides Me there is no saviour.*" ' (Isaiah 43:11)

Furthermore, the notion of reincarnation is foreign to the Bible, for the New Testament tells us:

> '... *it is appointed for men to die once, but after this the judgment, so Christ was offered once to bear the sins of*

*many. To those who eagerly wait for Him He will appear a
second time, apart from sin, for salvation.'*
(Hebrews 9:27–28) [187]

If you are seeking the truth, then be persuaded that Jesus is
'the Way, the Truth and the Life'. Indeed, He is not simply
another of the Hindu gods, but He is the Son of the only God
and the Saviour of the world.

Finally, if you are an agnostic, then closely examine the
ancient prophecies that have been fulfilled. There has been a
tremendous assault on the veracity of the Holy Scriptures in
this century. Many have claimed to have disproved the Bible,
yet it continues to be the world's number one bestseller. The
sceptics – including those in the church establishment – have
a basic motive for discrediting the Bible, and that is because
they are not prepared to be accountable to its divine author.
Despite what the sceptics say, modern biblical archaeology
and the fulfilment of prophecy after prophecy bear witness to
both the accuracy and the authenticity of the Bible as the
Word of God. The years to come will see even more prophecies – some of which we have discussed in this book – being
fulfilled as this present age comes to a close. The question
you need to consider is this: Do you *want* to have your name
written in the Lamb's Book of Life?

'Pray for the Peace of Jerusalem'

The destiny of Jerusalem is vital to all of us, whether we are
Jewish or not. It will impact not only the destiny of the
Jewish nation, but the destiny of every nation in the world.

The destiny of Jerusalem is foretold in the declared Word
of God. There is no escaping what is to come, but we can
prepare ourselves for it. The prophetic Word is there to warn
us. In His love and mercy to us, God has forewarned us so
that we may be forearmed and so that we may set the
priorities in our lives accordingly.

During the holocaust that will envelop the Middle East –
and indeed the whole world – in the years to come there will
be security for those who have put their trust in the Lord and
His Anointed One, Yeshua. He has promised to be with us

until the end of the age. We have eternal life in Him, and sooner or later we will go to be with Him forever.

The City of Peace will have to endure the most horrific time in its long and turbulent history – until the Prince of Peace returns to it, and takes up the throne of David. Then, and only then, will there be true and everlasting peace. For then there will be peace in Zion. And Zion the city, Zion the land and Zion the people will be truly united forever. And then the earthly Jerusalem shall fade into the glory of the heavenly Jerusalem.

Until the Prince of Peace returns, we have been encouraged to pray for that peace to come.

> *'Pray for the peace of Jerusalem,*
> *"They shall prosper that love thee."'*   (Psalm 122:6, KJV)

Notes

Chapter 1: The Status of Jerusalem in the Bible

1. Lance Lambert *The Uniqueness of Israel* (Eastbourne, UK: Kingsway, 1976), pp. 151–3.

2. The Messiah is central to both the Jewish and Christian religions. However, Judaism and Christianity have very different ideas about what or who the Messiah may be. Orthodox Christianity identifies Jesus of Nazareth to be the Messiah – the arguments for which are clearly put forward in this book. Furthermore Christians believe that Jesus Christ is the Son of God, and part of a holy Trinity – Father, Son and Holy Spirit. Judaism, on the other hand, clearly rejects the concept of Jesus being the Messiah or the Son of God, or even the possibility of a Trinity. Historically, this disagreement has been the major cause of the gulf that has existed between Christians and Jews with very sad consequences for both sides. The Jewish concept of the Messiah varies among the different branches of Judaism. However, there is a broad consensus within Judaism that the ultimate destiny of Jerusalem is linked with the Messiah, whoever or whatever the Messiah might be. Most religious Jews look forward to the Messianic Age believing that it will bring universal and everlasting peace to the world. Many Evangelical Christians share this view as well. For further comments on the origin and meaning of the designation 'Messiah' or 'Christ', see note 21.

3. The Holy Bible is holy to both Christians and Jews. It is split into two portions, the Old Testament (or more literally *Old Covenant*) and the New Testament (or more literally *New*

Covenant). Unfortunately, some Christians hold little regard for the Old Testament, and the overwhelming majority of Jewish people do not recognise the New Testament as Scripture. For more about what orthodox Jewish people and Christians each regard as Scripture, see note 7.

4. There are five covenants in the Bible which relate to the nation of Israel, of which the Abrahamic Covenant, which is unconditional, is historically the first, and the foundation to the others. The next covenant is known as the Mosaic Covenant, which contains God's specific call to the nation of Israel as His 'covenant people' (Exodus 19:5–6). The Mosaic Covenant is spread through the last four Books of Moses and much of it relates to the 'Promised Land'. This part of the Mosaic Covenant is sometimes known as the 'Land Covenant', the 'Canaanic Covenant', or the 'Palestinian Covenant' (a misnomer – see note 31). The main text of the Land Covenant is found in Leviticus 26 and Deuteronomy 28–30. The promises of blessing contained therein are conditional on the Israelis' obedience to the Lord. The Land Covenant, which relates to their residency and prosperity in the Promised Land, does not cancel the Israelites' inheritance, i.e. their title to the land promised in the Abrahamic Covenant. The other two covenants are: (1) the Davidic Covenant (2 Samuel 7:14–17 and 1 Chronicles 17:7–14), which relates to the everlasting nature of the dynasty of David's throne; (2) the New Covenant (Jeremiah 31:31–34, see also Matthew 26:26–29). Further discussion on the covenants and their final consummation is found in Chapter 10. A knowledge of these covenants, and the context in which God made them, is essential for a proper understanding of God's plan and purpose for both the Jewish people and the Church. Understanding the covenants will also assist the believer in understanding his/her personal relationship to God. *The Covenants and Promises* by K.A. Macnaughton (50 pages) is recommended reading. It is published by the David Press, PO Box 25, Carnegie, Victoria 3163, Australia.

5. For further investigation of this aspect of the Abrahamic Covenant, see Joseph H. Hunting, *Curse or Coincidence?* (The David Press, 1969).

6. The other Bible references concerning the Jewish inheritance of the Land of Israel are as follows: Genesis 24:7, 26:3, 50:24; Exodus 6:8, 13:5, 13:11, 32:13, 33:1; Numbers 11:12, 14:16, 14:23, 32:11; Deuteronomy 1:8, 1:35, 6:10, 6:18, 6:23, 7:13, 8:1, 9:5, 10:11, 11:9, 11:21, 19:8, 26:3, 26:15, 28:11, 30:20,

31:17, 31:20, 31:21, 31:23, 34:4; Joshua 1:6, 5:6, 12:43; Judges 2:1; 1 Chronicles 16:15–18; Nehemiah 9:15; Psalm 105:8–11; Jeremiah 11:5, 32:22; Ezekiel 20:6, 20:28, 20:42 47:14. In three of these references God's *'oath'* is joined with His *'covenant'*, and in three places it is explicitly stated that Israel's possession of the land is to be *'for ever'*, or *'everlasting'*. (Courtesy Derek Prince, *The Destiny of Israel and the Church*, Word (UK) 1992.) The absence of any reiteration of this promise explicitly in the New Testament is often used as an argument that neither Jesus nor the Apostles endorsed it. However, this is an argument from a position of silence. It would be just as valid to say that because the precept of the land being the everlasting inheritance of the Jewish people is so well established in the Old Testament, there is no need to raise it in the New Testament.

7. The *Tanakh* encompasses the whole of the Jewish Scriptures, and includes the *Torah* (the five books of Moses known to Christians as the Pentateuch), the *Nevi'im* (the Prophets) and the *Kethuvim* (the Writings, which includes the Psalms, Proverbs, Ecclesiastes and the Song of Solomon). For the Jews the *Tanakh* is the whole Bible. It is basically what Christians call the Old Testament, although it is presented in a different order. Judaism places the greatest emphasis on the *Torah*. Christians regard the New Testament as part of the Bible.

8. In modern-day Jerusalem, Mount Zion is situated outside the south-west corner of the Old City walls, where the Zion Gate is situated. Two of Jerusalem's main tourist attractions are on present-day Mount Zion – David's Tomb and the Upper Room, the traditional location marking where the Last Supper took place. However, this location in King David's time was well outside the city walls and is not the Mount Zion of the Bible. Biblical Mount Zion was almost certainly the Temple Mount.

9. It is interesting that the description of the Person who is dwelling in Zion seems to vary from prophecy to prophecy. Psalm 132 talks about the Person being the Lord's Messiah, while Psalm 2 mentions the Person as being the Lord's chosen King, who is also identified as His Son. The Scripture texts we have here from Joel 3:17 and Jeremiah 3:17 (along with other Scriptures to be considered later on) speak of the Lord God Himself dwelling in Jerusalem. Could they in fact be the same Person?

10. The term 'saint' in this book is used in a biblical sense rather than the ecclesiastical sense. In other words, this author's definition of a saint is not someone who has been venerated

or 'canonised' by the church establishment. The Unger's *Bible Dictionary* definition of a saint is summarised as follows: positionally – all New Testament believers, members of the Body of Christ are saints by virtue of their *position* 'in Christ'; experientially – a person eminent for piety and virtue: a consecrated person. In the Old Testament the term 'saint' is used of pious Israelites, and of the 'godly' in general. The New Testament refutes the idea of a special class of 'saints'. It is true that the *experience* of some believers may be more 'holy' than others, yet in their position before God, all believers are 'sanctified', i.e. saints by virtue of what they are 'in Christ'.

Chapter 2: The History of Jerusalem in the Bible

11. An appearance of the Messiah in pre-incarnate form is referred to as a 'Christophany' by Christian theologians. There are several such appearances in the Old Testament, and this one is chronologically the first. The Letter to the Hebrews says: *'This Melchizedek was the king of the city of Salem, and also a priest of the Most High God. When Abraham was returning home after winning a great battle against many kings, Melchizedek met him and blessed him; then Abraham took a tenth of all he had won in the battle and gave it to Melchizedek. Melchizedek's name means "Justice," so he is the King of Justice; and he is also the King of Peace because the name of his city is Salem, which means "Peace". Melchizedek had no father or mother and there is no record of any of his ancestors. He was never born and never died but his life is like that of the Son of God – a priest forever'* (Hebrews 7:1–3, Living Bible). The rest of the chapter goes on to talk about Melchizedek and his priesthood. For an explanation of the meaning of the Hebrew text 'U'MALKI-TZEDEK MELLEK SHALLEM' (which is translated 'And Melchizedek king of Salem'), see an article by Dov Chaikin entitled 'After the Order of?' in *Tishrei*, Volume 1, Number 2, Winter 1992/93, published by Dr Clifford Denton, The Orchard, 5 The Street, Gillingham, Beccles, Suffolk, NR34 0LH.

12. Joseph H. Hunting, *Jerusalem! Jerusalem!* (Melbourne: The David Press, 1973), p. 10.

13. *Diaspora*, which comes from the Greek word meaning 'dispersion', refers to the Jewish people living outside the Land of Israel. By implication, it also refers to the period of time the Jewish people have been dispersed from the land since the destruction of Jerusalem by the Romans.

14. The original 'Cyrus Cylinder' resides in the British Museum in London. Unfortunately the notes accompanying the artefact fail to mention the Decree of Cyrus found in the Bible specifically. However, an exact replica of the artefact, which resides in the Tower of David Museum in Jerusalem, does mention it – in fact that is the very reason for having it there.

15. Dr Arnold Fruchtenbaum writes: 'Many English versions [of the Bible] have translated the phrase to read "seventy weeks". But this translation is not totally accurate and has caused some confusion about the meaning of the passage. Most Jews know the Hebrew for "weeks" because of the observance of the Feast of Weeks, and that Hebrew word is *shavu'ot*. However the word which appears in the Hebrew text is *shavu'im*, which means "sevens". The word refers to a "seven" of anything, and the context determines the content of the seven. Here it is obvious that Daniel is thinking in terms of years – specifically the 70 years of the captivity. Daniel had assumed both that the captivity would end after 70 years and that the [Messianic] kingdom would be established after 70 years. But here Gabriel was using a play upon words in the Hebrew text, pointing out that insofar as Messiah's kingdom was concerned, it was not "70 years", but "70 sevens of years" – a total of 490 years.' Quoted from Dr Arnold Fruchtenbaum, *The Messianic Time Table* (Ariel Ministries, 1985).

16. The term 'Evangelical' is used to describe Christians who believe that the original manuscripts of the Bible i.e. the whole of the Old and New Testaments (but excluding the Apocrypha) contain the entire infallible 'Word of God'.

17. There are some scholars who believe that the decree of Cyrus, which is generally believed to have taken place in 538 BCE, marks the beginning of the 'Seventy Weeks'. This would bring the end of the sixty-ninth 'week' to around 55 BCE. However, authors E.J. Young and Dr David Lurie believe the Hebrew word *shavu'im* can refer to a period of seven years or periods of time which can be any integer multiple of 7 years – e.g. 7 years, 14 years, 49 years or 140 years. 'Armed with this new insight on the length of Daniel's weeks,' Dr Lurie writes, 'we can go ahead and make sense of the "seven weeks and "sixty-two weeks" which, according to the prophecy, must elapse from *"the command to restore and build Jerusalem until Messiah the Prince"* (Daniel 9:25). To see this, all we need to do is take 7 "weeks" of fourteen years and 62 "weeks" of seven years.' This calculation brings us to the year 6 BC, which Dr Lurie believes

is the year Messiah the Prince was born. See David Lurie, *The Covenant, The Holocaust and The Seventieth Week* (Coral Gables, Florida, USA, Messianic Century, 1988), pp. 21 and 22.

18.   Some scholars, including Herman Goldwag, believe the date of this decree by King Artaxerxes was nine years earlier in 454 BCE. The end of the 69-week period of seven years each (a total of 483 years) would then be in 29 CE.

19.   Fruchtenbaum, *The Messianic Time Table*. Some of the modern translations of the Bible render a different translation. For instance the New International Version says, *'the Anointed One will be cut off and will have nothing.'* Dr Fruchtenbaum says that the Hebrew text can legitimately be translated either way. The Living Bible, which is a paraphrase as distinct from a literal translation of the Scriptures, renders this phrase as follows: *'the Anointed One will be killed, His Kingdom still unrealised . . . '*

20.   Hunting, *Jerusalem! Jerusalem!*, pp. 18 and 19. Sir Robert Anderson calculated the start date of the 69 weeks as 1 Nisan in the Jewish calendar (14 March 445 BCE). Based on the Lunar or prophetic year of 360 days, 483 years would amount to 173,880 days which would bring us to 10 Nisan – the precise day on which the Messiah is recorded as entering Jerusalem (Matthew 21:1–9) in 32 CE. Working on a standard solar year, the period from 14 March 445 BCE to 6 April (10 Nisan) 32 CE also adds up to 173,880 days. There is considerable difference of opinion among Christian Bible scholars over the date of the crucifixion of Jesus Christ, but all agree it was at Passover, and nearly all agree it was between the years 29 and 33 CE.

21.   *Yeshua HaMashiach* is the original Hebrew name of the One whom Christians believe to be the Messiah. The name literally means 'Jesus the Messiah'. The Lord's name, Jesus – as it is commonly used throughout the English-speaking Church – is an anglicised transliteration of His name, *Iesous*, which was used in the Greek New Testament. However, He was Jewish from the line of David and He was given a Hebrew name. His parents were told to call Him *'Yeshua'*, *'for He shall save His people from their sins'* (Matthew 1:21). The name *Yeshua* is a contracted form of *Y'hoshua* which means 'YHWH is salvation' or 'YHWH – the eternally existing One – saves'. In the Jewish New Testament the Lord's Name is rendered as *Yeshua*. The Lord's title – 'Christ' – which Christians commonly use, is derived from the Greek word *Christos* which is equivalent to the Hebrew word *Mashiach*. *HaMashiach* literally means 'the Anointed One'. For a further study of the Name of the

Almighty, and the Messiah, the author recommends *The Name Above All Names*, written by Don Stanton and published by the Maranatha Revival Crusade, Secunderabad, India.

22. This was not Yeshua's first visit to the Temple. His first visit was when He was dedicated to the Lord after the completion of His mother's purification according to the *Torah* (Jewish Law). He went on to visit and teach in the Temple a number of times, so this prophecy was fulfilled on more than one occasion. The second Temple, which was being rebuilt by Herod at the time, and was from all accounts more spectacular than even Solomon's Temple, had neither the Presence of the Lord nor the Ark of the Covenant dwelling in it as Solomon's Temple had. However, the Lord did visit the Temple in the person of the Messiah in fulfilment of Malachi 3:1.

23. Yeshua is referred to as *'the Lamb of God'* in many parts of the New Testament. The Apostle Paul says: 'For indeed Messiah, our Passover, was sacrificed for us' (1 Corinthians 5:7). Perhaps unknown to most Jewish people, Yeshua's death, burial and resurrection are all symbolised in the traditional Jewish Passover Seder. Most significantly, the sacrificing of a lamb without blemish and the shedding of its blood is a picture of His atoning death for the sins of the world. The Cup of Redemption is the cup He described as symbolising the New Covenant (Jeremiah 31:31–34) which was ratified by the shedding of His own blood for the remission of sins. This not only fulfils the prophecy in Daniel 9:24, but also the requirement for the atonement for sin found in the *Torah* in Leviticus 17:11, in which the Lord God of Israel states: *'For the life of the flesh is in the blood, and I have given it to you upon the altar to make atonement for your souls; for it is the blood that makes atonement for the soul.'*

24. The *Torah*, or Law of Moses, which constitutes the first five books of the Jewish Scriptures, commanded the Jewish people to keep seven feasts, which are listed in Leviticus 23. During three of the feasts, *Pesach* (Passover), *Shavu'ot* (The Feast of Weeks or Pentecost), and *Sukkot* (The Feast of Tabernacles), all Israeli males had to appear before the Lord (Exodus 23:14–17) in the Tabernacle. When the Temple was built in Jerusalem, that was where they had to go.

25. Among Evangelical Christians (see note 16) there are three main eschatological viewpoints concerning the return of Jesus Christ and what is often termed as 'the Millennium'. 'The Millennium' refers to the reign of the Messiah upon the earth

which was implied repeatedly by the prophets of Israel. A number of times in Revelation 20 the reign of Jesus Christ on the earth is identified as being one thousand years long, hence the term 'Millennium'. The 'pre-millennial' view is that Christ will return to earth before the Millennium and reign from Jerusalem for a thousand years, which is what Revelation 20 indicates. The 'post-millennial' view is that the Millennium happens before the return of Christ. Those who hold this view believe that the Church will rule the world for a thousand years while Jesus rules in heaven. The theory is that the Church will evangelise the world and that there will be mass revival to the extent that evil on the earth will be virtually eradicated, and that the Church will hand over a near-perfect world to Christ when He returns. And the 'a-millennial' view is that there is no Millennium at all, and no earthly reign of Christ. This view is popular among those Christians who believe that God has finished with Israel.

26. The main precedent for believing there can be an indefinite time gap between two parts of a prophecy is taken from an example given by Yeshua in Luke 4:16–21, where He was identifying Himself as the fulfilment of Isaiah 61:1–2. Yeshua closed the book after quoting the passage from Isaiah 61:2 that says *'to proclaim the acceptable year of the Lord'* and left out the following part of the verse that says *'and the day of vengeance of our God'*. Clearly *'the acceptable year of the Lord'* was His fulfilment of the prophecy during the time in which He was living, and *'the day of vengeance of our God'* – also part of the same prophecy – He would fulfil at some time in the future, when He returns to judge the earth (see Matthew 25:31–46).

27. Herman Goldwag, *Daniel's 70 Weeks Prophecy,* pp. 33 and 36.

28. Thomas Ice and Randall Price, *Ready to Rebuild* (Eugene, Oregon, USA: Harvest House Publishers, 1992), p. 70.

29. Ibid.

Chapter 3: Jerusalem and the Diaspora

30. Shimon Bar Kokhba was one of the first of a long line of people, some Jewish and others Gentile, who was to be proclaimed Messiah. Some still have great followings today, such as Mohammed and Buddha. The twentieth century saw its share of both spiritual and political 'Messiahs'. The Baghwan Rajneesh and Adolf Hitler are two examples. The most recent Jewish example was Lubavitcher Rebbe Menahem Mendel

Schneerson, who was proclaimed to be the Messiah by his ultra-orthodox sect. He died in 1994, aged 92, having never actually set foot in Israel. In Matthew 24, Yeshua warns of false Messiahs and false prophets who would deceive many, especially in the end-times. As we will examine later, the greatest of the false Messiahs is yet to come.

31. The Holy Land was never known as 'Palestine' until the Bar Kokhba revolt was quelled by the Romans in 135 CE. Before that the Roman provinces in the Holy Land were known by their historical names, i.e. Judea, Samaria and Galilee. The Romans plainly intended to insult the Jews by the choice of the name 'Syria Palaestina' which was derived from the Philistines, Israel's ancient enemy who dwelt on the coastal plain where Gaza is today. See David Dolan, *Israel at the Crossroads* (Grand Rapids, MI, USA: Fleming H. Revell, a division of Baker Book House Company, 1998), p. 65. (A previous version of this book was first published under the title *Holy War for the Promised Land*, Hodder and Stoughton, 1991.)

32. This prophecy is often confused with the Babylonian exile, which was basically to one city and one country a few hundred miles to the east of Jerusalem – Babylon. Lamentations 1:3 tells us that this exile is to be *'among the nations'* plural, and therefore must refer to the *Diaspora* that began in 70 CE.

33. *Letter to the Community of the Jews*, No. 51, 396–398, in W.C. Wright, *The Works of the Emperor Julian*, 1913–1923, 3 Vols.

34. Thomas Ice and Randall Price, *Ready to Rebuild* (Eugene, Oregon, USA: Harvest House Publishers, 1992), p. 30.

35. 'Replacement Theology' takes the view that the Church has become 'the new Israel' and has replaced the Jewish people – 'the old Israel' – in the purposes of God. This theological standpoint not only denies the literal fulfilment of many of the promises of God to the nation of Israel found in the Old Testament (including the New Covenant) but it also contradicts the teaching of the New Testament concerning Israel, particularly what the Apostle Paul has to say in Romans 9, 10 and 11 – this will be discussed further in Chapter 10 of this book. Sadly, 'Replacement Theology' lies at the root of anti-Semitism practised by the Church through the centuries. The Crusades and the Spanish Inquisition are examples of this. One of the great leaders of the Reformation, Martin Luther, believed that God had finished with the Jews, and his theological

position seems to be one of the excuses offered for the Third Reich's 'final solution'. Unfortunately, 'Replacement Theology' continues to be popular in churches today despite the dramatic fulfilment of biblical prophecy in our generation, especially with the rebirth of Israel and the reunification of Jerusalem under Jewish sovereignty. For a biblical analysis of the teachings of 'Replacement Theology' we recommend a leaflet, *Is the Church the "New Israel?"* by Keith Parker, published by Prayer For Israel, PO Box 328, Bromley, Kent BR1 2ZS, UK.

36. Dolan, *Israel at the Crossroads*, p. 66.

37. Mark Twain, *The Innocents Abroad* (London, 1881).

38. Andrew Bonar, *Memoir and Remains of R.M. M'Cheyne* (London: Banner of Truth, 1966) p. 87.

39. Ibid., pp. 102–3. Robert Murray M'Cheyne once said in a lecture, '. . . we might anticipate an outpouring of the Spirit when our Church should outstretch its hands to the Jew as well as the Gentile.' In one letter he says: 'To seek the lost sheep of the house of Israel is an object very near to my heart, as my people know it has ever been. Such an enterprise may probably draw down unspeakable blessings on the Church of Scotland, according to the promise, "They shall prosper who love Thee" ' (p. 87). His words, it seems, were to be prophetic, for when he returned from the Holy Land, he found that Revival had broken out in Scotland (ibid., pp. 87–88).

40. Is it possible that the Lord's reference to Zion being inscribed on the palms of His hands is a prophetic insight to Yeshua's crucifixion, when the nails were driven through His hands, thus ratifying the New Covenant – the everlasting *'covenant of peace'* mentioned in Isaiah 54:10?

41. Interview with Teddy Kollek, former Mayor of Jerusalem, in the original version of the documentary film *Jerusalem, The Covenant City* (1981), produced by the author for David House Fellowship.

42. These prophecies that speak of the Lord returning to Zion, choosing Jerusalem again, and regathering the Jewish people from among the nations or, as in this prophecy, *'the four corners of the earth'*, are often misrepresented by those who hold the view that the nation of Israel no longer has any place in the purposes of God, and has been replaced by the Church. They say that these prophecies were fulfilled by the return of the Jews to Jerusalem from the Babylonian captivity. Might this be because if one applies these prophecies to the Church,

they obviously make no sense? For several reasons these prophecies cannot apply to the return of the Jews after the Babylonian captivity. Firstly, the prophet Zechariah was writing his book after the first wave of exiles had already returned to Jerusalem, and they were actually rebuilding the Temple at that time. If the 'replacement theologians' are to be believed, then Zechariah was prophesying (future tense) about something that had already happened, or was actually happening then and there. Secondly, as seen earlier in note 32, the exiles were taken to a location several hundred miles to the east of Jerusalem, and it was from this area that they came back under the leadership of Zerubbabel. Isaiah, in this prophecy, specifically tells us that not only are the exiles being gathered from *'the four corners of the earth'*, but they are being gathered *'again the second time'*. Later in the book we will see that the prophets – particularly Isaiah, Jeremiah and Ezekiel – speak of the exiles returning from 'among all the nations' where the Lord had scattered them – from the north, the west, the south, as well as the east. By their very description, these prophecies cannot possibly refer to the return after the Babylonian exile. And yet their description graphically coincides with the regathering we witnessed throughout the twentieth century, and continue to witness today. The God of Israel is fulfilling His Word before our very eyes!

43. The Apostle Jacob became known as James in the English-speaking world after the Reformation. His actual Hebrew name was Ya'akov. All of the twelve Apostles were Jewish and most of their names have become anglicised. For example, Matthew's name was Mattityahu, John was Yochanan, Peter was Kefa, Paul (or Saul) Sha'ul. All the New Testament writers were Jewish with the possible exception of Luke.

Chapter 4: Jerusalem and the Rebirth of the Nation

44. Robert St. John, *The Tongue of the Prophets* (New York: Country Life Press, 1952), pp. 45 and 46.

45. *Aliyah* is a Hebrew word which means 'to go up' or 'ascend'. 'Making *aliyah*' is the term used by Jewish people when they emigrate and go home to Israel.

46. St. John, *The Tongue of the Prophets*.

47. This interpretation of the fulfilment of this prophecy is one held by many pre-millennial Evangelical Christians, and is probably quite legitimate. However, the prophecy may also

have other applications. The Hebrew word *saphah*, translated in this verse as 'language', is also used in Isaiah 6:5, and translated as 'lip'. The implication here is that the people will be cleansed of profanity, rather than necessarily speaking the Hebrew language. Another possible (and more ambitious) interpretation of the prophecy according to some, which could have its ultimate fulfilment in the Messianic era, is that all the peoples – including Gentiles – will be speaking Hebrew when they come to worship the Lord. In other words Hebrew may replace English as the common world language. Or it may even be the language of heaven! Whether this is correct or not remains to be seen.

48. Murray Dixon, *Whose Promised Land?* (New Zealand: Heinemann, 1991), p. 8.
49. Ibid., p. 8.
50. St. John, *The Tongue of the Prophets,* p. 249.
51. Dixon, *Whose Promised Land?* p. 17.
52. Ibid., p. 16.
53. From the documentary film *The Last Generation* (1977) produced by the author for David House Productions.
54. Dixon, *Whose Promised Land?,* pp. 20 and 21.
55. During the late nineteenth century and the first half of the twentieth century, it was the Jewish people living in Palestine – including those who had made *aliyah* – who were referred to as 'the Palestinians'. Ironically it was a term rejected by the Arabs living in Palestine at the time.
56. Dixon, *Whose Promised Land?,* p. 26.
57. Ibid., p. 27.
58. Ibid., p. 28.
59. Part of a speech made by Winston Churchill in the House of Commons on 26 January 1949, taken from *In the Balance*, Speeches 1949–1950 by Winston S. Churchill, edited by Randolph S. Churchill (London: Cassel and Co. Ltd., 1951).
60. The *Haganah* was an armed Jewish resistance group formed to protect Jewish villages and settlements from armed attacks by Arabs. As such, under the British Mandate it was illegal for Jews in Palestine to bear arms, yet the British were often unwilling to defend them. While the British often turned a blind eye to Arabs who bore arms, Jews with weapons were often executed if caught.
61. By not voting for the Partition Resolution, Britain was openly reneging on both the Balfour Declaration and the terms of the Mandate given by the League of Nations in 1920. In effect, the

Britain that had been so sympathetic to the Jewish people had now double-crossed them. Her treatment of Jewish refugees, both before and after the Holocaust, can only be described as cruel, to say the least. The *Exodus* incident in 1947 was just one example of Britain's dealings with the Jewish people, and was one of the factors that influenced the UNSCOP Committee to recommend the formation of a Jewish State. An interesting observation about Britain's dealings with the Jews is that from 1947 the British Empire began to crumble. Could this be the outworking of the principle found in the Abrahamic Covenant (Genesis 12:3)? For further investigation of this, the author recommends *Curse or Coincidence?* by Joseph H. Hunting (The David Press, 1969). It seems that Britain's stance has not altered, for in May 1994 Prime Minister John Major said, 'The British Government does not recognise Israeli sovereignty over any part of Jerusalem.' This policy continued under Tony Blair, who endorsed a similar stand by the European Union.

62. This is part of a wider prophecy relating to the end-times in regard to the nations' dealings with Israel. No doubt, the dividing of the Lord's land by the nations of the world is a process that will continue until Messiah returns to judge the nations (Joel 3:12).

63. Dixon, *Whose Promised Land?*, p. 56.

64. This was said by Abdul Khader Husseini, cousin to the Mufti of Jerusalem. Quoted from *O Jerusalem!* by Larry Collins and Dominique Lapierre (George Weidenfeld and Nicolson Ltd, 1972).

65. For a fuller account of the history of this period the author recommends the very well-documented book *O Jerusalem!* by Larry Collins and Dominique Lapierre, paperback by Pan Books.

66. *Kibbutzim* is the plural of the Hebrew word *kibbutz*. A kibbutz is a co-operative venture which is owned by the members of the community who work it and live in it. Most of them were co-operative farms in which all possessions and equipment were purchased and owned by the community rather than by individuals. Nowadays many of them have branched out from agriculture into other forms of industry, including tourism. The *kibbutzim* were the backbone of the agricultural and economic development in Palestine in the first half of the twentieth century. For security reasons they were often established near borders or in exposed parts of the country.

67. The Living Bible rendition reads: *'Who has heard or seen anything as strange as this? For in one day, suddenly, a nation, Israel, shall be born, even before the birthpains come. In a moment, just as Israel's anguish starts, the baby is born; the nation begins'* (Isaiah 66:8–9). Some Bible scholars believe this prophecy refers to the spiritual rebirth of Israel rather than the physical rebirth. The author is of the opinion it could apply to either or, more likely, both.

68. Dixon, *Whose Promised Land?*, p. 54.

69. Ibid., p. 54.

70. Quoted from a speech by Ezer Weizman made 26 years later – on the occasion of his signing The Jerusalem Covenant, as the newly-elected President of Israel on *Yom Yerushalayim* (Jerusalem Day), 19 May 1993. Courtesy of Hatikvah Film Foundation.

71. Joseph H. Hunting, *Jerusalem! Jerusalem!* (Melbourne: The David Press, 1973), p. 24.

72. Part of a speech made by Winston Churchill in the House of Commons on 26 January 1949, quoted from Churchill (ed.), *In the Balance*.

Chapter 5: The Reunification of Jerusalem

73. Quoted from President Ezer Weizman's speech on the occasion of his signing The Jerusalem Covenant on *Yom Yerushalayim*, 19 May 1993. Courtesy of Hatikvah Film Foundation.

74. From an interview by Jimmy de Young with Gershon Salomon, 24 June 1991, quoted in Thomas Ice and Randall Price, *Ready to Rebuild* (Eugene, Oregon, USA: Harvest House Publishers, 1991), p. 121.

75. The reunification of Jerusalem in 1967 was at least a partial fulfilment of the conclusion of the Lord's prophecy in Luke 21:24. However, I believe its final and complete fulfilment lies in the future for two reasons. Firstly, while the Temple Mount in theory is under Jewish sovereignty, in practice it is under the control of the *Waqf*. The Jews are still denied access to it and, as long as it remains as a holy shrine to the Moslem religion, it is still being trampled on by the Gentiles. Secondly, the prophetic Scriptures tell us that the anti-Christ will control (and defile) the Holy Place and ravage the Holy City for a period of three and a half years prior to the Messiah's return, which will be discussed further in Chapter 9. As a result, it seems possible that the Jewish State may lose its sovereignty

over Jerusalem for that period. Recently, there have been moves afoot to revive UN Resolution 181 of 1947 to make Jerusalem international territory, and it is always possible these moves may be revived as a result of the 'final status' negotiations over Jerusalem. The Vatican, among others, favours this scenario (the Vatican's aspirations for Jerusalem will be discussed in Chapter 7).

76. David Dolan, *Israel at the Crossroads* (Grand Rapids, MI, USA: Fleming H. Revell, 1998), p. 137.

77. Victor Mordechai, *Is Fanatic Islam a Global Threat?* (January 1995) and *Christian Revival for Israel's Survival* (July 1999). This also applies to UN Resolution 338 which was passed after the 'Yom Kippur' War of 1973.

78. Those three States are Egypt, Jordan and Morocco. On 19 November 1977, President Anwar Sadat of Egypt made history by visiting Jerusalem and stretching out the hand of peace to Israel. A formal Peace Treaty was signed between the two countries at Camp David on 26 March 1979. Subsequently, Israel returned all territory gained from Egypt in the Six-Day War, with the exception of the Gaza Strip which Egypt did not want. Anwar Sadat was assassinated in October 1981. On 25 July 1994, on the lawns of the White House in Washington, King Hussein of Jordan and Prime Minister Yitzhak Rabin signed a 'Non-Belligerency' Agreement with a view to normalising relations. A formal Peace Treaty between the two nations was signed in the Jordan Valley three months later. Previously, Jordan had waived its right to the territory it lost to Israel in the Six-Day War in favour of the PLO, which recognised Israel in a similar ceremony on the lawns of the White House on 13 September 1993. At the time of writing Syria had begun a dialogue with Israel after a long silence, while at the same time continuing to build up her offensive weaponry, including a nuclear capability. Western leaders are optimistic that the ailing Syrian president, Hafez al-Assad, finally wants to make peace with the Jewish State if he can get back all of the Golan Heights, which he lost to Israel in 1967. However, some Middle East analysts seriously doubt Assad's good intentions, believing he wants the Golan purely for its strategic advantage in a war against Israel. It is interesting to note that there is a prophecy in Isaiah 17:1 which tells us that Damascus, one of the oldest continuously inhabited cities of the world, will cease to be a city and become a heap of ruins. This prophecy has never yet been fulfilled.

79. For the first time since its destruction by Nebuchadnezzar, in 1967 Jerusalem was under the control of the Jews as a sovereign nation. However, it has had four brief periods under Jewish control: firstly, the Maccabees in the second century BCE; secondly, the rebellion against Rome in 66 to 70 CE; thirdly, the Bar Kokhba revolt in 132–5 CE; and fourthly, three years under the Persians between 614 and 638 CE.

80. Quoted from Joseph H. Hunting in the documentary film *The Last Generation,* produced by the author for David House Fellowship in 1977.

81. *'Olim'* is the plural of the Hebrew word *'oleh'* which means immigrant.

82. Ma'ale Adumim and Mevasseret Zion, at the time of writing, adjoin the municipal boundaries of the city of Jerusalem. Another suburb which was very much in the international spotlight in the late 1990s, Har Homa, is inside the municipal boundaries. Har Homa will be discussed on pp. 159–161.

83. Victor Mordechai, *Is Fanatic Islam a Global Threat?* (January 1995) and *Christian Revival for Israel's Survival* (July 1999). Israel returned half of the Golan Heights to Syria (2 per cent of the total territory won by Israel in 1967) after the Yom Kippur War in 1973. Then all of the Sinai was returned to Egypt in 1981 (91 per cent of the total territory won by Israel in 1967) following the signing of a peace treaty (see Appendix F, maps 5 and 6). At the time of writing, Israel was in the process of withdrawing from further territory in Judea and Samaria as part of the Oslo Accords and subsequent agreements.

84. The Knesset is the Parliament of Israel. The single House, situated in West Jerusalem, has 120 seats. At that time the right-wing Likud party was in power under Prime Minister Menachem Begin.

85. These comments from Shimon Peres and Yitzhak Rabin were quoted from interviews in the original version of the documentary film *Jerusalem, The Covenant City* produced by the author for David House Productions in 1981. Yitzhak Rabin (as Prime Minister of Israel) reiterated his remarks on several later occasions.

86. A number of nations, including Great Britain, already had their embassies in Tel Aviv.

87. Quoted from an interview with Johann Lückhoff filmed by the author in April 1981 for the original version of the documentary film *Jerusalem, The Covenant City.*

88. This is quoted from a publication of the International Christian Embassy, Jerusalem. The ICEJ has held a celebration of the Feast of Tabernacles every year since, attended by up to 6,000 pilgrims from more than 100 nations. Further information about this can be obtained from the ICEJ, PO Box 1192, Jerusalem 91010, Israel.

89. Christian organisations involved in this sort of ministry include: Ebenezer Emergency Fund, Ebenezer House, 5a Poole Road, Bournemouth, BH2 5QJ, England – tel.: +44 1202 294455, fax: +44 1202 295550; Christian Friends of Israel, PO Box 1813, Jerusalem, 91015, Israel – tel.: +972 2 626 4172; the ICEJ, PO Box 1192, Jerusalem 91010, Israel – tel.: +972 2 566 9823; Bridges For Peace, 7 Shaul Adler, Jerusalem, Israel – tel.: +972 2 624 5004, fax: +972 2 624 6622. All of these organisations have national offices in some western countries. A Messianic Jewish organisation with a similar ministry is: Vision For Israel, PO Box 7265, Jerusalem 91073, Israel – tel.: +972 2 570 4010, fax: +972 2 570 4011.

90. *'Eretz Yisrael'* is the Hebrew for the 'Land of Israel'.

91. The words of the late Israeli Prime Minister on that occasion are singled out for rebuke by the Lord in the *Tanakh*, for He says: *'What you have in your mind shall never be, when you say, "We shall be like the Gentiles, like the families in other countries . . . "'* (Ezekiel 20:32).

92. Quoted from an article by Michele Chabin in *The Australian Jewish Times*, 29 May 1992.

93. Quoted from a speech by Ezer Weizman on the occasion of his signing The Jerusalem Covenant, as the newly-elected President of Israel on *Yom Yerushalayim*, 19 May 1993. Courtesy of Hatikvah Film Foundation.

94. Moslems may claim that Allah is the same God as YHWH, the God of Israel. The God of the Koran, Allah, is so different to the God of the Hebrew Scriptures, not only in terms of his character, but also his dealings with human beings, that to all intents and purposes he is not the same God as YHWH at all. Allah is portrayed as having discarded the covenants of promise because of the unfaithfulness of the Christians and Jews. However, YHWH is a God who will keep all His covenants, particularly the Abrahamic and New Covenants which are unconditional and everlasting.

95. Excerpts from an article in the 'Opinion' column of *The Jerusalem Post* (International Edition, week ending 29 May 1993) entitled 'Battle for the Holy City', written by Eliyahu Tal.

Chapter 6: Jerusalem – the Capital of Palestine?

96. Murray Dixon, *Whose Promised Land?* (New Zealand: Heinemann, 1991), p. 98.

97. The Palestine Liberation Organisation (PLO) was formed in January 1964 when President Nasser of Egypt called together Arab heads of state and revolutionaries to discuss the problems of the Palestinian Arabs and Israel. The gathering voted to appropriate finance for the new organisation and a total of 422 representative members of the Palestinian Arab people were appointed to the Palestine National Council that ruled the PLO, and still does today. Later in 1964 the Palestine National Council held its first conference in East Jerusalem (then under Jordanian control) and resolved to 'liberate Palestine'. The *Palestinian National Covenant*, which calls for the liquidation of the State of Israel, was adopted as the basic law of the PLO. This covenant states 'the partition of Palestine in 1947 and the establishment of the State of Israel are entirely illegal', 'the Balfour Declaration, the Mandate for Palestine and everything based upon them, are deemed null and void', 'the demands of security and peace, as well as the demands of right and justice, require all states to consider Zionism an illegal movement'. The covenant goes on to state the means to achieve this end: 'Armed struggle is the only way to liberate Palestine … The Palestinian Arab people assert their absolute determination and firm resolution to continue their armed struggle and to work for an armed popular revolution for the liberation of their country and their return to it.' Quoted by Murray Dixon in *Whose Promised Land?* (New Zealand, Heinemann, 1991), p. 80. At the fifth National Council meeting in February, 1969, in Cairo, Yasser Arafat was elected chairman of the PLO. The PLO was active in pursuing these aims with many horrific terrorist attacks in Israel and around the world over the next three decades. Following the signing of Oslo I and Oslo II, Yasser Arafat was under pressure to renounce terrorism publicly, as a means to achieve his aims.

98. Ibid., p. 90.

99. Ibid., quoted from an interview with Abu Iyad, deputy leader of the PLO in the Lebanese newspaper *Al-Safir* on 25 January 1988. In view of the stated aims of the PLO (see note 97) the term 'the entire territory of Palestine' can only be interpreted to mean the whole of the Land of Israel.

100. It is not possible within the scope of this book to examine fully how and why the bias of reporting of Middle East affairs by the media became so 'anti-Israel'. However, these are two brief examples of such bias: (1) the emergence and activities of another radical Islamic terrorist organisation – HAMAS – went more or less unreported until the upsurge in terrorism against Israel following the signing of the Declaration of Principles in late 1993; (2) the murder by HAMAS and the PLO of many hundreds of Palestinian Arabs who would not support the *Intifada* went virtually unreported, as did the fact that HAMAS and the PLO killed many more Palestinian Arabs than the Israelis did.

101. From an interview by Jimmy de Young with Gershon Salomon, 24 June 1991, quoted in Thomas Ice and Randall Price, *Ready to Rebuild* (Eugene, Oregon, USA: Harvest House Publishers, 1991), p. 125.

102. Ibid., p. 123.

103. Ibid., p. 124.

104. David Dolan, *Israel at the Crossroads* (Grand Rapids, MI, USA: Fleming H. Revell, 1998), pp. 11–15.

105. Ice and Price, *Ready to Rebuild*, p. 16.

106. There have been reports that there is an ancient tunnel that leads under the Temple Mount to a place where the Temple treasures, including the Ark of the Covenant, are rumoured to be hidden. There is a shrine halfway along the Western Wall Tunnel that marks the point which archaeologists and rabbis believe is the closest accessible point (for Jews) to where the Temple stood. At that point there is a sealed entrance known as Warren's Gate, behind which there is an ancient tunnel leading under the Temple Mount. This tunnel was explored by the late Rabbis Schlomo Goren (former Chief Rabbi) and Yehuda Getz in 1981 (see Ice and Price, *Ready to Rebuild*, chapter 11). The two rabbis were prevented from completing their investigations after being attacked by Moslems. The ancient tunnel was then sealed and archaeologists have since been refused permission to explore under the Temple Mount. Consequently, it may be a long time before we find out what, if anything, is hidden there. The Western Wall Tunnel is open to the public and a visit is strongly recommended. It is necessary to book a tour several days in advance. Bookings can be made with the Western Wall Heritage Foundation on (02) 627 1333 in Jerusalem.

107. Quoted from interviews with Yasser Arafat on 25 September 1996, shown on both American Broadcasting Corporation and Israel Television news bulletins.

108. Iraq's possession of chemical and biological weapons was a proven fact, as Saddam Hussein had already slaughtered thousands of Iraqi Kurds with them. However, it was not until 1995, when two of Saddam's daughters fled Iraq with their husbands to seek asylum in Jordan, that the extent of Iraq's nuclear programme was finally revealed. When debriefed, Saddam's sons-in-law, one of whom had been in charge of Iraq's nuclear development programme, informed Western intelligence experts that Iraq was only weeks from exploding her first nuclear device when the Allies started bombing Iraq in January 1991. Saddam's sons-in-law were later lured back to Iraq and murdered.

109. The Feast of *Purim* (Esther 9:26) commemorates the occasion when the Jewish people were delivered from genocide at the hands of Haman, the son of Hammedatha the Agagite, during the Babylonian exile. The deliverance occurred due to the vigilance of Mordecai as well as the fasting and intercession of Queen Esther.

110. The Phased Plan was adopted by the PLO in June 1974. Its aim is to destroy Israel in stages – in accordance with the Palestinian National Covenant (see note 97), often referred to as the Palestinian Charter. Article 2 of this plan calls for the establishment of a Palestinian State on any territory vacated by Israel. Article 8 calls for the subsequent use of that State as a base for a combined Arab assault against the geographically truncated State of Israel.

111. Edom was the area east of the Dead Sea, now situated in modern Jordan. The Edomites were descendants of Jacob's twin brother, Esau. Today, the area is mostly inhabited by Palestinian Arabs who make up about 70 per cent of Jordan's population.

112. From an article entitled *'Jihad* for Jerusalem' by Tony Pearce in *Prophecy Today*, volume 10, no. 5, published by Prophetic Word Ministries ISSN 0267–9000, London.

113. Ibid.

114. This prophecy is a word from the Lord to the 'Philistines'. At the time Isaiah lived, the Philistines were approaching extinction as an identifiable ethnic entity. Certainly today there are no identifiable descendants of the Philistines. However, there is a people who bear the name of the Philistines (see note 31)

and they are the modern 'Palestinian' Arabs, some of whom claim they are descended from the Philistines. Interestingly enough, the area inhabited by the Philistines – Gaza – is now almost entirely populated by 'Palestinian' Arabs, who have autonomous government there. Is it possible that the Lord was speaking to a future people who would bear the name of the Philistines? Another interesting aspect to this particular prophecy is that it follows on from another end-time prophecy in the same chapter – against Lucifer (Isaiah 14:12–17), which we shall consider in Chapter 9.

115. At that time, January 1996, Shimon Peres had been Israel's Prime Minister for two months following Yitzhak Rabin's assassination. Yossi Beilin was a minister in the Rabin government, and at the outset had been the main architect of the 'Oslo' process, acting under the authority of Shimon Peres as Foreign Minister.

116. *Christian Friends of Israel News Digest*, March 1996, written by David Dolan. This monthly journal is written by Christian journalists living in Jerusalem and published by Christian Friends of Israel, PO Box 1813, Jerusalem 91015, Israel. Alternatively you can visit their website at: www.cfijerusalem.org

117. Ibid., June 1996.

118. Ibid.

119. Ibid., January 1999.

120. Quoted from an interview with David Bar-Illan by David Dolan, filmed for the documentary *Jerusalem, The Covenant City*, 2 December 1999.

121. Quoted from an interview with the Mayor of Jerusalem by David Dolan, filmed for the documentary *Jerusalem, The Covenant City*, 2 December 1999.

Chapter 7: Jerusalem Becomes a Burdensome Stone

122. 'Peres Sells Jerusalem To The Vatican' in *Prayer For Israel – New Zealand – Newsletter* Number 79, November/December 1994. Courtesy: Inside Israel, Israel's Investigative News Source.

123. From *The Feast Of Tabernacles* video (1993) filmed by the International Christian Embassy Jerusalem. This was a statement he reiterated in a BBC television interview with Jane Corbin in June 1994 and again at a similar Feast of Tabernacles gathering during the *Jerusalem 3000* celebrations in October 1995, just a month before his assassination. However, there

were many in the audience on that last occasion who doubted the Prime Minister's sincerity.

124. 'Peres Sells Jerusalem To The Vatican' in *Prayer For Israel – New Zealand – Newsletter* Number 79, November/December 1994. Courtesy: Inside Israel, Israel's Investigative News Source.

125. *Christian Friends of Israel News Digest*, September 1994, written by David Dolan.

126. From an article by Ariel Sharon entitled 'A Sickness in Jerusalem' published in *The Jerusalem Post* (International Edition, week ending 20 August, 1994).

127. *YESHA* stands for 'The Council of Jewish Communities in Judea, Samaria and Gaza' and the name is often used to identify the communities who live in the towns and cities in those areas. In the media, the *YESHA* communities are generally referred to as 'settlers', and the towns or cities in which they live as 'settlements'. These terms, which unfortunately are often used by Israelis as well as the media, can be misleading and tend to de-legitimise the existence of these communities – hence the popular PLO usage of the term 'settlement activity'.

128. Quoted from a speech given by Binyamin Netanyahu at the International Christian Embassy's Feast of Tabernacles' celebration in the International Conference Centre, Jerusalem, on Wednesday 11 October 1995.

129. *Christian Friends of Israel News Digest*, April 1997, written by Julie Stahl.

130. Ibid.

131. One of the main antagonists in the stand against Israel over Har Homa – the UN – has their Middle East headquarters on another hill south of the Old City which has a prophetically significant name. This other hill was the site originally chosen as the administrative headquarters during the British Mandate, and the United Nations took it over in 1948. The Hebrew name for the hill they chose – inadvertently one assumes – means 'the Hill of Evil Counsel'!

132. *ICEJ News*, 9 April 1999, compiled and written by Patrick Goodenough. This news bulletin is published two or three times every week and transmitted by e-mail. To subscribe, e-mail a blank message to: icej-news-service-subscribe@icej.org.il – and their monthly *Middle East Digest* is available on the Internet at http://www.icej.org.il

133. Christian Action For Israel Third Quarter Newsletter 1999, quoting *Jerusalem Dispatch*, August 1999.

134. *ICEJ News*, 3 December 1999, compiled by David Parsons for the International Christian Embassy, Jerusalem. Sources: *The Jerusalem Post, Israel Line, Ha'Aretz, CNN, Reuters, Associated Press, Arutz 7, Washington Post, Daily Telegraph*.

135. Quoted from an interview by Sir David Frost with Ehud Barak in *Breakfast With Frost* broadcast by BBC Television in Britain on Sunday 28 November 1999.

136. This does not mean that Israel will be wiped off the map or the Jewish people annihilated. The Lord has promised *never* to allow that to happen (Jeremiah 31:35–37). What many Christian intercessors fear is that Israel could pay very dearly for the 'peace' process, when it finally collapses, in terms of loss of life and damage to the nation's infrastructure.

137. Doubtless there are many other spiritual forces arrayed against both the natural and the spiritual seed of Abraham, Isaac and Jacob. One which is often mentioned in the Old Testament, and also in the Book of Revelation, is Babylon. Depending on the context, 'Babylon' sometimes refers to the literal Babylon – i.e. the place and the people. However, it can also refer to a demonic principality, which may or may not be the same as the 'Prince of Persia'. In the Book of Revelation, it seems that 'Babylon' is a powerful and wealthy counterfeit religious system. This may be either Islam or the apostate church establishment that has embraced 'New Age' religion, which is elsewhere described as 'the great harlot' (Revelation 17:5). Some Evangelical Christians regard Babylon as the source of most, if not all, false religion – i.e. 'religion' that is not sanctioned by the God of Abraham, Isaac and Jacob. As the literal city of ancient Babylon has been deserted for many centuries, following the fulfilment of Jeremiah 50:3, the city mentioned in Revelation 18 could refer to the city where the religious system has its seat of power. If this is not literal Babylon, then it could refer to Rome.

138. The Koran – the Islamic holy book – does not record Mohammed ever actually visiting Jerusalem during his lifetime. In fact he died six years before Jerusalem fell to the Arabs under Caliph Omar in 638 CE. Islam's claim to the Temple Mount, and particularly the rock over which the Dome of the Rock stands, is based on the legend that Mohammed rode on his magical winged steed, *al-Baraq*, from 'the sacred mosque' in Arabia to 'the farthest mosque' and on to heaven (Sura 17, the Koran). It was not until many years after the Koran appeared that Moslems began to claim that this 'farthest mosque' was in

Jerusalem, and so elevate the city to the third holiest in Islam, after Mecca and Medina. Even Islamic scholars differed over the issue for centuries. Jerusalem does not rate a single mention by name in the Koran, whereas it is mentioned many hundreds of times in the Hebrew Bible.

139. There are a number of differing theories among students of eschatology as to the timing of the fulfilment of the prophecy in Ezekiel 38/39 in relation to the Great Tribulation and the return of the Messiah. One theory is that it will be fulfilled between now and the start of the Great Tribulation, which many pre-millennial Evangelical Christians believe is the seven-year period known as the Seventieth Week of Daniel (which will be discussed further in Chapter 9) or 'the time of Jacob's trouble'. A second theory is that it will come to pass in the early part of the seven-year period. A third theory is that it will take place in the final three-and-a-half years (after the abomination of desolation has been set up in the Temple) and shortly before Armageddon. Another theory is that the Ezekiel 38/39 invasion is a description of the actual Battle of Armageddon, and yet another is that this prophecy describes the great rebellion led by Satan at the end of the thousand-year reign of Messiah on earth (Revelation 20:7–9); the reason put forward for this is that the passage in Revelation is the only other place in the Bible where 'Gog and Magog' (which also appear to be spiritual principalities) are mentioned together. However, the author believes that the latter scenario is unlikely and the fulfilment of this prophecy may well be quite soon.

140. The King James Version says in Ezekiel 39:2: ' "*And I will turn thee back and leave but the sixth part of thee . . .* " ' The Living Bible also refers to 85 per cent, but many of the modern versions, e.g. the New King James and the New International Version, do not give the percentage which perish, implying perhaps that all of the invading troops are killed (see v. 4). Verse 12 informs us that it will take seven months for Israel to bury the dead (see also vv. 17–20). Verse 9 tells us that the enemy weapons will provide fuel for Israel for the following seven years.

141. Bruce D. Reekie, *The Holy Spirit and Israel* (Tonbridge, England: Sovereign World, 1993), pp. 168 and 169.

Chapter 8: Jerusalem and the Rebuilding of the Temple

142. The Temple that the Jewish people are planning to rebuild is often referred to as 'the third Temple'. King Solomon built the

'first Temple', and the 'second Temple' was built by Zerubbabel in 515 BCE and destroyed by the Romans in 70 CE. There were in fact at least two, and possibly three, Temples on the site in the period from Zerubbabel to Herod. Zerubbabel's Temple was cleansed and rededicated by Judas the Maccabee in 164 BCE after Antiochus Epiphanes had defiled it. Some historians believe the Temple was actually rebuilt then. Herod the Great began rebuilding the Temple in 20 BCE, a project that was not completed until shortly before it was destroyed ninety years later. However, official Temple worship and sacrifices continued throughout the period of the 'second Temple' except for the three-year interruption by Antiochus Epiphanes.

143. Thomas Ice and Randall Price, *Ready to Rebuild* (Eugene, Oregon USA: Harvest House Publishers, 1991), p. 105.

144. Ibid., pp. 106–7.

145. *Ready to Rebuild* by Thomas Ice and Randall Price is a well-researched history of the Temple Mount from Solomon's time to the present day, and includes documentation of the preparations for the third Temple.

146. For a more graphic look at the three theories on the position of the second Temple, see the video *Walkabout Zion* – a personal diary filmed by the author in 1997. This video also contains a walk through the Western Wall Tunnel. Available from: Evangelical Films, Danbury Common Old Mission, The Common, Danbury, Chelmsford, Essex CM3 4EE, England; Embrace Israel Ministries, PO Box 10077, Cedar Rapids, Iowa 52410–0077, USA; Hatikvah Film Foundation, PO Box 545, Balcatta, WA 6194, Australia.

147. Ice and Price, *Ready to Rebuild*, p. 152, quoting from Kathleen Kenyon, *The Bible and Recent Archaeology* (London: The British Museum, 1978), pp. 85–6.

148. Ibid., p. 152.

149. Ibid., pp. 161–2.

150. The common Christian theological position on the Jewish Temple is that there is now no need for a Temple in Jerusalem because the Church is the Temple or dwelling place of the Spirit of the Lord. It is, of course, absolutely true that a believer who has received Yeshua as Lord and Saviour, and consequently been baptised in the Holy Spirit, is a 'Temple of the Holy Spirit' (1 Corinthians 3:16, 2 Corinthians 6:16 and Ephesians 2:21) and there is no further sacrifice required for atonement of sin (Hebrews 9:12–28). The question is: is this

sufficient reason to negate a literal fulfilment of the prophetic Scriptures which clearly seem to indicate there will be another Temple in Jerusalem?

151. There are approximately twenty Hebrew words which are translated 'BRANCH' in the *Tanakh*. The Hebrew word used in Zechariah 6:12 is *tsamech* and is only used in reference to the Messiah. *Tsamech* is also used in Zechariah 3:8, Isaiah 4:2 and Jeremiah 23:5 and 33:15. This prophecy in Zechariah 6:12, by the way, has had a spiritual fulfilment in the Church (see previous note), but it is the author's view that it will have a literal fulfilment too.

152. There are some Messianic Jews in Israel who believe that the third Temple will be a very low-key affair. Some are of the view that it may be a temporary structure like the Tabernacle in Moses' day. There are others who judge that nothing more than the altar is required so that the offerings and sacrifices can be carried out as happened when the exiles returned from Babylon. They built an altar, commenced the offerings and sacrifices and continued them for some years before the second Temple was completed (Ezra 3). Some Evangelical Christians refer to the third Temple as the 'Antichrist Temple'. This term is somewhat misleading. It is true that it will be defiled by the Antichrist, but the first Temple was defiled by Nebuchadnezzar, and the second Temple by Antiochus Epiphanes and then Titus in 70 CE, who were all 'types' of the Antichrist. The site of the Temple was then defiled by Hadrian who built a pagan temple there, and then by the Moslems to this day. However, Yeshua referred to 'the holy place' in Matthew 24:15 and Paul referred to it as 'the Temple of God' in 2 Thessalonians 2:4. The same term is used in Revelation 11:1. This suggests, rather than being an 'Antichrist Temple' (which could easily describe the structures standing on the Temple Mount at present), the third Temple will have the Lord's sanction, and it will be what the Scriptures say it will be.

153. Quoted from a videotaped interview with the author on 11 October 1999.

154. Excerpts quoted from the key-note address given at the ICEJ Feast of Tabernacles celebration in Jerusalem, by Rev. Malcolm Hedding on 21 October 1997. Tapes on this subject by Malcolm Hedding are available from Christian Action for Israel, PO Box 51065, Musgrave 4062, Kwazulu, Natal, South Africa.

155. Quoted from an interview with Ofer Amitai by the author for the documentary film *Jerusalem, The Covenant City* on 11 October 1999.

156. Ibid.

157. If you wish to support the Messianic Believers in Israel, the following organisations have a specific ministry to the Messianic congregations, financially and in prayer: in Britain: Prayer For Israel, PO Box 328, Bromley, Kent BR1 2ZS; in Australia: Prayer For Israel, PO Box 7077, Toowoomba Mail Centre, Queensland 4352; in New Zealand: Prayer For Israel, PO Box 1032, Palmerston North; in the USA: Embrace Israel Ministries, PO Box 10077, Cedar Rapids, Iowa 52410–0077. Another ministry, which is based in Israel, financially assists believers with 'no interest' loans to get started in business (they also give grants to believers in need): The Nehemiah Trustees Covenant Fund, PO Box 64, Ma'aleh Adumim, 98100, Israel.

Chapter 9: Jerusalem and the Coming of the Messiah

158. Rebbe Menahem Mendel Schneerson was recognised by the Lubavitchers as the 'Provisional' Messiah as he had not actually fulfilled all the requirements of the Messiah, which many in the sect believed he would. There have been a number of 'Provisional Messiahs' proclaimed in past generations as they hold the view that each generation produces a potential 'Messiah'. They believe that when the aggregate number of *mitzvot* (good deeds) for the Jewish nation is complete, then the Messiah will finally be made manifest. There were some Lubavitchers who proclaimed Rebbe Schneerson to be the 'actual' Messiah before his death. His followers claim that the Rebbe is still performing miracles from his grave in New York.

159. There are certain ultra-Orthodox sects, particularly the Haredi, who do not recognise the present State of Israel, as they believe that the Messiah must establish the only legitimate State. Unfortunately, some of the more radical sects are actually working for the destruction of the State.

160. Yeshua said: *'I am the light of the world. He who follows Me shall not walk in darkness, but have the light of life'* (John 8:12). The Apostle John bears witness that Yeshua is *'the true Light which gives light to every man who comes into the world. He was in the world, and the world was made through Him, and the world did not know Him. He came to His own* [place], *and His own* [people] *did*

not receive Him' (John 1:9–11). His own place, of course, is the Land of Israel, and His own people are the Jews.

161. Bruce D. Reekie, *The Holy Spirit and Israel* (Tonbridge, England: Sovereign World, 1993), pp. 170 and 171.

162. There is possibly another striking similarity between Antiochus Epiphanes and the Antichrist to come. As we discussed in Chapter 7, Epiphanes was a Hellenist and as such believed in the supremacy of the human race. Their common ideology will prove to be humanism in its most radical form – they think themselves to be God.

163. The only other person in the Bible referred to in such a way was Judas Iscariot, the disciple who betrayed Yeshua (John 17:12), into whom Satan had entered (Luke 22:3).

164. The Apostle John goes on to say that anyone who denies the Father and the Son has the spirit of Antichrist: *'Who is a liar but he who denies that Jesus is the Messiah? He is antichrist who denies the Father and the Son. Whoever denies the Son does not have the Father either; he who acknowledges the Son has the Father also'* (1 John 2:22–23). Without doubt, John believed there was a figurehead coming who would be known as 'the Antichrist' (v. 18).

165. One popular theory among some teachers of eschatology in recent decades is that the restrainer is the Church – or, more precisely, the Holy Spirit resident in the Church. Paraphrased, this interpretation of verses 6 and 7 might read something like ' . . . you know that the Church is holding [the Antichrist] back, so that he may be revealed at the proper time . . . the Holy Spirit who now restrains will do so until He is taken out of the way. And then the lawless one will be revealed.' In other words the Church is removed from the earth, or 'raptured' before the Antichrist is revealed. While this could possibly be a valid interpretation, it is neither what the text actually says, nor even necessarily implies. A problem arises because Revelation 7 tells of a great multitude of Gentile believers standing in heaven – many of them martyrs – who have come out of the great tribulation. A multitude of believers, clothed in white robes, is by definition part of the Church. That being the case, the power of the Holy Spirit must be present on earth for them to become believers and live as believers. Furthermore, Yeshua gave this promise to believers under persecution: *'whatever is given you in that hour, speak that; for it is not you who speak, but the Holy Spirit'* (Mark 13:11). Is it not more likely that the 'restrainer' in 2 Thessalonians 2:6–7 may be an angelic being

similar to those found in Revelation who are sent out at specific times to perform various tasks?

166. Revelation 13 gives further insight about the satanic 'godhead' prophesied by the Old Testament. Some Christian scholars have likened it to a counterfeit 'Trinity'. Certainly the fallen angel Lucifer, otherwise known as Satan, is the empowering force in this counterfeit godhead containing himself, the Antichrist (the Beast) and the False Prophet, who many Christian eschatologists believe may be the dominant world religious leader or guru of the time. Another revelation which would identify the Antichrist is the apparently miraculous healing of a mortal wound. Whether this happens before or after the Antichrist is revealed is not clear. The False Prophet is able to perform apparent miracles and erects a graven image of the Antichrist which can actually speak. It may be this image that is referred to as the *'abomination of desolation'*. The False Prophet also orders all people to receive a mark on the right hand or forehead which will indicate allegiance to the Antichrist. Refusal to accept the mark or to worship the image will result in denial of life's essential provisions and end in death. The Scriptures do warn us, however, that anyone who receives the mark of the Antichrist, the number of which we are told is 666, and worships him, will not enter the Kingdom of God.

167. As noted in Chapter 8 and note 150, the subject of the rebuilding of the Temple and the reintroduction of the offerings and sacrifices is a highly controversial one among Christians. Many Christians, quite validly, object to such a notion on theological grounds because the finished work of the Messiah on the cross makes the sacrificial system obsolete (see Hebrews 8–9). However, one must acknowledge that, when they made these predictions that the Temple would be in use at the time the Antichrist defiles it, both Yeshua (Matthew 24:15) and the Apostle Paul (2 Thessalonians 2:4) had a complete understanding of the significance of the finished work of Messiah's sacrifice on the cross. Furthermore, they made these predictions knowing of the imminent destruction of the Temple by the Romans. There are Christian Bible scholars who argue that the Temple which the Antichrist defiles will be the 'Spiritual Temple', i.e. the Church. While I agree that the apostate church establishment of the time will be defiled by their acquiescence to the Antichrist's regime, and the True Church – the Body of Christ – persecuted and violated for its resistance, this again does not negate a literal fulfilment

of these New Testament prophecies. The Apostle John, in his apocalyptic vision (which was given about twenty years after the destruction of the second Temple in 70 CE), is told to take a measuring rod and measure the Temple, the altar, and the worshippers (Revelation 11:1). This hardly makes sense if the Temple is merely a spiritual entity, and not a physical building.

168. There are differing views among Christian Bible scholars about the timing of the 'Time of Jacob's Trouble' or Great Tribulation as it is often called. One view is that these prophecies were fulfilled between 67 and 70 CE. In the Olivet Discourse the disciples raised two questions with Yeshua following His remark concerning the Temple that *'not one stone shall be left upon another'* (Matthew 24:1–3, Mark 13:1–3, Luke 21:5–7). In the first question they asked Him when this would take place, and in the second they asked Him about the signs concerning His return and the end of the age. The Luke account seems to deal more fully with the destruction of Jerusalem by the Romans, while the other two accounts seem to concentrate more on the end of the age. While there appear to be some similarities between the two sieges of Jerusalem, and there was undoubtedly great tribulation when the city was destroyed, many of the other accompanying signs were not fulfilled at that time. Two particular signs that would herald the end of the age and the Great Tribulation, Yeshua said, would be that the gospel would be preached throughout the world and that we would see the *'abomination of desolation'* (Matthew 24:14–15). Another view is that the Holocaust of World War II was the Great Tribulation. The problem with this view is that the Olivet Discourse indicates that the Great Tribulation will be *immediately* followed by signs in the heavens and the return of the Messiah (Matthew 24:29–30). This did not happen at the end of World War II. Also Jeremiah 30:3 seems to indicate that the 'Time of Jacob's Trouble' would take place after the people were established in *Eretz Yisrael*. There are many other prophecies in the Old and New Testaments that speak of a time of unprecedented horror immediately prior to the coming of the Messiah, some of which we will consider. I have therefore come to the conclusion that the Great Tribulation, which Yeshua and the other prophets speak of, is still to come.

169. As discussed in Chapter 8, another important role of the two witnesses may well be to proclaim the meaning of the death of the Messiah, thus preparing the nation of Israel for repentance.

170. In his novel *The End Of Days*, David Dolan portrays the two witnesses as being disciples of Yeshua. One is the Apostle John (Yochanan), the author of the Book of Revelation, and the other Nathanael (Natan-el). His novel, which is based on end-time biblical prophecy, makes very interesting and thought-provoking reading.

Chapter 10: Jerusalem and the Consummation of the Covenants and Promises

171. A further exposition of what the atoning death of Yeshua HaMashiach means in relation to the New Covenant can be found in Hebrews 8–9.

172. There are some church groups who have made a move towards repentance of past crimes against the Jewish people. On 1 November 1999, in London, a group of committed Christians met with representatives of the House of Lords to encourage such an act of repentance. This was held simultaneously with a public meeting in Westminster. A petition with three thousand signatures was sent to Her Majesty Queen Elizabeth II, requesting that the British monarchy publicly denounce all acts of anti-Semitism past, present and future, and especially in relation to the expulsion of all Jews from England by King Edward I in 1290 CE. On the other side of the world, an encouraging statement was made by the Council of Presidents of the Lutheran Church of Australia in 1996. In part, it reads as follows: 'We need to recognise that Christians over the centuries have often mistreated and persecuted the followers of Judaism and so have failed to live by the faith they profess. We Lutherans acknowledge that the anti-Jewish writings of Martin Luther were used by the persecutors of Jews to justify their positions and practices ... It is true that before and during World War II, our Lutheran church papers naïvely and un-critically published German propaganda against the Jews. We declare that all forms of anti-Semitism are contrary to the Christian way of life. We urge the members of the Lutheran Church of Australia to repent of and confess our silence over the Holocaust and other such attacks on Jews, and our sins of prejudice and misunderstanding over against the Jewish people. We call on members of the Lutheran Church of Australia to make the following commitment: (1) to respect and defend the rights of the Jewish community to observe the faith of their ancestors; (2) to live out their Christian faith by

showing love and understanding toward Jewish people; (3) to engage in open and honest dialogue with Jewish people about our common Old Testament heritage and our distinctive religious beliefs; and (4) to oppose in word and action religious bigotry of whatever form both within the church and the wider community ... At the same time, since we believe that Jesus is the Saviour of all people, let us all continue to confess Him publicly as God's promised Messiah.'

173. This depends upon exactly to what the 'river of Egypt' in Genesis 15:18 refers. Some Bible scholars believe it to be the Nile, while others believe it refers to the Great Wadi which runs from south to north roughly halfway across the Sinai Peninsula. If the latter is the case, then Israel's territory to the south-west would only take in about half the Sinai Peninsula and none of Egypt.

174. Many Bible scholars believe that when the term 'David their king' or 'David My Servant' is used prophetically, as in this case, it is referring to the Messiah (see also Jeremiah 30:9 and Ezekiel 37:24). In the view of some scholars, however, such passages refer to the historical King David, and they suggest that he will reign over Israel as consort to the Messiah. However, there do not seem to be any Scriptures that allude to the two actually reigning together.

Chapter 11: Jerusalem, the City of the Great King

175. It appears there are three main judgements that will take place. Firstly, there will be the judgement of the nations on earth when the Messiah returns to earth. Secondly, there is what the Apostle Paul refers to as the 'Judgement Seat of Christ' (Romans 14:10 and 2 Corinthians 5:10). It appears this judgement will take place after the 'first resurrection' (Revelation 20:5–6) and will be specifically for believers, who will be judged for what they have done in the body and be rewarded for it accordingly – whether good or bad. It is not clear which of these two judgements will occur first, but many eschatologists believe the latter will take place in heaven prior to the Lord's return. The third judgement will take place after the 'second resurrection' (Revelation 20:11–15) and is often referred to as the 'Great White Throne Judgement'. This judgement will involve every person who has ever lived. *'And anyone not found in the Book of Life was cast into the lake of fire.'* Some Christian Bible scholars believe these judgements are in

fact one and the same, while others are of the opinion that because God is a God of love, there will be no judgement and subsequent retribution at all. The latter view is totally inconsistent with the revealed Word of God.

176. There has been some debate among Christians as to who these 'brethren' are. Some hold they are the Jews, and the Joel prophecy quoted would seem to confirm this view. Others are of the view they are Christians who suffer misfortune, hardship and persecution, while others believe it refers to anyone who suffers innocently at the hands of evil men. If one takes into account the parable of the Good Samaritan, then the more universal interpretation, which would include both Jews and Christians, may be the correct one.

177. References to the Messiah ruling the nations with a 'rod of iron' are found chiefly in the Book of Revelation – e.g. 2:27 (quoting Psalm 2:8–9), 12:5 and 19:15. The Scriptures also speak of a sharp sword or rod coming out of His mouth, implying that His words will express righteous indignation and judgement against evil. References include Isaiah 11:4, Revelation 1:16 and 19:15.

178. There are Bible scholars who believe that the restoration of the animal kingdom will take place after the new heavens and new earth are created (Isaiah 65:17 and Revelation 21:1). The passage quoted here in Isaiah 11 appears to link this restoration with that of the Messiah's Kingdom on earth, while a similar passage found in Isaiah 65:25 follows the promise of new heavens and a new earth. While the prophetic Word seems clear that the restoration of the animal kingdom **will** take place, only time will tell **when** it will take place.

179. The issue of Creation versus Evolution is beyond the scope of this book. I strongly recommend *The Genesis Record* by Professor Henry M. Morris. This book and other excellent material on this subject is available in the United States from either The Institute of Creation Research, PO Box 2667, El Cajon CA 92021 or Answers in Genesis, PO Box 6330, Florence, Kentucky 41022. Also in Australasia from Creation Science Foundation, PO Box 6302, Acacia Ridge DC, Qld 4110, Australia.

180. The New Testament has quite a lot to say about the resurrection of believers. Apart from Revelation 20, two other key passages are found in 1 Thessalonians 4:13–18 and 1 Corinthians 15. It will be in 'spiritual bodies' (1 Corinthians 15:44) that the resurrected believers will reign with Yeshua (Revelation 20:4) in the Messianic Kingdom.

181. Some Bible scholars believe that some of these prophecies refer to the New Jerusalem after the new heavens and new earth are created (Isaiah 65:17 and Revelation 21:1–2). These prophecies will certainly be literally fulfilled then, but most likely during Messiah's earthly reign too.

182. This prophecy was given prior to the Babylonian exile and much of what is prophesied in the following chapter was fulfilled shortly afterwards. Many Bible scholars ascribe this prophecy to the return of the Babylonian exiles. If this is the case then the promise concerning Jerusalem's ongoing security was never fulfilled. Therefore the fulfilment of this prophecy must lie in the future, after the return of the Lord Yeshua.

183. Some believe that Ezekiel's vision of the Temple will be part of the New Jerusalem. There cannot be a Temple as such in the New Jerusalem, for in Revelation 21:22 the Apostle John tells us: *'I saw no temple in it, for the Lord God Almighty and the Lamb are its temple.'*

Chapter 12: The New Jerusalem

184. It is interesting that the twelve gates have the names of the twelve tribes of Israel inscribed on them, and that the twelve foundations of the city walls have inscriptions of the names of the twelve apostles. This surely signifies that the destiny of Israel and the Church, which now appears to be separate on this earth, will ultimately be unified in the eternal Kingdom of God.

185. Peter was quoting a prophecy found in Psalm 118:22 which graphically foretold that the Jewish religious leaders would reject the Messiah. What is also interesting is that the resurrection of Yeshua, which had taken place only a few months before, could have easily been disproved by them if it was a false claim. The authorities were unable to do this. The resurrection of Yeshua and the healing of the blind man by the power of the risen Messiah endorses His claim to be the only way to the Father.

186. For Jewish readers, *The Jewish New Testament* translated into English by David Stern is recommended. This translation expresses the New Testament's original and essential Jewishness and corrects mistranslation resulting from anti-Jewish bias in some other translations. Gentile Christians will benefit from reading it too.

187. Like Hindus, Christians believe that there is life after death. But beyond that basic concept, any similarity ceases. Nowhere does

the Bible teach, or even suggest, that human beings return to earth in the form of other creatures or even other humans. Those who are 'in Christ' will be resurrected to everlasting life, and those who refuse to put their faith in Him to everlasting damnation. One of the best passages explaining the resurrection of those 'in Christ' is found in 1 Corinthians 15.

Appendix A

Notes on the Prophecy of the 'Seventy Weeks'

by Herman Goldwag

'Seventy weeks are determined upon thy people and upon thy holy city, to finish the transgression, and to make an end of sins, and to make reconciliation for iniquity, and to bring in everlasting righteousness, and to seal up the vision and prophecy, and to anoint the most Holy.

Know therefore and understand, that from the going forth of the commandment to restore and to build Jerusalem unto the Messiah the Prince shall be seven weeks, and threescore and two weeks: the street shall be built again, and the wall, even in troublous times.

And after threescore and two weeks shall Messiah be cut off, but not for himself: and the people of the prince that shall come shall destroy the city and the sanctuary; and the end thereof shall be with a flood, and unto the end of the war desolations are determined.

And he shall confirm the covenant with many for one week: and in the midst of the week he shall cause the sacrifice and the oblation to cease, and for the overspreading of abominations he shall make it desolate, even until the consummation, and that determined shall be poured upon the desolate.' (Daniel 9:24–27, KJV)

This prophecy, recorded in Daniel 9:24–27, is often mentioned nowadays by Christian preachers and believers. However, I cannot fully reconcile to Scripture the exposition of the majority of them after a serious study of the Hebrew text, especially concerning the 70th week (the last), in which

Messiah was crucified (v. 26), and in which He mightily strengthened the covenant (v. 27). Furthermore, the events at Messiah's first Advent fully correspond to the Hebrew text of verse 27.

The first part of verse 27, which clearly refers to Christ, is often interpreted as speaking of Antichrist (seemingly 'the future ruler' mentioned in verse 26), who supposedly will make a peace treaty in the Middle East for seven years in the near future. According to this interpretation, the 70th week will come to fulfilment some two thousand years after Messiah's crucifixion.

These four prophetic verses so perfectly fit the events known to us about Christ's first advent, that taking the first part of verse 27 out of context and applying it to Antichrist, is like taking the heart out of this outstanding prophecy. As far as I can see, the seventy-week period was fulfilled in one uninterrupted sequence. The Hebrew text and the historical events conclusively support this. However, if this part of verse 27 is mistakenly interpreted (partly due to the translators' failing to follow closely the Hebrew text) as referring to other than Christ, this remarkable prophecy is infinitely diminished. I have concentrated on these four verses without being diverted by eschatology. I leave it to you to prayerfully assess my findings. My translation of the Hebrew text of Daniel 9:24–27 is as follows:

24. Seventy weeks have been decreed upon thy people and upon thy holy city, to restrain [1] the transgression, and to make an end of sins, and to atone [2] for iniquity, and to bring in everlasting righteousness, and to seal [3] vision and prophet, and to anoint Holy of Holies. [4]

25. Know, therefore, and understand, that from the emergence of the word to restore and to build Jerusalem until [5] Messiah [6] Ruler [7] (shall be) seven weeks [8] and sixty-two weeks, and she will be restored and rebuilt, street and moat, but in troubled times. [9]

26. And after the sixty and two weeks [10] shall Messiah be cut off, and he is not, [11] and the city and the sanctuary will be destroyed by nation of the future ruler, and its end [12] shall come with flood-like devastation, [13] and until the end of war, desolations are determined.

27. And (he) shall mightily strengthen[14] covenant for many[15] one week,[16] and in the midst of this week (he) shall terminate sacrifice and offering,[17] and abominations on wing shall cause desolation,[18] until total extermination be decreed on desolator.

Notes

1. *Lechale* in Hebrew: to restrain, withhold, imprison.
2. *Lechaper* in Hebrew: 'to atone' – King James Version (KJV) 'to make reconciliation' is incorrect.
3. *Lachtom* in Hebrew: to sign, to seal, to stamp, etc. – KJV 'to seal up' is misleading.
4. Most Holy.
5. *Ad* in Hebrew: 'until' – KJV 'unto' is inexact.
6. *Mashiach* in Hebrew: 'Messiah' or 'Christ' (*Christos* in Greek) – both mean 'Anointed One'.
7. *Nagid* in Hebrew: 'ruler' or 'leader'.
8. The seven weeks (49 years) mentioned most likely refers to the time of rebuilding the city and the Temple after the return from Babylon.
9. Opposition of the local people to the rebuilding of the city and the Temple mentioned in the records of Ezra and Nehemiah.
10. Actually, after sixty-nine weeks (483 years), after adding the previous seven weeks mentioned in verse 25.
11. *Ve ein lo* in Hebrew: literally 'and he does not have', but here rendered 'he is not', as Hebrew commentaries confirm (KJV 'but not for himself' is misleading).
12. *Vekitzo* in Hebrew: 'and his end' – refers to 'the nation' – *am* in Hebrew (masculine).
13. This could refer to the desolation of the Roman Empire by the barbarians.
14. *Vehigbir* in Hebrew: 'And [he] shall mightily strengthen' – (KJV 'And he shall confirm' is not precise).
15. *Larabim* in Hebrew: 'for many' or 'to many' (mistakenly translated 'with many' in KJV).
16. The KJV reads: 'for one week' but there is no 'for' in the Hebrew text. The 'one week' should be understood as meaning during the week. Hebrew Bible commentaries confirm this. It is obvious this is the last (70th) week.
17. *Zevah umincha* in Hebrew: 'sacrifice and offering' – refers to the Old Testament sacrificial system in its entirety.
18. Desecration of the Temple by the Roman army after the siege of Jerusalem (Josephus, *The Wars* 6.6.1).

This prophecy of seventy weeks indicates not only the precise time of Christ's first coming but also His ministry, the establishment of the New Covenant, His crucifixion and the anointing of the Most Holy. The seventy weeks of 490 days actually refer to 490 years. Each day of the week stands for one year (Ezekiel 4:6). Hebrew scholars support the view that it refers to 'weeks of years'.

It has to be emphasised that the 69 weeks (483 years) bring us, not to the birth of Jesus, but to His appearance as Messiah, which means 'anointed one'. This happened immediately after His baptism in the River Jordan, when He was anointed by the Holy Spirit coming from heaven and alighting upon Him in the form of a dove. The voice of God proclaimed, 'This is My beloved Son in whom I am well pleased' (Matthew 3:16, Acts 10:37, 38). Only there did He become Messiah, the anointed one.

Although there is an interpretation suggesting that when it says 'unto Messiah the Prince...' in verse 25 it refers to the later ministry of Christ close to His crucifixion, I can see no good reason for it, nor scriptural support for it. The prophecy clearly states that with the termination of 69 weeks, we come to Messiah (the anointed one), the Prince, having been born of the royal family and destined to be ruler and king (Isaiah 9:7). This prophecy obviously brings us to Messiah, the Prince's appearance on the world scene, and not to His crucifixion three and a half years later, otherwise it would have sufficed to mention Him only once, stating: '...from the emergence of the word to restore and rebuild Jerusalem until Messiah Ruler's cutting off...'

The date of the beginning of John the Baptist's ministry, when he was of age (30 years according to the Law – Numbers 4:3), is clearly stated in Luke as being in the fifteenth year of Tiberius Caesar (Luke 3:1–3). Although, during the last ten years of Caesar Augustus' reign, Tiberius was virtually co-regent, he only became Caesar on the death of Augustus in 14 AD. The fifteenth year of his reign would be 29 AD, the year in which Luke states that John began his ministry. Jesus began His ministry when He was of age (at least 30 years according to the Law – Luke 3:23), after being anointed by

God. His ministry lasted three and a half years from the age of about 30.

As the crucifixion took place at Passover, around April, it means that Christ began His three-and-a-half-year ministry in October 29 AD, the year that John the Baptist began his ministry. It therefore follows that Christ was crucified in April 33 AD.

We know that the 'emergence of the word' to rebuild Jerusalem was granted to Nehemiah (Nehemiah 2) in the twentieth year of the rule of Artaxerxes, which was 454 BC. Counting the prophesied 483 years (69 weeks) from this date, we come to the anointing of Jesus in October 29 AD. Then the prophecy: '... until Messiah the Ruler...' was fulfilled.

I believe that the dates quoted herein are correct. If there are any discrepancies, they will be marginal and will not affect the evidence that the last (70th) week of this prophecy took place during Messiah's first advent.

In verse 26 it reads: 'And after the sixty and two weeks shall Messiah be cut off...'. It is clear from this statement that the crucifixion of Christ took place in the 70th week. 'And after...' (*ve'acharei*) does not necessarily mean immediately after, as confirmed by other mentions of this word in Scripture. When it says 'And after...', it is obvious that some years could have passed, and that is what actually happened. As we know, the crucifixion of Christ (in the middle of the 70th week) took place three and a half years after His anointing and becoming Messiah the Ruler.

Clear confirmation of this comes in verse 27 where it reads: 'and in the midst of this week' (at the end of three and a half years of the 70th week) 'he shall terminate sacrifice and offering'. As we know, this was accomplished when Christ offered His precious life-blood on the cross as a paschal lamb and, in so doing, terminated the annual sacrifices and offering forever.

Verse 26 explains that after Messiah's crucifixion, the destruction of the city and Temple will follow: 'and the city and the sanctuary will be destroyed by nation of the future ruler'. This actually happened in 70 AD after Christ's crucifixion when the Roman army under Titus completely destroyed the city and the Temple. This destruction of the city was also prophesied by Christ: *'Verily I say unto you, there shall not be left one stone upon another, that shall not be thrown down'* (Matthew 24:2).

Verse 27 says: *'Vehigbir brit larabim shavua echad...'* – 'And [he] shall mightily strengthen covenant for many one week...' and **not** '**for** one week...' as the KJV says, but rather **during** the seventieth week. *'Vehigbir'* is in the masculine form and obviously refers to a man, even though the pronoun 'he' is not quoted in the Hebrew. If the pronoun 'he' was included in the Hebrew, it would tend to point to the 'future ruler' mentioned in verse 26. Without it, it can refer to someone else, but knowing the facts, it obviously refers to Messiah mentioned in verses 25 and 26. *'Vehigbir'* – 'and [he] shall mightily strengthen', is from the same Hebrew root as *'gibbor'*, which was used as one of the attributes of Christ – *El Gibbor* (God Mighty – Isaiah 9:6). It is noteworthy that the verb in this form – *vehigbir* – appears only once in the Bible, in this very verse. The KJV translates *'Vehigbir brit larabim...'* as 'And he shall confirm the covenant with many...'. Although 'confirm' is synonymous with 'strengthen', the marginal reference is mistaken in stating that 'confirm the covenant' means 'make a firm covenant', which is the generally accepted rendering. *'Vehigbir brit'* clearly refers to strengthening an **existing** covenant. A further mistake in the KJV reads: 'And he shall confirm the covenant **with** many...' when the Hebrew text actually says '**for** many', which Christ actually declared at the Last Supper: 'For this is My blood of the new covenant, which is shed **for** many for the remission of sins' (Matthew 26:28 – NKJV). There is a very great difference in making a worldly covenant **with** individuals or nations and a voluntary covenant **for** many, which Christ did. We can fully comprehend the significance of that small word 'for' when we realise that Christ shed His precious blood **for** many (Matthew 20:28 and Mark 14:24).

'And [he] shall mightily strengthen covenant for many one week...'. In the first half of the week (three and a half years), Jesus Christ was laying the foundation of the New Covenant, teaching His disciples, showing in every way that He was the promised Messiah, by powerful words such as were never spoken before (John 7:46, Matthew 13:54), performing miracles, raising the dead and even calming the storm. All these things greatly strengthened them. By the time of the Last Supper they wholeheartedly accepted the New Covenant made for them by their Messiah (Matthew 26:28). Furthermore, after His crucifixion, He mightily strengthened the New Covenant confirmed by Him at the Last Supper – by His resurrection, His appearances to His disciples and by sending the Holy Spirit to anoint them at Pentecost. This was essential bearing in mind that the apostles were in disarray after His crucifixion. ' ... smite the shepherd and the sheep shall be scattered ... ' (Zechariah 13:7).

' ... and in the midst of this week [he] shall terminate sacrifice and offering ...'. Thus, by His crucifixion as a paschal lamb making atonement for sin for ever, the sacrifice and offering was terminated. The everlasting righteousness (justification from sin) was laid down – as mentioned in Daniel 9:24. Thence, the animal sacrifices and offering for sin were no longer valid. The KJV incorrectly reads in verse 27: ' ... and he shall make it desolate ... ', thus making it appear to refer to the one who strengthens the covenant. In the Hebrew text there is no 'he', so the one who strengthens the covenant has no connection with the destruction which follows.

Knowing that (1) Christ's ministry lasted three and a half years, (2) that He established the New Covenant and (3) He terminated the sacrifice and offering by His death on the cross, who can doubt that this was a fulfilment of the prophecy in verse 27 which clearly mentions these three events?

It is noticeable that verse 27 is, in a way, a repeat of verse 26 but with additional details. Verse 26 speaks about the crucifixion of Christ (in the middle of the 70th week), and the subsequent destruction of Jerusalem and the Temple. Verse 27 speaks about the establishment of the New Covenant and the termination of the sacrifice and offering after the crucifixion, mentioned in verse 26, and it repeats the calamity also mentioned in verse 26 which was to follow. Verse 27 also mentions Christ's ministry before the crucifixion and the mighty strengthening of the New Covenant after His resurrection, which took place during the 70th week.

The prophecy of the 70 weeks speaks only about the people of Israel: 'Seventy weeks have been decreed upon **thy** people...'. When we come to the crucifixion in the middle of the 70th week there are three-and-a-half years (half a week) of the 70 weeks remaining. During this period the preaching of the gospel was exclusive to the Jews. After the 70th week the gospel was opened up to all nations, starting with Cornelius. As the Holy of Holies refers to a place, what could better fit the reality of it than the temple made up of living stones, the twelve apostles and the first disciples? (1 Peter 2:5, 9) Weren't they the most Holy amongst the whole nation of Israel, having direct fellowship with the Son of God? In direct fulfilment of the last part of verse 24: '...and to anoint the Holy of Holies', the Holy Spirit fell upon the whole body of believers at Pentecost (Acts 2).

The exact timing of Christ's coming; His mighty ministry to establish the New Covenant; His sending of the Holy Spirit to empower the believers and restrain transgression; His sealing up of sins and bringing in everlasting righteousness by His atonement for iniquity, in offering Himself as the Paschal Lamb; His fulfilling in Himself many prophecies concerning Him, even to His death on the cross, thereby putting a seal (guarantee) on the fulfilment of all vision and prophecy, and the anointing of the Holy of Holies were all accomplished in His first advent.

The foregoing therefore demonstrates how the whole of the 70-week period was fulfilled in one unbroken sequence. The mistaken interpretation of verse 27 – due in part to mistranslation of the original Hebrew text – greatly diminishes the truth of this remarkable prophecy.

This prophecy revealed by God to Daniel is so outstanding in its inclusion of all the main events concerning the Messiah that it is unsurpassed by any other prophecy concerning Jesus Christ.

Daniel's 70 Weeks Prophecy by Herman Goldwag is obtainable from:

    H. Goldwag, PO Box 97,
    Cheltenham GL53 0YY,
    England.

Postscript:

It has recently been found that the Hebrew name *Yeshua* is often encoded in the original Hebrew Scriptures where the context refers to the Messiah. Several experts suggest that the equidistant sequences of the Hebrew letters forming significant words is most unlikely to occur by chance and that if this is the case, then it is of God's doing. I concur.

I discovered the name *Yeshua* – formed from the four Hebrew letters *yod, shin, vav* and *ayin* – encoded twice in the four verses Daniel 9:24–27:

1. In Daniel 9:24, starting from the *yod* in *'iyr'* (city), counting every 79th letter three times right to left (the Hebrew way), with the last letter *ayin* in *'ve'ad'* (and until) in verse 26.
2. In Daniel 9:25, starting from the *yod* in *'shishim'* (sixty), counting every 61st letter three times right to left, with the last letter *ayin* in *'ve'ad'* (and until) in verse 27.

A third encoding was found by Yacov Rambsel, mentioned in his book *Yeshua*:

3. In Daniel 9:26, starting from the *yod* in *'ve'ah'iyr'* (and the city), counting every 26th letter three times from left to right, with the last letter *ayin* in *'ve'shavuim'* (and weeks) in verse 25.

I believe that that these encoded mentions of Yeshua in the Hebrew Scriptures are very significant as they occur in Daniel's 70 Weeks prophecy, and especially as *Yeshua* is embedded in verse 27 which mainly refers to Christ, and not to Antichrist as many mistakenly interpret it.

Herman Goldwag

Appendix B

The Jerusalem Covenant

AS OF THIS DAY –

Jerusalem Day, the twenty-eighth day of the month of Iyar in the year five thousand seven hundred and fifty-two; one thousand nine hundred and twenty-two years after the destruction of the Second Temple; forty-four years since the founding of the State of Israel; twenty-five years since the Six Days War during which the Israeli Defence Forces, in defence of our very existence, restored the Temple Mount and the unity of Jerusalem; twelve years since the Knesset of Israel re-established Jerusalem, "unified and whole", as the "Capital of Israel"; "the State of Israel is the State of the Jewish People" and "the Capital of Israel is the Capital of the People of Israel."

WE

have gathered together in Zion, sovereign national officials and leaders of our communities everywhere to enter into a covenant with Jerusalem, as was done by the leaders of our nation and all the people of Israel upon Israel's return to our land from the Babylonian exile wherein the people vowed to "dwell in Jerusalem, the Holy City."

ONCE AGAIN

"our feet stand within your gates, O Jerusalem – Jerusalem built as a city joined together" which unites the people of Israel "to one another" and "links heavenly Jerusalem with earthly Jerusalem."

WE HAVE RETURNED

to the place that the LORD vowed to bestow upon the descendants of Abraham, Father of our Nation; to the City of David, King of Israel; where Solomon, son of David, built a Holy Temple and a Capital City; which with time became the Mother of all Israel; a City and a Mother of all enactments of Justice and Righteousness, and for the wisdom and insights of the ancient world; where a Second Temple was erected in the days of Ezra and Nehemiah.

IN THIS CITY

the prophets of the LORD prophesied; in this City our Sages taught Torah; in this City the Sanhedrin convened session in its stone chamber. "For here were the seat of Justice and the Throne of the House of David," "for out of Zion shall go forth Torah, and the Word of the LORD from Jerusalem."

TODAY AS OF OLD

We hold fast to the truth of the words of the prophets of Israel, that all the inhabitants of this world shall enter within the gates of Jerusalem: "And it shall come to pass in the end of days, the mountain of the House of the LORD will be well established at the peak of the mountains and will tower above the hills, and all the nations shall stream towards it."

Each and every nation shall live by its own faith: "For all the peoples will go forward, each with its own Divine Name: We shall go in the name of the LORD our God forever and ever." And in this spirit the Knesset of the State of Israel has enacted a law establishing: the places holy to the peoples of all religions shall be protected from desecration and from any restriction of free access to them.

JERUSALEM

peace and tranquillity shall reign in the city: "Pray for the peace of Jerusalem; may those that love you be tranquil. May there be peace within your walls, and tranquillity within your palaces." Out of Jerusalem a message of peace went forth and shall yet go forth again to all the inhabitants of the earth: "And they shall beat their swords into plowshares, *and their spears into pruning-hooks; Nation will not lift up sword against nation, nor shall they learn war any more." Our sages, of blessed memory have said: "In the future The Holy One, the Blessed can comfort Jerusalem only with peace."*

FROM THIS PLACE

We once again take our vow: "If I forget thee, O Jerusalem, may my right hand lose its strength; may my tongue stick to my palate if I do not remember you, if I do not raise up Jerusalem at the very height of my rejoicing."

AND WITH ALL THESE UNDERSTANDINGS,

we enter into this Covenant and write:

We shall bind you to us forever; we shall bind you to us with faithfulness, with righteousness and justice, with steadfast love and compassion. We love you O Jerusalem with eternal love, with unbounded love, under siege and when liberated from the yoke of oppressors; we have been martyred for you, we have yearned for you, we have clung to you. Our faithfulness to you we shall bequeath to our children after us. For ever more, our home shall be within you.

IN CERTIFICATION OF THIS COVENANT, WE SIGN:

Appendix C

The Olivet Discourse

The Account in the Gospel of Matthew

Now as He sat on the Mount of Olives, the disciples came to [Yeshua] privately, saying, 'Tell us, when will these things be? And what will be the sign of Your coming, and of the end of the age?'

And Yeshua answered and said to them: 'Take heed that no one deceives you. For many will come in My name, saying, "I am the Messiah," and will deceive many. And you will hear of wars and rumours of wars. See that you are not troubled; for all these things must come to pass, but the end is not yet.

'For nation will rise against nation, and kingdom against kingdom. And there will be famines, pestilences, and earthquakes in various places. All these are the beginning of sorrows.

'Then they will deliver you up to tribulation and kill you, and you will be hated by all nations for My name's sake. And then many will be offended, will betray one another, and will hate one another. Then many false prophets will rise up and deceive many.

'And because lawlessness will abound, the love of many will grow cold. But he who endures to the end shall be saved. And this gospel of the kingdom will be preached in all the world as a witness to all the nations, and then the end will come.

'Therefore when you see the "abomination of desolation," spoken of by Daniel the prophet, standing in the holy place' (whoever reads, let him understand), 'then let those who are in Judea flee to the mountains. Let him who is on the housetop not come down to take anything out of his house. And let him who is in the field not go back to get his clothes. But woe to those who are pregnant and to those with nursing babies in those days! And pray that your flight may not be in winter or on the Sabbath.

'For then there will be great tribulation, such as has not been since the beginning of the world until this time, no, nor ever shall be. And unless those days were shortened, no flesh would be saved; but for the elect's sake those days will be shortened.

'Then if anyone says to you, "Look, here is the Messiah!" or "There!" do not believe it. For false messiahs and false prophets will arise and show great signs and wonders, so as to deceive, if possible, even the elect.

'See, I have told you beforehand. Therefore if they say to you, "Look, He is in the desert!" do not go out; or "Look, He is in the inner rooms!" do not believe it.

'For as the lightning comes from the east and flashes to the west, so will the coming of the Son of Man be. For wherever the carcass is, there the eagles will be gathered together.

'Immediately after the tribulation of those days the sun will be darkened, and the moon will not give its light; the stars will fall from heaven and the powers of the heavens will be shaken.

'Then the sign of the Son of Man will appear in heaven, and then all the tribes of the earth will mourn, and they will see the Son of Man coming on the clouds of heaven with power and great glory.

'And He will send His angels with a great sound of a trumpet, and they will gather together His elect from the four winds, from one end of heaven to the other.

'Now learn this parable from the fig tree: When its branch has already become tender and puts forth leaves, you know that summer is near. So you also, when you see all these things, know that it is near, at the very doors.

'Assuredly, I say to you, this generation will by no means pass away till all these things are fulfilled. Heaven and earth will pass away, but My words will by no means pass away. But of that day and hour no one knows, no, not even the angels of heaven, but My Father only.

'But as the days of Noah were, so also will the coming of the Son of Man be. For as in the days before the flood, they were eating and drinking, marrying and giving in marriage, until the day that Noah entered the ark, and did not know until the flood came and took them all away, so also will the coming of the Son of Man be.

'Then two men will be in the field: one will be taken and the other left. Two women will be grinding at the mill: one will be *taken and the other left. Watch therefore, for you do not know what hour your Lord is coming.*

'But know this, that if the master of the house had known what hour the thief would come, he would have watched and not allowed his house to be broken into. Therefore you also be ready, for the Son of Man is coming at an hour when you do not expect Him.'   (Matthew 24:3–44)

'When the Son of Man comes in His glory, and all the holy angels with Him, then He will sit on the throne of His glory. All the nations will be gathered before Him, and He will separate them one from another, as a shepherd divides his sheep from the goats. And He will set the sheep on His right hand but the goats on the left.

'Then the King will say to those on His right hand, "Come, you blessed of My Father, inherit the kingdom prepared for you from the foundation of the world: for I was hungry and you gave Me food; I was thirsty and you gave Me drink; I was a stranger and you took Me in; I was naked and you clothed Me; I was sick and you visited Me; I was in prison and you came to Me."

'Then the righteous will answer Him, saying, "Lord, when did we see You hungry and feed You, or thirsty and give You drink? When did we see You a stranger and take You in, or naked and clothe You? Or when did we see You sick, or in prison, and come to You?" And the King will answer and say to them, "Assuredly, I say to you, inasmuch as you did it to one of the least of these My brethren, you did it to Me."

'Then He will also say to those on the left hand, "Depart from Me, you cursed, into the everlasting fire prepared for the devil and his angels: for I was hungry and you gave Me no food; I was thirsty and you gave Me no drink; I was a stranger and you did not take Me in, naked and you did not clothe Me, sick and in prison and you did not visit Me."

'Then they also will answer Him, saying, "Lord, when did we see You hungry or thirsty or a stranger or naked or sick or in prison, and did not minister to You?" Then He will answer them, saying, "Assuredly, I say to you, inasmuch as you did not do it to one of the least of these, you did not do it to Me."

'And these will go away into everlasting punishment, but the righteous into eternal life.'   (Matthew 25:31–46)

Appendix D

The Eschatological Implications of a Past Fulfilment of 'The Seventieth Week of Daniel'

Most Evangelical Christians of a 'pre-millennial' persuasion believe that the 'Seventieth Week of Daniel' (Daniel 9:27) will be fulfilled at some time in the future. As we noted in Chapter 2, they believe that there is an indefinite time gap between the fulfilment of 'week sixty-nine', which had been completed by the time Jesus Christ was executed by the Romans (Daniel 9:26), and 'week seventy' (Daniel 9:27). To recap, the New King James Version of the Bible renders verses 26 and 27 of Daniel 9 as follows:

> ²⁶ *'And after the sixty-two weeks*
> *Messiah shall be cut off, but not for Himself;*
> *And the people of the prince who is to come*
> *Shall destroy the city and the sanctuary.*
> *The end of it shall be with a flood,*
> *And till the end of the war desolations are determined.*

> ²⁷ *Then he shall confirm a covenant with many for one*
>   *week;*
> *But in the middle of the week*
> *He shall bring an end to sacrifice and offering.*
> *And on the wing of abominations shall be one who*
>   *makes desolate,*
> *Even until the consummation, which is determined,*
> *Is poured out on the desolate.'*

Broadly paraphrased, the general belief among 'pre-millennial' Evangelical Christians is that verse 27 makes the following predictions:

(1) The Antichrist (*'the prince who is to come'* in verse 26) will make or confirm a covenant or treaty 'with many' for a period of 'one week' or seven years (the last of the seventy weeks of the prophecy). In all probability this covenant or treaty will be a comprehensive peace treaty in the Middle East involving Israel and her Arab neighbours.

(2) In the middle of this seven-year period, he (the Antichrist) will break the covenant or treaty by bringing the offerings and sacrifices to an end.

(3) He will set up an image of himself in the Temple so that people will worship him instead of the Lord.

(4) He will continue to regard himself as God until he is judged and dealt with at the return of the Messiah at the end of the seven-year period, or 'Great Tribulation'.

This verse is often interpreted in conjunction with the other verses in Daniel that we considered earlier in Chapter 9, and other prophetic passages of Scripture which refer to the events in the 'Great Tribulation'. Daniel 9:27 has become one of the pillars of eschatology in determining the timing and chronology of events in the last days before the Lord's return.

There are other Christians who would object to the above interpretation on the grounds that any possibility of the Temple being rebuilt is utter nonsense. Many of these Christians would also hold the 'Replacement Theology' view concerning Israel, and believe that Old Testament prophecy, especially anything concerning Israel, is now irrelevant.

However, as we noted towards the end of Chapter 2, there are a number of Hebrew-speaking Messianic Jews and some pre-millennial Evangelical Gentile Christians who would not agree with the above interpretation of Daniel 9:27, simply because they believe that the original Hebrew text does not support it.

For that reason, alone, I believe they should be listened to, and their view prayerfully considered. Furthermore, I believe it needs to be prayerfully considered in isolation to our own theological persuasion. For this reason an interpretation of 'Daniel's 70 Weeks Prophecy' by Herman Goldwag is included in Appendix A.

As we noted, for many pre-millennial Evangelicals Daniel 9:27 is one of the pillars of eschatology. So what would be the ramifications if in fact the 'Seventieth Week of Daniel' had already been fulfilled in and by Yeshua HaMashiach, as Mr Goldwag and others suggest?

Before answering this question, I would agree with many Bible scholars that it is a very sound rule, when interpreting the Bible, not to build a doctrine or theological position on one verse of Scripture alone. This is especially true when dealing with a verse where the original language (the Hebrew text) is somewhat ambiguous and the English translation is obscure, as is the case with Daniel 9:27.

So let us apply this rule of thumb to Daniel 9:27.

First of all Daniel 9:27 is the only verse in the Bible in which the Antichrist appears to be making or confirming a covenant or treaty 'with many'. This being the case, it is perhaps unwise to be dogmatic in applying this verse to the possibility of the Antichrist signing a comprehensive peace treaty in the Middle East. In other words, the world leader who is ultimately responsible for bringing about such a peace treaty, if it ever happens, may not be the Antichrist.

Secondly, it is the only verse in the Bible which implies that 'the Great Tribulation' will be a period of seven years, due to the fact that it is often equated with the 'Seventieth Week of Daniel'. In many other Bible verses, specifically in the Books of Daniel and Revelation, the time span for 'the Great Tribulation' is three-and-a-half years. So the concept of 'the Great Tribulation' remains, but not necessarily a seven-year one.

Thirdly, the 'Seventieth Week of Daniel' – or final seven years before the return of the Messiah – is also significant for those who hold the view that the Church will be 'raptured' seven years before the Lord returns to rule on earth. This is often referred to as the 'pre-tribulation rapture' viewpoint. The 'rapture' itself is a certainty and is mentioned a number of times in the New Testament (e.g. Matthew 24:40, 1 Corinthians 15:51–52, 1 Thessalonians 4:13–18). However, the timing of the rapture in relation to the return of the Lord is sometimes a subject of heated debate among some Christians who hold dogmatic views, and sadly has been known to cause division. It is my belief that the Lord's statements in Deuteronomy 29:29 and Mark 13:32 should be the final word on this debate. However, if the 'Seventieth Week of Daniel' has already been fulfilled, obviously the theory that the Church will spend a period of seven years in heaven partaking in the Marriage Supper of the Lamb (Revelation 19:7–10), while the 'Great Tribulation' rages on earth, will need some reconsideration too.

Fourthly, the cessation of the offerings and sacrifices mentioned in Daniel 9:27 is also mentioned in Daniel 8:11 and 12:11. It is also implied in Matthew 24:15 and 2 Thessalonians 2:4, which more specifically talk about the Temple being defiled. However, it is possible that the mention of it in Daniel 9:27 may be speaking of something entirely different – i.e. the superseding of the sacrificial system by the atoning death of the Messiah.

In formulating a view on whether or not the 'Seventieth Week of Daniel' has already been fulfilled, or whether its fulfilment lies in the future, I believe that the real meaning of the Hebrew text in Daniel 9:24–27 needs to be the only consideration, not the eschatological implications.

Appendix E

A Prayer for Salvation

Dear Lord God,
I come to You now because I believe that You are the only true God, that Yeshua is Your only begotten Son, that He was born of the Virgin Mary and lived here on earth. I believe that He died on a cross, then rose from the dead and is now alive and seated at Your right hand on Your throne in heaven.

I believe that it is only through the perfect sacrifice of Yeshua dying on the cross that You are able to cleanse me of all my sin and adopt me into Your family as Your child.

I confess before You, Lord God, Creator of the universe, that I am a sinner, and as such I am separated from You. I ask You now to forgive my sin and to give me a new start in life by cleansing the stain of my sin with the precious Blood of Yeshua the Messiah, which He shed for me.

I choose deliberately to turn away from sin and by faith I now acknowledge You, Yeshua, as my Lord and Saviour. I ask You, Heavenly Father, to accept me as Your child and I now surrender my life to You because through Yeshua's sacrifice He took my place and paid the price, which You required, to redeem me and to make me righteous and acceptable in Your sight. I ask that instead of me living my own life for myself, Your will now be done in my life. I believe that by the power of Your Holy Spirit, the third Person of the Godhead now dwelling within me, You will lead me and guide me for the rest of my life here on earth.

I thank You, Lord God, that through Your wonderful grace and mercy, which I did nothing to deserve, but which You have chosen to show me through the death and resurrection of Yeshua HaMashiach, my name is now written in the Lamb's Book of Life and I will live with You throughout eternity.

Amen.

If you have prayed this prayer with sincerity and you genuinely want God's will for your life – and He knows whether you do or not – then your name is now written in the Lamb's Book of Life. You have now become a partaker of the New Covenant. Not only have you been forgiven from all your sin – whether or not you actually *feel* forgiven – but the Lord has put His Spirit within you. This is what Yeshua referred to as being *'born of the Spirit'* (John 3:5–6). This is not something that you do – it is something supernatural that God does within you. The Holy Spirit is now abiding **in** you and He will abide with you forever (John 14:16). As you read the Bible – and this is essential for the growth of your faith – you will find that the Holy Spirit illuminates the Scriptures in a way you have never seen before. This is the outworking of the promise of Yeshua to all His disciples: *'The Holy Spirit, whom the Father will send in My name, He will teach you all things, and bring to your remembrance the things I have said to you'* (John 14:26).

I would urge you to find a church or congregation in your area. Just as a young child needs to be nurtured and fed, so does a young disciple of Yeshua. The Book of Acts tells us that the disciples *'continued steadfastly in the apostles' doctrine and fellowship, in the breaking of bread* [Holy Communion], *and in prayers'*.

There is no one particular denomination of the Christian Church that is better than the others, but there are many individual churches right across the denominational spectrum who are faithful to the Word of God. If you make this a matter of prayer, the Lord will guide you to a fellowship where you can grow in your faith.

The transaction you have just made with God is the beginning of eternal life for you. You have joined the company of millions of people who have been redeemed by the Blood of the Lamb. The walk here on earth will not be easy, but it will be an adventure. And the Lord has promised never to leave you or forsake you. You are in a covenant relationship with Him, which He will never break.

> *'May the Lord bless you and keep you, may the Lord make His face shine upon you, and be gracious to you; may the Lord lift up the light of His countenance upon you and give you His peace, now and forever.'*

Amen.

Appendix F

Maps of the Middle East Conflict

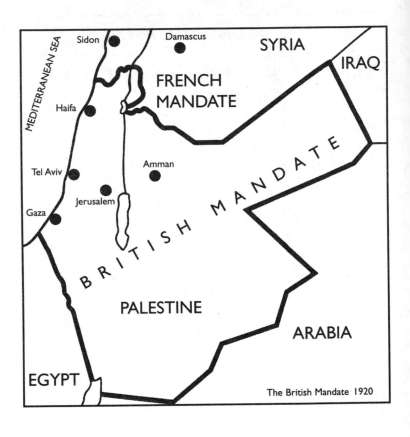

Map 1   The British Mandate in Palestine.
Area allocated for Jewish national home –
San Remo Conference 1920.

GOLAN HEIGHTS Ceded to the French Mandate of Syria in 1923 and captured by Israel in 1967

Map 2 The British Mandate in Palestine.
Great Britain's division of Palestine in 1922.

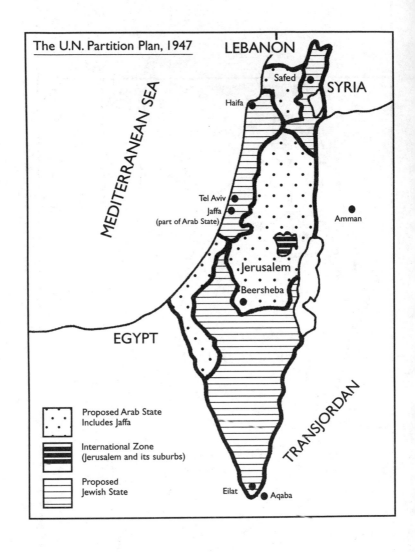

Map 3 The British Mandate in Palestine.
The Partition Plan, 1947 – UN Resolution 181.

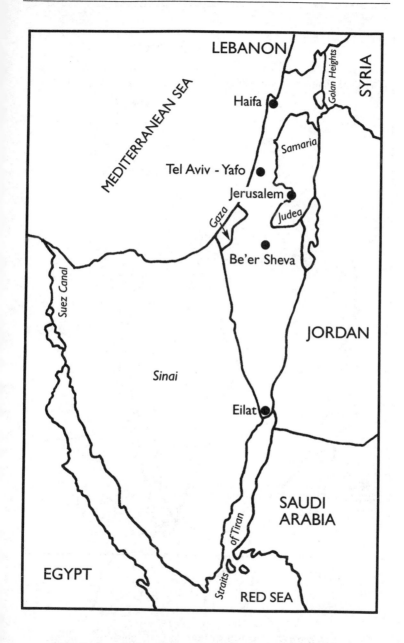

Map 4 Israel's border before the Six-Day War in 1967.

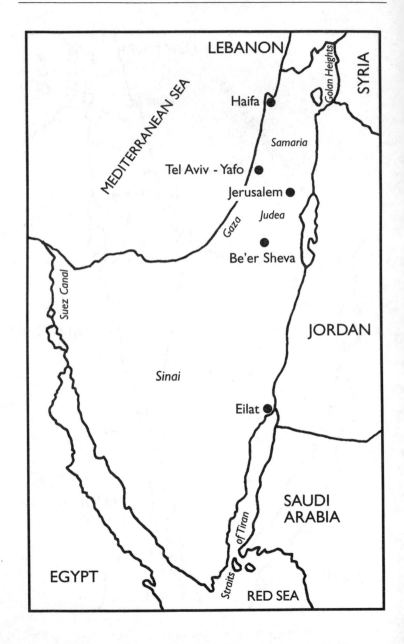

Map 5   Cease-fire lines after the Six-Day War in 1967.

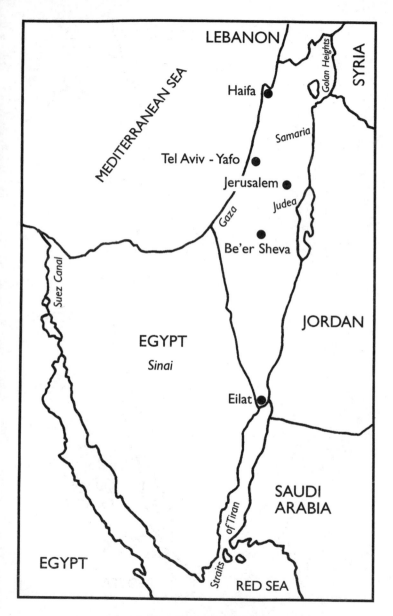

Map 6 Israel's borders following
peace treaties signed with Egypt and Jordan.